ADVANCED Composites

Cindy Foreman

Cindy Foreman
© Copyright 1990, 2002, 2016

Published by Avotek Information Resources, LLC.
All Rights Reserved

International Standard Book Number 1-933189-55-X
ISBN 13: 978-1-933189-55-0
Order # T-ADVCOM-0101
For Sale by: Avotek
A Select Aerospace Industries, Inc. company

Mail to:
P.O. Box 219
Weyers Cave, VA 24486
USA

Ship to:
200 Packaging Drive
Weyers Cave, VA 24486
USA

Toll Free: 800-828-6835
Telephone: 540-234-9090
Fax: 540-234-9399

Printed in the USA

www.avotek.com

PREFACE

Since the first edition of this textbook there have been many advances in the manufacture and use of composite components. There have been fewer advances in the field of composite aircraft repair. Advances in composite repair is largely dependent on the manufacturers to include these advances into the Structural Repair Manuals.

Materials are still not standardized, meaning that there are so many types of materials and resin systems available, stocking enough materials and resin systems for one type of aircraft would be at an enormous cost to the operator or repair station. If the materials were more standardized, the stocking of materials for aircraft repair could be reduced considerably. The actual cost of the materials would also go down, because of less testing and over-testing of the materials, which now takes place with each and every engineer who designs a part constructed with composites.

The FAA has been concerned with the conformity and documentation of parts since the "bogus parts" problems came to the forefront. This increases the cost for many ethical small quantity distributors because there is no part designation of the fabric. The industry could take a lesson from the days of old if they would print the spec number on the selvage edge of rolls of material every 3 feet, as it was required in the days of dope and fabric. Now, information is not always sent with the materials and must be requested separately. Material Safety Data Sheets are often more than 5 years old, making more paperwork problems.

The FAA requires that the expiration date of a material be complied with. Many times there is no expiration date listed. Frequently there is no time limit listed on how much time out of the freezer is allowed.

Recordings of temperature during the cure are sometimes required, but this produces a false sense of security that the part has been repaired correctly. Composite repair is so process dependent that there are many things that could go wrong within the repair procedure that a printout of the cure temperature cannot represent. The process itself should be under scrutiny, not just the recording of the temperature.

There are many misconceptions about what is involved in composite maintenance and repair. Working with composites falls into three categories, Manufacturing, Re-manufacturing, and Repair.

The manufacturing of composites differs greatly from the maintenance of composites, yet many believe the techniques used in manufacturing are also used in maintenance. When composite components are manufactured, the process is accomplished in a number of procedures. Most components that can be repaired are manufactured by laying pre-impregnated fabric onto a mold, many times with a core structure. To cure the part, it is put into an oven or an autoclave to apply extra pressure and heat.

The second category, re-manufacturing or rebuilding a component, is when very large damage has occurred that is outside the limits of the Structural Repair Manual. To re-manufacture a part, molds, vacuum bags, ovens, or autoclaves are also used.

The third category is the repair to composites where the damage is within the limits of the Structural Repair Manual. This is the type of damage that is covered in this book. Frequently the component can be repaired on the aircraft. Repairs such as these differ from remanufacturing. The part is usually cured by vacuum bagging and using hot bonding equipment. These parts are not cured in an oven or autoclave. The manufacturing and rebuilding of composite components is different than repairing composites. Many people tend to think that to repair a composite you need all the equipment that a manufacturer uses. This is completely false.

In ten years of training technicians in advanced composite repair, I have found that with proper training, composites are not hard to work with; they are just different. Learning this simple fact is the primary purpose of this textbook.

Table of Contents

Chapter 1 INTRODUCTION 1-1
What Is A Composite Structure? 1-1

Chapter 2 REINFORCING FIBERS 2-1
Fiberglass 2-2
Aramid 2-3
Carbon/Graphite 2-4
Boron 2-5
Ceramic 2-6
Fiber Science 2-7
Fiber Orientation 2-8
Glass Fiber Terminology 2-10
Aramid Fiber Terminology 2-10
Carbon/Graphite Tows 2-10
Fabric Styles 2-10

Chapter 3 MATRIX MATERIALS 3-1
Matrix Systems 3-1
Thermoplastic 3-1
Thermosets 3-2
Working With Resins & Catalysts 3-7
Pre-Impregnated Materials 3-11
Resin Systems Used On Some Pre-preg Materials 3-15
Adhesives 3-15
Fillers 3-17
Metal Matrix Composites 3-18

Chapter 4 CORE MATERIALS 4-1
Honeycomb 4-3
Foams 4-4
Wood Cores 4-6

Chapter 5 MANUFACTURING 5-1
Heat & Pressure 5-2
Manufacturing Methods..................................5-2
Molds Or Tooling 5-6
Lightning Protection 5-12
Electrical Bonding 5-13
Painting The Composite Part 5-14

Chapter 6 COMPOSITE SAFETY 6-1
Material Safety Data Sheets 6-1
Personal Safety With Chemicals and Matrices 6-5

Solvents: Usage And Safety 6-7
Use & Storage of Matrix Materials 6-8
Personal Safety While Machining 6-11

Chapter 7 APPLYING PRESSURE 7-1
Methods 7-1
Vacuum Bagging Process 7-4

Chapter 8 METHODS OF CURING 8-1
Room Temperature Curing 8-1
Heat Curing 8-1
Heating Equipment 8-5

Chapter 9 MACHINING COMPOSITES 9-1
Cutting Uncured Fabrics 9-1
Machining Cured Composites 9-2
Fasteners 9-6
Sanding 9-15
Trimming Cured Laminates 9-16

Chapter 10 SETTING UP SHOP 10-1
Facilities Required 10-2
Cost Considerations 10-6
Tools and Equipment 10-7
Training 10-11

Chapter 11 ASSESSMENT & REPAIR 11-1
Classification of Damage 11-1
Types of Damage 11-4
Inspection Methodology 11-5
Repair Operation 11-9
Repair Procedures 11-12
Lightning Protection 11-35
Recording Your Work 11-38

Chapter 12 TYPES OF REPAIR 12-1
Repair Failures 12-2
Typical Repair Procedures 12-2
Delaminations 12-7
Damage to Laminate Structures .12-10
Repairs to Sandwich Structures .12-18
Propeller Repairs 12-31
Homebuilt Aircraft Repairs 12-31
Author's Note 12-33

COMPOSITE TERMINOLOGY .G-1

Chapter 1
Introduction

The use of composite materials for aircraft manufacturing has elicited a variety of reactions among members of the aviation industry.

- Aircraft manufacturers hail composites as a very durable, highly manufacturable material.

- Aircraft owners regard the new composite aircraft as lightweight and more cost effective than their metal counterparts.

- Aircraft technicians all too often regard composites as either another name for traditional fiberglass, or as a mystery material only engineers can understand.

Composite materials are quickly becoming recognized as the most advanced substance for fabrication of aircraft parts. Composite structures are made from a combination of fabrics, fibers, foams, and honeycomb materials bonded by a matrix or resin system.

WHAT IS A COMPOSITE STRUCTURE?

The term composite is used to describe two or more materials that are combined to form a structure that is much stronger than the individual components. The simplest composite is composed of two elements: a matrix that serves as a bonding substance, and a reinforcing material.

Prior to combination, the matrix is generally in liquid form and the reinforcing material is a solid. Many times a core material is also added. All of these materials are combined and cured to make a structure that is stronger than each was originally.

The concept of composite materials is not new. The oldest man-made building material, adobe, is a composite formula. Adobe is produced by combining two dissimilar components, mud and straw, to form building bricks. After the bricks are cured in the sun, the resulting building block is substantially stronger and more durable than the original components were alone. The centuries old ruins of the Anasazi Indians in southwestern Colorado bear eloquent testimony to the durability of this simple composite material.

A more contemporary example of composite material is the traditional dope and fabric airplane. In this instance, nitrate or butyrate dope is combined in proper proportions with *grade A* cotton fabric, producing a strong, lightweight skin covering. The strength and simplicity of the dope and fabric airplane has endured through the years and is still a favorite airframe material for hand-crafted classic and high-performance aerobatic airplanes. The smooth lines and meticulous workmanship of the dope and fabric airplane can be seen in such high-performance airplanes as the Stinson, Beech Staggerwing and the Christen Eagle, all of which perform at summer air shows throughout the world. [Figure 1-1]

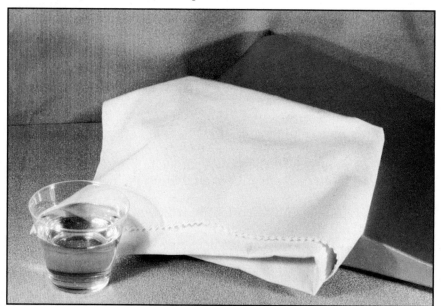

Figure 1-1. Dope and fabric is a type of composite material that is still in use today.

World War II fighters and early airliners, such as the DC-3, used dope and fabric materials on control surfaces such as elevators, rudders, and ailerons. The technology of composite materials progressed with the introduction of Butyrate dope, fiberglass, and polyester resins. In the 1940s and 1950s, fiberglass fabric was impregnated with polyester resin and used for fairings, radomes, and other nonstructural components. In the 1950s, epoxy resins were introduced and have been used very successfully with fiberglass reinforcing materials.

Fiberglass parts were found to reduce the weight of an aircraft considerably when used to replace their metal counterparts. Fiberglass parts have been used in such places as wing tips, radomes, tail cones, and many other nonstructural parts. The success of these lightweight parts lead to the increased use of composites on newer models of airplanes. For example, the 747 has over 10,000 surface square feet of fiberglass composite structure.

When carbon/graphite was introduced as a reinforcing material in the early 1960s, a minor resurgence in the use of new composites occured. Carbon/graphite composites were used experimentally and on military aircraft during the 1960s and 1970s. Now, it is a very common advanced composite building material. Kevlar®, an aramid fiber material, was first produced in the 1970s and is now found extensively in many aircraft. Concurrent with the development of new reinforcing materials has been the development of new chemical bonding formulas that create improved matrix materials.

During recent years, many manufacturers, working with development grants from the government, have made major advancements in the fields of structural science. The resulting new developments in materials technology have made it possible to design and build aircraft that perform better and operate more efficiently than previously thought possible.

Aviation composites technology has advanced to the point that it is strong enough to be used in primary airframe components. In some cases whole airframe assemblies are constructed of advanced composite materials. It can be seen then that as more manufacturers equip their aircraft with composite parts, the need for trained aviation technicians to fabricate, inspect, and maintain these aircraft also increases.

Advanced composites have evolved as a result of combining developments in chemical bonding formulas with new or existing forms of solid structural materials to form the high-strength lightweight components used structurally in aircraft. These components may sometimes be referred to as a Fiber Reinforced Plastic, or FRP. This term is not widely used with the general public, as people do not want to think they are flying in plastic airplanes. Plastic, (which is actually what the resin matrix material is made of) has the bad connotation of cheap little toys that break into millions of pieces. Because of this, the term composite or advanced composite is used with the public.

A common misconception of advanced composites is that they can be repaired in the same way as the older fiberglass structures. A very dangerous temptation in the industry has been to relegate composite repairs to the fiberglass shop. Fiberglass, in the past, has been used mostly for nonstructural components such as fairings, spinners, etc..

It makes sense to repair a composite component instead of scrapping it, even if the damage is substantial. The damage may be so extensive that it exceeds the limits stated in the structural repair manual, but to send it out to a re-manufacturing facility will save money over purchasing a new component. If you compare the cost of repairing the damage against the cost of materials and labor involved in fabricating a new component, it is usually more economical to repair the component.

The newer advanced composites use stronger fabrics and resin matrices, which cannot be repaired in the same way as fiberglass and still produce the greatest strength. To repair an advanced composite part using the materials and techniques that have traditionally been used for fiberglass repairs may result in an unairworthy repair because such traditional repairs allow for excessive weight, increased susceptibility to material fatigue, and decreased flexibility.

Advanced composites are being used structurally because of their strength and adaptability to withstand stresses. These composites differ in the repair procedures because the part must replace the structural integrity of the component. Excessive weight should not be added by applying excessive resin material, and the drilling of holes into a composite structure can weaken the load carrying characteristics of the fibers. The fabric type, weave, and positioning of the fabric patches are extremely important in distributing the stresses imposed on a repair.

Again, proper training and a strong understanding of the type of structure you are working with are very important. Follow all manufacturer's instructions carefully, using the proper materials and procedures.

ADVANTAGES

The greatest advantage of using composites is the high strength-to-weight ratio. Since weight is one of the key considerations for the use of any material in aircraft construction, if it can be saved, more cargo, fuel or passengers can be carried.

A composite part can be designed as strong as a metal part, but with considerable weight savings. Typically, 20 percent or more weight reductions are achieved when aluminum parts are replaced with composite structures.

When designing with composite materials, the weight savings are the primary pursuit. However, the composites also lend themselves well to the formation of complex, aerodynamically contoured shapes. The parts do not have to be flat, but can have smooth, sweeping contours that would be difficult and expensive to fabricate from sheet metal. The reduced drag produced by these contoured shapes, in combination with the weight savings, enables an aircraft's range to be extended significantly.

The number of parts and fasteners may be reduced by the use of composites, as well, simplifying construction and reducing cost. In some cases, very large structures can be manufactured in one piece, eliminating the riveting and seams.

Composites are becoming increasingly cost effective as materials and manufacturing technologies mature. Composites may be designed to be very flexible, resisting vibrations, thus eliminating the problem of stress fatigue found in metal structures.

Composites don't corrode like metal does, either. However, they do have their own problems, which will be discussed in later chapters. Many people talk as if composites are indestructible. If this were the case, a book on the repair to composites would not have to be written, as they would never fail or break.

Reduced wear is another advantage of using composites. Composites will flex in flight without producing stress cracks like metal. For example, helicopter rotor blades in flight have many stresses imposed on them. When made of composites, the wear is less, because the fibers can take the bending and twisting forces without developing metal fatigue.

Many articles written on composite materials state that a composite part can be built many times stronger than a metal part. This is true, but when working with aircraft components, weight is also a very big factor. If the part has as sufficient strength as a metal component, the composite part can be made with the same strength while saving considerable weight.

If you are using composite materials to build something other than an aircraft, such as a bridge, weight would not be an issue and the component could be made many times stronger than metal. The strength of the composite depends on the type of fibers used, the bonding materials used, and how the part is engineered to take specific stresses.

In short, composites are years ahead of traditional aluminum alloy and are the closest thing yet to an ideal aircraft material.

USES

Composites today are being used throughout the world. On helicopters, military aircraft, commercial aircraft and homebuilts. Composites are being used in the powerplants as well as the airframe designs. This book concentrates on the airframe uses of composites. European and other foreign aircraft manufacturers may be utilizing more composite materials in their designs than American designers, but this difference in design philosophy may be due in part to the more conservative policies of the American Federal Aviation Administration (FAA).

Military

The military has been using composites longer than the civilian market. Many military helicopters and aircraft are presently using composite components, however, only the more exceptional aircraft will be included in this section. Boron, a common composite material used in many military applications, is expensive and very dangerous to work with. Many accidents have occurred from mishandling Boron. Because of this, civilian aviation manufacturers shy away from the use of Boron. However, it is still used to construct a variety of components on many military aircraft. [Figure 1-2 on page 1-6]

COMPONENT	MANUFACTURER	METAL EQUIVALENT	WEIGHT SAVINGS%	STATUS
F-15 Horizontal and Vertical Stabilizers Boron Epoxy 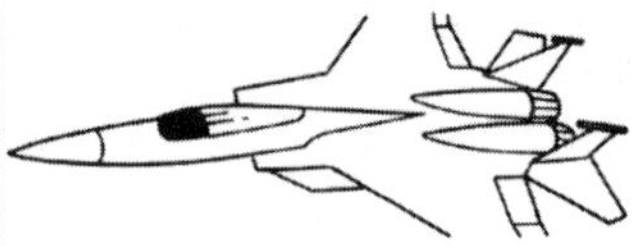	McDonnell-Douglas Mitsubishi Heavy Industies	Titanium	22% Estimated	Production
F-14 Horizontal Stabilizer Boron Epoxy 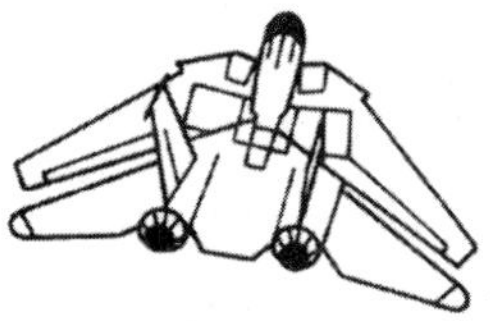	Grumman Aerospace Corp.	Titanium	19%	Production
B-1B Reinforced Longeron Boron Epoxy 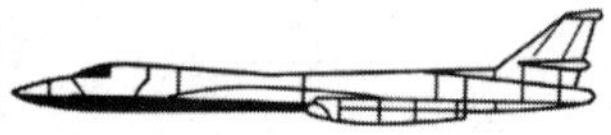	Rockwell International	Steel-Titanium	44%	Production

Figure 1-2. Boron composite aerospace applications.

Figure 1-3 shows the construction of the F-14 horizontal stabilizer, which uses boron materials primarily in the stabilizer skin panels.

ACAP

The objectives of the U.S. Army's Advanced Composites Airframe program, or ACAP, were to achieve a 22 percent weight reduction and a 17 percent cost reduction using an all composite airframe on U.S. Army helicopters. Under the ACAP program, Bell helicopter produced a successful example using carbon/graphite for the forward roof, bulkheads, cowlings, frame, and beam caps. Kevlar was used in the fuselage shell and outside skins. A hybrid of carbon/graphite and Kevlar was used to construct the nose, canopy, vertical fin, horizontal stabilizer, fuel compartment, bulkheads, and floors. Fiberglass was used for the tail boom skin and cargo floor.

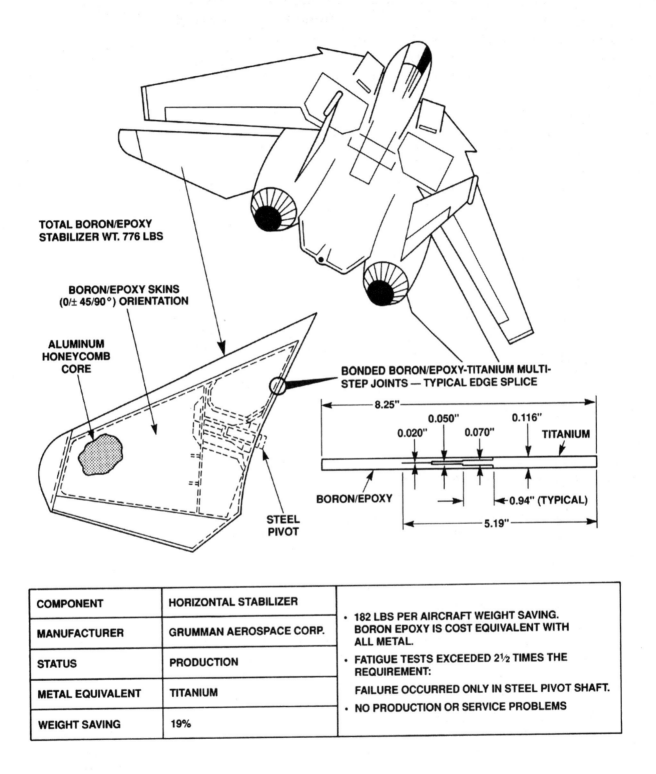

Figure 1-3. F-14 Horizontal stabilizer – *first boron composite production unit.*

Grumman X-29

Grumman's X-29 forward swept wing design requires extraordinary rigidity and torsion resistance. This is accomplished by employing carbon/graphite filament in a complex fiber pattern. In flight, the X-29's aerodynamic forces tend to twist upward on the leading edge. The orientation of the fibers limits the twist and allows the wing to return to its original configuration once the load is removed. [Figure 1-4]

Figure 1-4. The composites used in the forward-swept wing design of the X-29 withstand extraordinary stresses.

If made of traditional sheet metal, the wing could not withstand the imposed stresses. To provide adequate strength, 156 fiber layers are laminated together, with each layer running in slightly different directions. Although it is a thin wing, this design produces a very strong structure that has a very low profile.

AV-8B Harrier

The AV-8B, known as the Harrier, is made of 26 percent (by weight) carbon/graphite and epoxy materials. The Harrier was the first military aircraft with an all-composite wing. [Figure 1-5]

B-2

The B-2 Advanced Technology bomber, known as the Stealth Bomber, is designed for minimum radar detectability. Although the information is still classified, it is believed that the frame and skin are composed of carbon/graphite fiber with epoxy resin to form the composite material.

V-22

The V-22 Osprey was the first tilt-rotor airplane in production. It combines the vertical-lift capabilities of a helicopter with the

Figure 1-5. The AV-8B, known as the Harrier, was the first military aircraft with an all-composite wing.

high-speed fuel efficiencies of a fixed-wing turboprop plane. The V-22's airframe consists of carbon/graphite and epoxy laminate, and its propeller/rotors are an advanced fiberglass composite.

F-22

Twenty-six percent of the F-22 airframe is made of composite components, meaning more than 200 composite parts are manufactured for the aircraft, mostly of carbon and epoxy.

C-17

The C-17 cargo plane, developed for the Air Force, uses approximately 15,000 pounds of composite materials. Of this, 40 percent is carbon fiber, 40 percent is aramid, and 20 percent is fiberglass. These materials are used in the manufacturing of the secondary structures.

AIRLINERS

A large number of commuter airliners are manufactured in foreign countries using many composite components. These airline manufacturers include SAAB, Dornier, Embraer, and Canadaire, among others. The physical size of the components may not be as big as the larger airliners, however, the total amount of composites is quite large on these smaller airliners.

L-1011

Lockheed's use of composites on the L-1011 consists of 1,300 pounds of woven fabric for the fairings, ailerons, vertical stabilizer, leading edges of the wings, and other components.

Lockheed succeeded in recognizing substantial weight savings in the L-1011 by using composites to fabricate the vertical fin. The composite part reduced the weight by 28 percent as compared to the metal counterpart, and a lower cost was achieved by reducing the number of internal ribs and fasteners. [Figure 1-6]

	Aluminum	Composite
Weight	858	622
Number of ribs	17	11
Number of parts	716	191
Number of fasteners	40,371	6,311
Weight savings of 28%		

Figure 1-6. L-1011 composite vertical fin compared to an aluminum fin. The composite fin uses fewer parts and is easier to assemble, while also being lighter than the aluminum fin.

Boeing

Boeing's use of composites in the past has been mainly with ailerons, elevators, rudders, and spoilers. Boeing is now using carbon/graphite, hybrid mixtures, and Kevlar for most of their newer applications. Boeing was the first to use a carbon spoiler and the first to use Nomex® honeycomb on their aircraft.

Boeing 737

The Boeing 737 uses approximately 1,500 pounds of composite material, providing a weight savings of approximately 600 pounds when compared to conventional sheet metal construction. Composites of graphite, Kevlar, fiberglass, and hybrids of these materials are used in the secondary flight control surfaces, fairings, landing gear doors, and interior paneling. [Figure 1-7]

Boeing 757

The Boeing 757 uses composite materials in almost all of their secondary structural components, which has increased fuel efficiency dramatically. Graphite/epoxy is used on primary control surfaces and spoilers. Hybrids of Graphite/Kevlar are used on the access panels, undercarriage doors, wing/fuselage fairings, and cowlings.

The design of the 757 saved 1,000 pounds per aircraft by using advanced composite components. Substantial amounts of composite material are used structurally as a replacement for aluminum.

Boeing 767

For the Boeing 767, fiberglass reinforced plastics are used on the main deck floor panels, radome, and the fixed leading edge panels. Fiberglass is used for its light-weight, sonic and buffet resistance, and corrosion resistance. [Figure 1-8, 1-9 and 1-10].

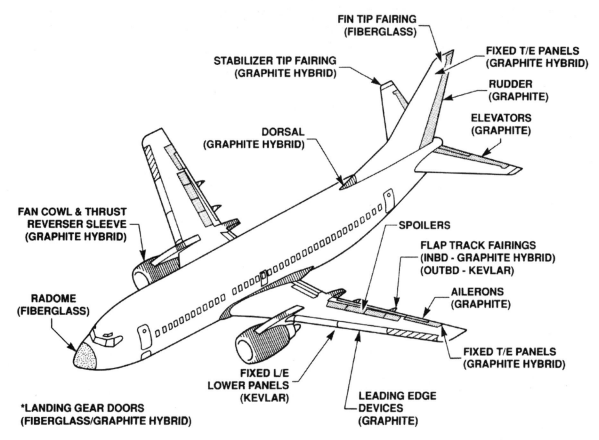

Figure 1-7. Composite materials on the Boeing 737-300.

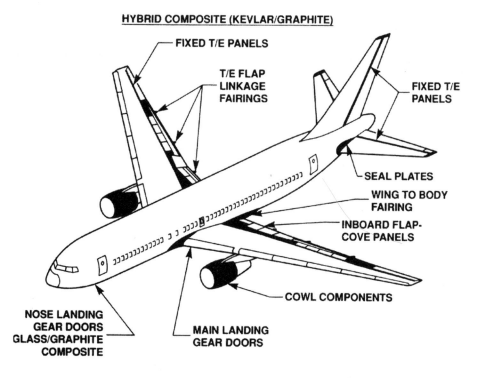

Figure 1-8. Hybrid composite use on the Boeing 767. A hybrid is formed by combining two or more types of reinforcing materials into a composite structure.

1-11

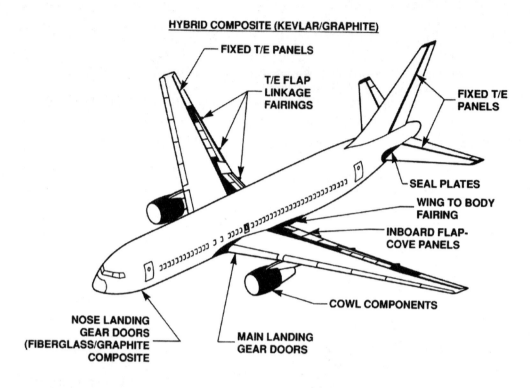

Figure 1-9. Graphite/Epoxy use on Boeing 767.

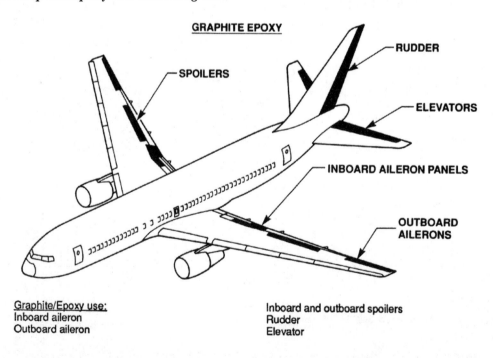

Figure 1-10. Kevlar use on Boeing 767.

The flooring construction of the 767 varies with location and application. Under the seat area, a Nomex core with fiberglass reinforced plastic is used as the skin. The main aisles and galleys use a higher density of Nomex core, but with the same fiberglass reinforced skins. These floors are corrosion resistant panels, which have been sealed in the entry-ways, galleys, and lavatories. The floor panels are replaceable without removing any major components (galleys, lavatories, etc.). The lavatory floors are reinforced for extra strength. [Figure 1-11 and 1-12]

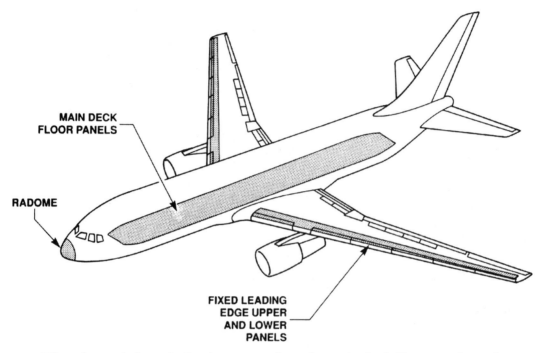

Figure 1-11. Fiberglass reinforced plastics are used on the main deck floor panels, radome, and the fixed leading edge panels.

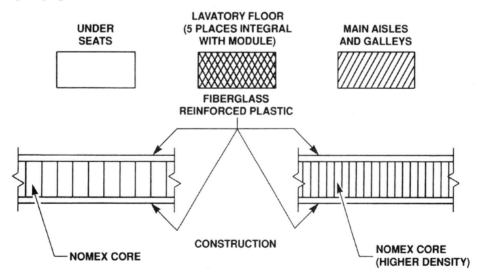

Figure 1-12. The flooring construction of the 767 varies with location and application.

BOEING 777

The newest of the Boeing fleet, the 777, uses composites for 9 percent of its structural weight as compared to about 3 percent on other Boeing Jets. The 777 has a 43 foot tall composite vertical fin box made of carbon and fiberglass. It also utilizes carbon fiber floor beams throughout the fuselage. The engine cowlings are made of carbon fiber and epoxy skins covering a core of Nomex honeycomb. [Figure 1-13]

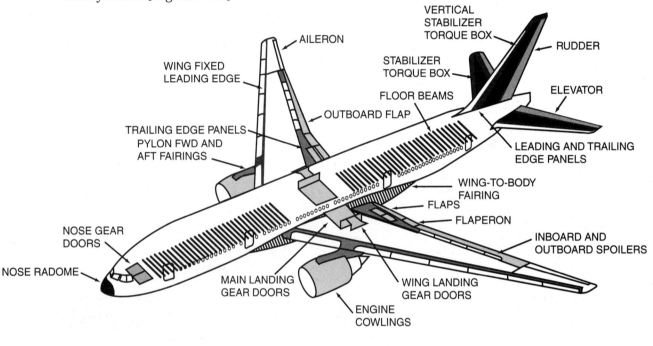

Figure 1-13. Composite material use in the Boeing 777-200.

AIRBUS

The Airbus 300, 310, and 320 are a joint effort of British Aerospace and Aerospatiale. Extensive amounts of Nomex, graphite, and Kevlar are used on the control surfaces as well as other components.

Composites were first introduced on the Airbus by using fiberglass reinforced plastic components. In 1978, carbon fiber components were tried on the A399 and later removed for extensive testing and evaluation. This led to the use of carbon fiber on their aircraft.

Aramid and carbon are used extensively on the A310-200. All new Airbus models now include an all carbon-fiber vertical fin.

The new A300-600 utilizes composites on the radome, nose landing gear doors, outer wing trailing edge, as well as other traditional areas such as the rudder, airbrakes and spoilers, main landing gear doors, thrust reversers, and fan cowl.

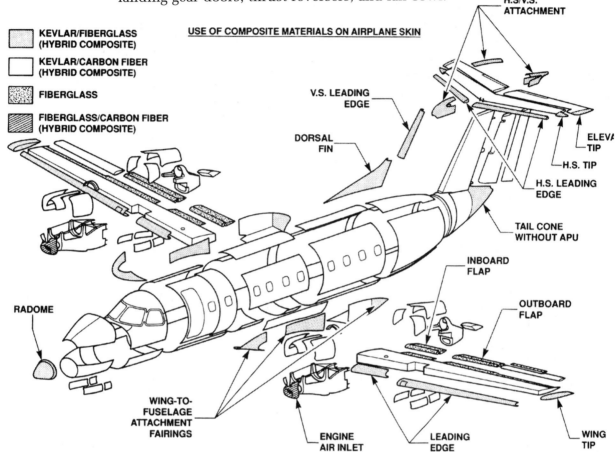

Figure 1-14. Embraer EMB 120 Brasilia composite material application.

BUSINESS JETS

Composite materials are used on many secondary structures and flight control surfaces. Fiberglass, carbon fiber, and Kevlar are used, as well as hybrid materials. Sandwich structures of Nomex honeycomb core are used extensively on the aircraft.

Composite materials used on the Saab SF 340 are used extensively. Kevlar and Nomex sandwich structures are used on the flap leading edge, trailing edge, flap cove, nacelle heat/ex. fairing, aileron skin, aileron trim tabs, aileron tab control fairing, elevator skin, elevator trailing edge, elevator fairings, elevator trim tabs and fairings, rudder skin, rudder cove, rudder leading edge, rudder trim tab and fairings, wing/fuselage fairing and doors, and main landing gear doors. Kevlar laminate is used on the aileron cove, flap hinge fairing, radar door, dorsal fairing, and tail cap. The propeller blades are fabricated of fiberglass skins with laminated carbon fiber spars, with a core of polyurethane foam. [Figure 1-14 and 1-15]

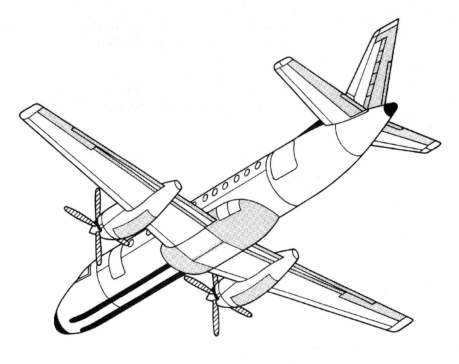

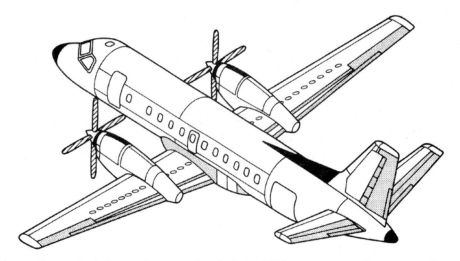

Figure 1-15. Composite materials used on the Saab Fairchild 340 are used extensively.

HELICOPTERS

Sikorsky's S-76 helicopter uses thermoset matrix around extensive amounts of Kevlar sheet and Kevlar honeycomb. This conserves weight while providing a vibration dampening effect. Sixty percent of the total airframe is considered composite. The main and tail rotors are made of fiberglass with a honeycomb core and are considered bearingless rotors.

Kevlar 49 is used and saves about 30 percent in the weight of the S-76 airframe components. The first production line S-76 was delivered in February of 1979.

The Sikorsky UH-60, or the Blackhawk, uses 400 lb. of Kevlar/carbon. It has a composite rear fuselage, carbon main rotor blades, and composite rotor head.

The Bell Helicopter Model 222 main rotor is made of fiberglass/Nomex.

By refitting the CH-53 Super Stallion with composites, a 40% cost reduction was possible. Using composite materials eliminated approximately 10,000 fasteners.

Chapter 2
Reinforcing Fibers

When combined with a matrix, the reinforcing fibers give the primary strength to the composite structure. There are three common types of reinforcing fibers: fiberglass, aramid, and carbon/graphite. Other fibers that aren't quite as common include ceramic and boron. All of these fibers can be used in combination with one another (hybrids), woven in specific patterns (fiber science), in combination with other materials such as rigid foams (sandwich structures), or simply in combination with various matrix materials. Each particular composite combination provides specific advantages. The following information details each of the five common types of reinforcing fibers and their characteristics. [Figure 2-1]

Figure 2-1. Each reinforcing fiber comes in a variety of weaves and may be used in combination with other materials to produce the desired result.

FIBERGLASS (GLASS CLOTH)

Fiberglass is made from small strands of molten silica glass (about 2,300° F) that are spun together and woven into cloth. Glass fibers are somewhat fragile, so a sizing is used as a protective shield during the weaving process. After it is woven, the sizing may be removed, and a finish applied, which makes the fibers more compatible with the matrix or resin system to be used. There are many different weaves of fiberglass available, depending on the particular application. Its widespread availability and its low cost make fiberglass one of the most popular reinforcing fibers. [Figure 2-2]

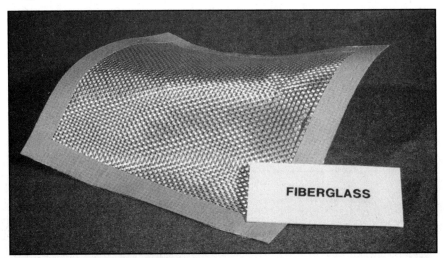

Figure 2-2. Fiberglass can be recognized as a white gleaming cloth. It is considered to be the most economic reinforcing fiber of advanced composites.

Fiberglass weighs more than most other composite fibers, but has less strength. In the past, fiberglass was used for nonstructural applications; the weave was heavy and polyester resins were used, making the part brittle. Recently, however, newly developed matrix formulas have increased the benefits of using fiberglass.

The three common types of fiberglass are E-glass, S-glass (S2-glass), and C-glass. In structural applications, E-glass and S-glass are the most common.

E-glass, also known as "electric glass" for its high electrical resistance, is a borosilicate glass commonly used for reinforcement because of its low cost and good strength characteristics.

S-glass is a magnesia-alumina-silicate glass that is up to 40 percent stronger than E-glass and retains its strength characteristics at higher temperatures. S-glass is used where a very high tensile strength fiberglass is needed.

C-glass is used in materials that require chemical resistance.

When used with the newer types of matrices and with the proper use of fiber sciences, fiberglass is one of the best reinforcing fibers used in today's advanced composite applications. Some of the new fiberglass composites compare favorably in terms of strength to weight ratios with traditional aluminum materials. By using some very clever methods of combining fiberglass with other, more expensive fibers, such as Kevlar® or carbon/graphite, a hybrid material can be produced that yields a low cost, high-strength material. This mixing of fibers to form hybrids is an exacting science that allows very little room for error.

ARAMID

An aramid, or aromatic polyamide fiber, is usually characterized by its yellow color, light weight, tensile strength, and remarkable flexibility. Kevlar® is a registered trademark of the EI DuPont Company and is the best-known and most widely used aramid. Kevlar will ordinarily stretch a great deal before it breaks. The tensile strength of alloyed aluminum is about 65,000 psi, or about one-fourth that of Kevlar composite. However, the objective in aviation is not necessarily to have a stronger part, but rather to have a part that weighs much less. By using a Kevlar reinforcing fiber, a component can be fabricated with the strength of a metal counterpart, at a fraction of the weight. [Figure 2-3]

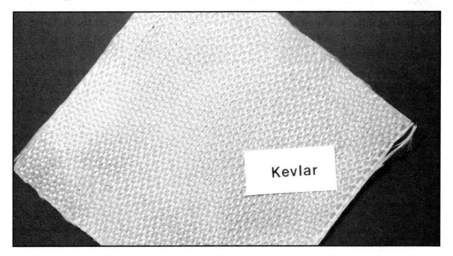

Figure 2-3. Kevlar is the most widely used aramid fiber. It has a tensile strength approximately four times that of aluminum alloy. As with most reinforcing fibers, Kevlar comes in various grades and weaves for different uses.

The aircraft structural grade of Kevlar fiber is known as Kevlar 49. Kevlar 29 is used for boats and Kevlar 129 is bulletproof material. A common misconception about Kevlar is that if Kevlar fabric is bulletproof, and an aircraft is made with Kevlar, then the aircraft is bulletproof. Bulletproof vest's made with Kevlar are typically made of a different weave, weight, and process than aircraft-type

Kevlar. A bulletproof vest also omits the matrix, which makes a part more brittle. A bulletproof vest is made with multiple layers of Kevlar fabric, which will stretch as the bullet impacts the fabric, preventing penetration.

Aramid is an ideal material for use in aircraft parts that are subject to high stress and vibration. For example, some advanced helicopter designs have made use of aramid to fabricate main rotor blades and hub assemblies. The flexibility of the aramid fabric allows the blade to bend and twist in flight, absorbing much of the stress. In contrast, a blade made of metal develops fatigue and stress cracks more frequently under the same conditions.

Aramid materials also have their drawbacks. Because aramid stretches, it can cause problems when it is cut. Drilling aramid, for example, can be a problem when the drill bit grabs a fiber and stretches it to the breaking point instead of cutting it. This material will look fuzzy. If the fuzzing material around fastener holes or seams is not sealed, it may act as a wick and absorb moisture. The moisture, in the form of water, oil, fuel, or hydraulic fluid, probably won't damage the aramid fibers, but it may cause problems with the resin system by causing them to deteriorate, causing layers of laminates to separate. The fuzzing around the drilled hole may also prevent a fastener from seating properly, which may cause the fastened joint to fail.

Some manufacturers recommend using fiberglass to repair aramid material because even a slight amount of moisture will prevent aramid from bonding properly. To combat any extra moisture in the fabric, the raw fabric may be vacuum bagged to dry out any excess moisture. Although aramid exhibits great tensile strength, it does not have as much compressive strength as carbon/graphite composites.

CARBON / GRAPHITE

Carbon fiber, also known as graphite fiber, is a very strong, stiff reinforcement. For many years, American manufacturers used the term graphite, while European manufacturers used the term carbon. Carbon correctly describes the fiber since it contains no graphite structure. Regardless of what you call it, you order it by number. If you order Carbon #584 you will get the same weight and weave as if you order Graphite #584. It is the same material. Some structural repair manuals may call for Carbon #584 in one area, and Graphite #584 in another. Recently, Carbon has become the favored term by both American and European manufacturers. There are still many structural repair manuals however, that use the term Graphite, so understanding that this material can be referred to in either way is still important to the maintenance technician.

This black fiber is very strong, stiff, and used for its rigid strength characteristics. Carbon/graphite fiber composites are used to fabricate primary structural components, such as ribs and wing skins. Even very large aircraft can be designed with a reduced number of reinforcing bulkheads, ribs, and stringers, thanks to the high strength and high rigidity of carbon fiber composites. Carbon/graphite is stronger in compressive strength than Kevlar, but it is more brittle. [Figure 2-4]

Carbon fibers are electrically conductive, have low thermal expansion coefficients, and have high fatigue resistance. The impact resistance of carbon fibers is less than some other composite materials, and may splinter or crack with high impact.

At one time, because of its conductivity, manufacturers didn't require lightning or static protection on the carbon fiber components. However, after many problems, the carbon components used today incorporate some kind of lightning protection. (See more in Chapter 12)

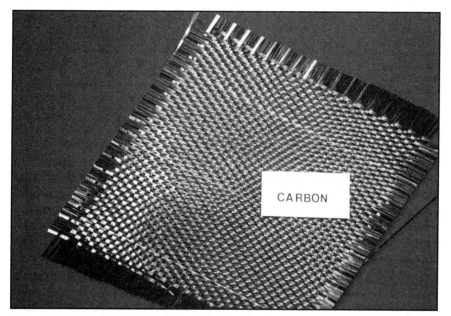

Figure 2-4. Carbon/Graphite. While the correct name is carbon, it is often referred to as graphite; frequently in the same publication. Whichever name is used, it is the same material.

Carbon/graphite has the problem of being corrosive when bonded to aluminum. Special corrosion control techniques are employed when carbon/graphite materials are in contact with aluminum components. Usually, a layer of fiberglass is used as a barrier, and the aluminum is anodized, primed, and painted prior to assembly.

BORON

Boron fibers are made by depositing the element boron onto a thin filament of tungsten. The resulting fiber is about .004-inch in diameter, has excellent compressive strength and stiffness, and is extremely hard. Because boron can be hazardous to work with, along with its high expense, it is not commonly used in civil aviation. Boron fibers were first used in the early 1960's for military application of the F-14, F-15, and B-1.

Boron fibers usually come in a unidirectional prepreg material. Boron composites have very high strength and stiffness in tension, compression, and bending stresses. The extent of these strengths, however, depends on the type of fiber science designed into the part.

At one time, boron fibers were used to see if they could help extend the life of the aging aircraft fleet. When aluminum wing skins developed tiny stress cracks, boron patches were bonded to the aluminum to prevent further cracking.

In designing a composite component that needs both strength and stiffness associated with boron, many civil aviation manufacturers are utilizing hybrid composite materials of aramid and carbon/graphite, instead of boron.

CERAMIC

Ceramic fibers are used when a high temperature application is needed. This form of composite retains most of its strength and flexibility at temperatures up to 2,200°F. The tiles on the space shuttle, for example, are made of a special ceramic composite that is heat resistant and dissipates heat quickly. Firewalls are often made of ceramic fiber composites to dissipate the heat. Ceramic fibers are often also used with a metal matrix.

FIBER USAGE

As composite materials gain use, new reinforcing fibers may be developed. Currently, the most frequently used reinforcing fibers are fiberglass, aramid, and carbon. This book focuses on the most common types of reinforcing fibers used in the aviation community.

Figure 2-5 is a chart of the different types of materials and their current uses, as well as their projected use in the coming years. Notice that boron is the only fiber that is declining in use. [Figure 2-5]

FIBER PLACEMENT

The strength of a reinforcing material in a matrix is dependent on the weave of the material, the wetting process (how the matrix is applied), filament tensile strength, and the design of the part.

Many books and articles report the tensile strengths of fabrics, but these numbers represent the raw fabric without the resin that is added during the wetting process. Since the aviation community

ITEM	1977	1987	1992 (estimate)	2000 (estimate)
Composite Materials	2,265	24,045	49,000	120,000
Aircraft/Aerospace	1,079	16,879	34,900	85,500
TYPES OF FIBERS				
Carbon/Graphite	532	4,953	10,800	28,530
Aramid	361	4,716	8,670	18,780
Boron	31	15	10	8
Other	2	8	20	82

Figure 2-5. U.S. demand for advanced composite fibers and materials (thousand lbs.).

uses composites that contain a resin material, the tensile strength decreases because the resins make the structure more brittle, causing it to break at a lower tensile strength.

To find the amount of strength in a laminate that is 50 percent fibers and 50 percent resin, add the tensile strength of the fibers to the tensile strength of the resin, and divide by two. This information is not really required by technicians, but it will give you an idea how strong the part may become.

$$\frac{275,000 + 20,000}{2} = 147,500 \text{ PSI}$$

FIBER SCIENCE

The selective placement of fibers needed to obtain the greatest amount of strength in various applications is known as fiber science. The strength and stiffness of a composite depend on the orientation of the plies to the load direction. A sheet metal component will have the same strength no matter which direction it is loaded.

For example, a helicopter rotor blade has high stress along its length because of centripetal forces. If the blade is made of metal, the strength is the same in all directions, giving strength in directions that are not needed. If fabricated of composites, however, the blade may have the majority of fibers running through its length to give more strength in the direction in which the most stress is concentrated. These vectors of strength might be referred to as zero degree plies (to react to axial loads like those to which a rotor blade is subjected), 45° plies (to react to shear vectors), or 90° plies (to react to side loads).

For example, if a wing in flight bends up as well as twists, the part can be manufactured so one layer of fibers runs the length of the wing, reducing the bending tendency, and another layer with the fibers running at 45° and at 90°, to limit the twist. Each layer may have the major fibers running in a different direction. The strength of the fibers are parallel to the direction the threads run. This is how designers can customize fiber direction for the type of stress the part might encounter. [Figure 2-6]

Figure 2-6. In flight, the structure tends to bend and twist. The fiber layers are laid in a way to limit the forces, thereby customizing a part to the type of stresses encountered.

Another example, the X-29 forward-swept wing experimental jet fighter, required extremely strong wings to withstand the aerodynamic forces that caused wing failure on similar all-metal aircraft. In order to withstand these multidirectional stresses, the wings were produced with 156 layers of unidirectional carbon/graphite and designed to use multidirectional fiber orientation.

FIBER ORIENTATION

Some of the terms used to describe fiber orientation are:

WARP

The threads that run the length of the fabric as it comes off the bolt are referred to as the warp. The warp direction is designated at 0°. In a woven application, there are typically more threads woven into the warp than the fill direction. Ultimately, a material is stronger in the warp direction than in the fill direction.

Since the warp direction is often critical in fabricating or repairing composites, it may be identified by inserting another type of thread at periodic intervals. The plastic backing on the underside of materials that have been pre-impregnated with resins (pre-pregs) may also be marked to identify the warp threads.

WEFT (FILL)

Weft threads are those that run perpendicular to the warp fibers. They are designated as 90°. The weft, or fill, threads are the threads that interweave with the warp threads.

SELVAGE EDGE

A tightly woven edge produced by the weaver to prevent the edges from raveling is referred to as the selvage edge. It is parallel to the warp threads. The selvage edge is removed for all fabrication and repair work because the weave is different than the body of the fabric and would not give the same strength as the rest of the fabric.

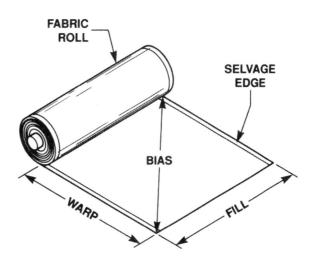

Figure 2-7. All design, manufacturing, and repair work begins with the orientation of the fabric.

BIAS

The bias is at a 45° angle to the warp threads. Fabric can be formed into contoured shapes by using the bias. Fabrics can often be stretched along the bias but seldom stretched along the warp or weft. This is important to keep in mind when it is necessary to wrap a fabric around a contoured shape. [Figure 2-7]

GLASS FIBER TERMINOLOGY

Glass fibers have two numbers that designate how the yarn is made. The strand count designates how many hundreds of yards of glass strand there are in a pound. The second number designates the number of strands that are twisted and plied together to make up the yarn, which is then woven into a specific style. An example of a yarn count might be 450 1/2. The first number set "450" means that the strand count of each strand is 450 X 100 yards, or 45,000 yards per pound. The 1/ indicates that there is just one strand, and the /2 indicates that two of these groups are plied together to make the final yarn. So, 1/2 indicates a yarn comprised of two single strands that have been twisted together to make a yarn. There are also number designations, which indicate the fabric style and weave. These will be discussed later in this chapter.

ARAMID (KEVLAR®) FIBER TERMINOLOGY

Aramid, or Kevlar, yarns are designated by the yarn denier. The Denier is a numbering system that designates how many grams 9000 meters of yarn weighs. Kevlar 49 yarn, which is aircraft quality, may have a designation of 1140de, which means that 9,000 meters of the Kevlar 49 yarn weighs 1140 grams. Aramid yarns are not twisted and plied as fiberglass yarns are.

CARBON/GRAPHITE TOWS

Carbon/Graphite yarns are designated in tows. A tow is a bundle of continuous carbon fiber filaments. Carbon-fiber tows are designated by the number of continuous filaments that make up the fiber bundle. A 3K tow means that 3000 carbon fiber filaments make up the tow. Carbon fiber tows usually do not have twist.

FABRIC STYLES

Materials used in aircraft construction are commonly found in three styles: a non-woven unidirectional fabric, woven fabric, or a mat.

UNIDIRECTIONAL

Fiber orientation in which all of the major fibers run in one direction, giving strength in that direction, are known as unidirectional. This type of fabric is not woven together. In other words, there is no weft. Sometimes, small cross threads are used to hold the major fiber bundles in place, but they are not considered woven together. Most of the time, they come in prepreg form, and the resin/curing agent holds the fibers in place. Occasionally, you may see a strand of a different type of fiber along with the major fiber. This fiber is used to maintain the correct fiber alignment. Unidirectional fabrics may be laminated together with the fibers of each layer running in a different direction than the first layer. [Figure 2-8]

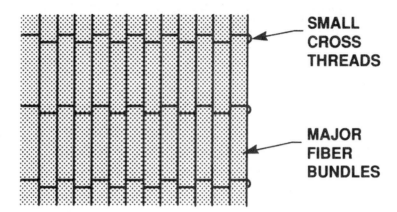

Figure 2-8. Unidirectional materials are constructed with the fibers running in one, uniform direction. The component's greatest strength is parallel to the fiber direction.

Tapes are unidirectional and are usually only made of carbon/graphite material. It is less expensive than fabric and creates a smoother surface. Tapes are sometimes replaced with fabrics for repair work. Unidirectional tapes are usually preimpregnated with resin, because unidirectional materials are difficult to saturate with resin manually.

BIDIRECTIONAL OR MULTIDIRECTIONAL

This type of fiber orientation calls for fibers to run in two or more directions (bidirectional). Usually, these are woven together and may be seen in many different weaves. Again, the warp threads have more fibers woven together than the weft, so it is important to line up the warp threads when doing a repair. In this arrangement, there usually is more strength in the warp direction than in the fill direction. [Figure 2-9]

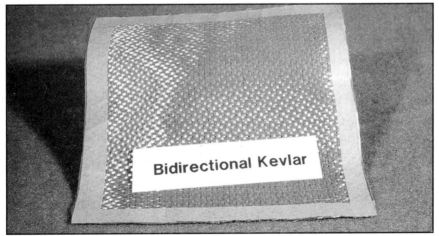

Figure 2-9. The major fiber bundles in bidirectional/multidirectional fabrics are woven in two or more directions.

MATS

Chopped fibers that are compressed together are often called mats. These mats typically are used in combination with other woven or unidirectional layers of fabric. A mat is not as strong as a unidirectional or woven fabric, and therefore is not commonly used in repair work.

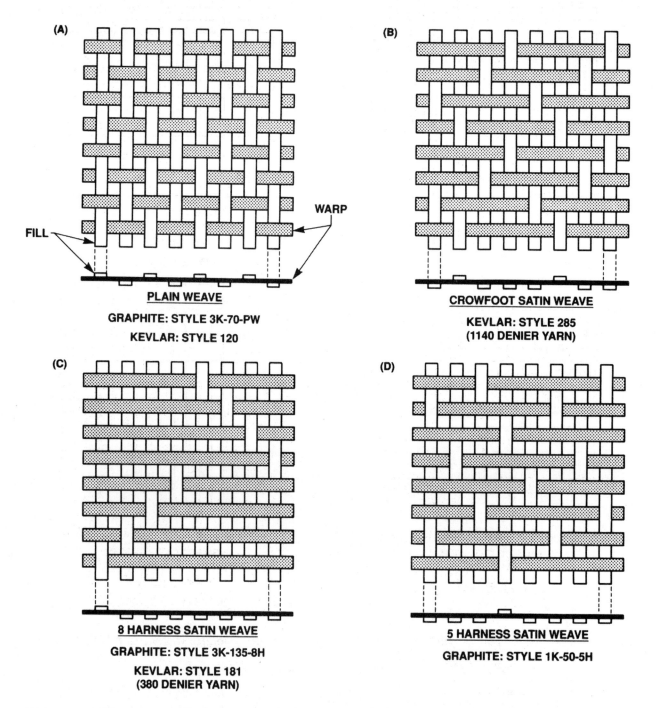

Figure 2-10. *The structural repair manual states which style fabric to use for a given repair.*

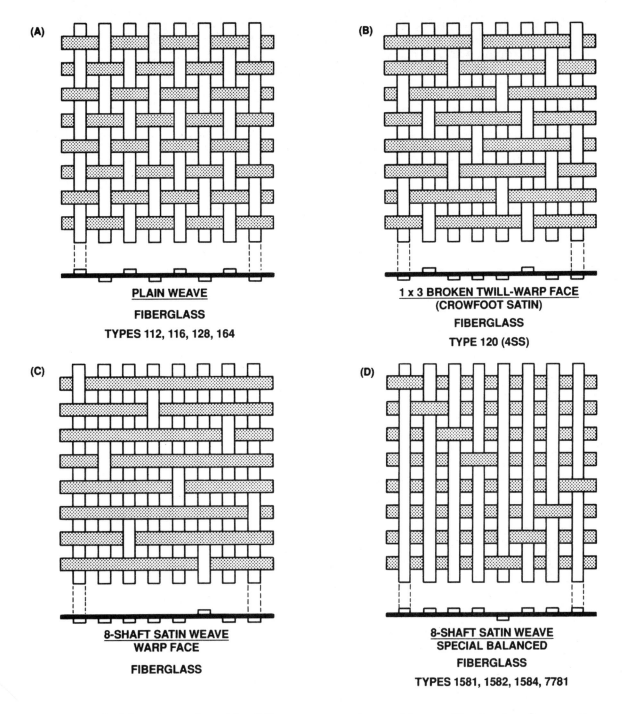

Figure 2-11. Each fabric is produced in different weaves to provide specific structural properties.

WOVEN FABRIC WEAVES

Fabrics are woven together in a number of weaves and weights. Fabrics are more resistant to fiber breakout, delamination, and more damage tolerant than unidirectional material. [Figures 2-10 and 2-11]

The most common weaves used in advanced composite aircraft construction are the plain and satin weaves. The Plain weave is a simple pattern in which the warp and fill yarns alternate over and under each other. Plain weave fabrics are popular for wet lay-up because they are easy to impregnate with resin. A basket weave is a type of plain weave in which multiple yarns are woven together as one. A 4x4 basket weave uses 4 yarns bundled together and woven with 4 yarns bundled together. This makes a heavier stable fabric.

Satin weaves are very common for repair applications. They are made by floating warp yarns over several fill yarns and under one fill yarn in a repetitious pattern. It is called a satin weave because it produces a satiny finish by exposing more warp threads on the front side of the fabric. Satin weaves contour better around a complex curve than a plain weave. The eight harness satin weave is woven by interlacing a thread over seven threads and under one thread, as shown in figure 2-10(c). Some typical styles of satin weaves for repair operations include the 7781, the 181, and the 1581. All have a 57 warp and 54 fill with a thickness of .009-inch. The differences in these fabrics is in the number of yarns used to produce the thread. The 7781 has 75 yarns warp and fill, the 1581 has 150 yarns warp and fill, and the 181 has 225 yarns warp and fill.

The four harness satin or crowfoot weave interlaces a thread over three threads and then under one. The style 120 has a 60 thread warp, 58 thread fill, with 450 yarns warp and fill, and a thickness of .004-inch.

The Style 120 for Kevlar and fiberglass, and the 3K-70-PW for carbon/graphite, are tight weaves, which makes them more resistant to moisture penetration. Because of this, they are often found in the construction of honeycomb panel structures. The eight harness and crowfoot satin weaves are looser weaves that drape easily around contours. The 1K-50-5H carbon/graphite weave is a thin fabric with good draping characteristics. Because of its expense, however, it is seldom used.

Each type of material (Kevlar, fiberglass, carbon/graphite) can be found in various weaves. Make sure you are using the correct type of material (Kevlar, carbon/graphite, or fiberglass), in the proper form (bidirectional, unidirectional, mats), and in the proper weight and weave for each application. These will be listed in the structural repair manual. Some common fabric styles and their data are included in the chart in figure 2-12.

Fabric styles are characterized by the yarn construction, count, weight, thickness, and weave. The yarn construction is the yield

Fabric Style	Weave	Weight Oz/Sq. yard	Thickness (mils)	Count Warp x Fill	Yarn Warp	Yarn Fill
FIBERGLASS						
120	Crowfoot	3.2	3.5	60X 58	450 1/2	450 1/2
7781	8-HS (Harness satin)	8.9	9.0	57 x 54	75 1/0	75 1/0
KEVLAR						
120	Plain	1.7	4.5	34 x 34	195 de	195 de
285	Crowfoot	5.0	10.0	17 x 17	1140 de	1140 de
CARBON						
584	8-HS	10.7	13.5	24 x 24	3K	3K

Figure 2-12. The structural repair manual often includes charts to indicate the style of fabric to use for repair work.

or denier, twist and ply level. The count is the number of yarns per inch of width in the warp and fill directions. The fabric's weight is measured in ounces per square yard, or grams per square meter. The thickness is measured in thousandths of an inch, or millimeters. And the weave style is plain, satin, crowfoot, etc.

FINISHES

Some fabrics have a finish to protect them during the weaving process, or to help bond the fibers and resins together. Different fabrics have different finishes. On fiberglass, the manufacturer may use a type of lubricant to protect the fibers during the weaving process, then this is burned off, and another type of finish may be applied to the fabric. Volan and Silane finishes are common on fiberglass. Kevlar does not need the lubricant during the weaving process, and is cleaned by a process known as scouring. There is no other type of finish used with Kevlar, but the mechanical properties in a laminate are higher if the material has been scoured. Carbon fabrics also do not have any type of finish on them. All the above materials are compatible with epoxy resin systems.

HYBRIDS

A manufacturer can design a part by using different types of fiber combinations (hybrid) to tailor a part for strength, or to reduce cost. This can be done in a number of ways. The different materials are combined to give the characteristics of each different fiber. For example, Kevlar may be combined with carbon/graphite to produce a structure that combines the flexibility of Kevlar with the stiffness of carbon/graphite. Another example would be a combination of Kevlar and fiberglass to produce a less expensive high-strength material. There are three common types of hybrid structures used in aviation today:

INTRAPLY HYBRID

Intraply hybrids utilize reinforcing material that is woven from two or more different fibers. The strength of the final structure can be designed based on the proportions of each fiber used. [Figure 2-13]

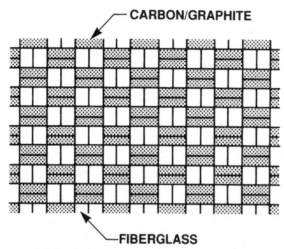

Figure 2-13. Intraply Hybrid – Two or more types of reinforcing fibers woven together to produce cloth.

INTERPLY HYBRID

An *interply hybrid* uses two or more layers of different reinforcing material that are laminated together. Each layer, in addition to being a different material, may be used in the form of unidirectional or bidirectional fabric. [Figure 2-14]

SELECTIVE PLACEMENT

Fibers may be selectively placed to give greater strength, flexibility, or reduced cost. The I-beam shown in figure 2-15 may use carbon/graphite if stiffness is desired, and blends in fiberglass to reduce the cost of the structure.

SUMMARY

When a part is manufactured, designers can decide on the fiber science, or the placing of the fibers, to produce the greatest strength for a specific stress. They can also use different types of fibers together as a hybrid to develop the characteristics of different fiber materials, or they may elect to use a core structure. As a result, designers use different types of fiber combinations to customize a part for their specific aircraft. Each aircraft part is made differently as opposed to sheet metal components, which are all typically the same type of material throughout the structure or throughout the entire aircraft skin.

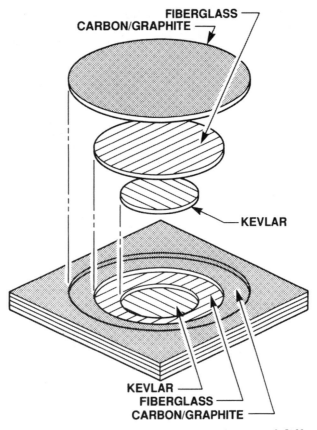

Figure 2-14. Interply Hybrid – Two or more layers of different reinforcing material which are laminated together. Each layer is of different material.

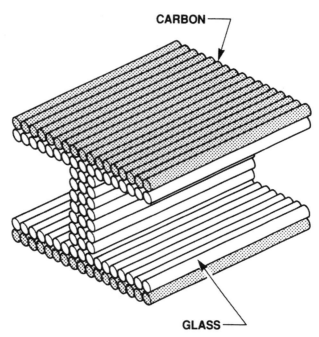

Figure 2-15. This I-Beam may use carbon/graphite where stiffness is desired, and blends in fiberglass to reduce the cost of the structure.

Chapter 3
Matrix Materials

The matrix is a bonding material that completely surrounds the fiber, giving it extra strength. The strength of a composite lies in the ability of the matrix to transfer stress to the reinforcing fibers. An advanced composite uses various manufacturing techniques and newer matrix formulas with newer reinforcing fabrics.

Polyester resin is an example of an early matrix formula used with fiberglass for many nonstructural applications such as fairings, spinners, and trim. The old polyester/fiberglass formulas did not offer sufficient strength to be used to fabricate primary structural members; it can be somewhat brittle. The newer matrix materials display remarkably improved stress distributing characteristics, heat resistance, chemical resistance, and durability. Most of the newer matrix formulas for aircraft are epoxy resins.

Resin matrix are two-part systems consisting of a resin and a catalyst, or hardener, which acts as a curing agent. The term resin often times means both parts together, not just the resin. For simplicity, this book uses the term resin to mean both parts together. Many times a maintenance manual may use the term catalyzed resin, meaning that the resin and the curing agent or hardener have been mixed, but not necessarily cured.

MATRIX SYSTEMS

Resin matrix systems are a type of plastic. Some companies refer to composites as fiber reinforced plastics. There are two general categories of plastics: thermoplastic and thermoset. By themselves, these resins do not have sufficient strength for use in structural applications, however, when used as a matrix and reinforced with other materials, they form the high strength, lightweight structural composites used today.

THERMOPLASTIC

Thermoplastic resins use heat to form the part into the desired shape; one that is not necessarily permanent. If a thermoplastic is heated a second time, it will flow to form another shape. Plexiglas®, which is used to form aircraft windshields, is an example of thermoplastic. The shape of the windshield is retained after it is cooled at the factory, but if the windshield is heated again, the plastic will flow to form another shape.

Thermoplastic resins may be found in overhead storage bins and nonstructural applications. However, with the advancements being made in composite science, thermoplastic resins are finding their way into the structural airframe applications, too. With the development of high temperature thermoplastic resins, these plastics can be used in more places, as long as the temperature does not exceed 750°F.

POLYESTER RESIN SYSTEMS

Polyester resins were developed in the 1930s by a chemist named Carleton Ellis. He patented the first process for making polyester resins in 1936. A year later, Ellis improved the basic design of polyester resin when he discovered what is still used today—combining unsaturated polyester alkyd with vinyl acetate or styrene, and curing it with a peroxide catalyst. The new formula was less viscous than the original, and it cured faster and more completely. The process for the new polyester resin system was patented in 1941.

Polyester resin was one of the core product advances that launched the modern plastics industry. Annual production of polyester resin in the United States is now at about one billion pounds per year.

CHEMISTRY OF POLYESTER RESINS

The reasons for the widespresad use of polyester resins are simple. Polyester resins are very stable at room temperature and can be kept in storage for years without affecting the quality of the materials. The resins cure at room temperature in just a few minutes when an inexpensive peroxide catalyst is added. Plus, no by-products are released, and the curing process actually produces additional heat, thus enhancing the curing process. Polyester resins are low in cost and are very versatile. They are not very resistant to alkali, however, nor are they strong enough to use as matrix material for structural components.

Different curing agents can be mixed with the basic polyester resins to provide different pot-life and cure times. Furthermore, accelerators combined with curing agents enhance the curing process. By varying the concentrations of the curing agent and accelerator, the rate of the cure process can be varied.

THERMOSETS

Thermosets use heat to form and set the shape of the part permanently. The plastic, once cured, cannot be reformed even if it is reheated. Most structural airframe applications are presently constructed of thermoset resins.

EPOXY RESIN SYSTEMS

Epoxies are a type of thermosetting plastic resin well known for their outstanding adhesion, strength, and their resistance to moisture and chemicals. They are very useful for bonding nonporous and dissimilar materials, such as a metal part to a composite component.

In 1946, an innovative company named Ciba (now known as Ciba-Geigy Corporation) introduced a new product called "Araldite" at the Swiss Industries Fair. This was the first formal introduction of epoxy resin to the manufacturing industry. Since that introduction, Epoxy resins have become one of the most widely used resin formulas in the world. Araldite is still widely used in the manufacturing industry.

Epoxy resins are among the most common matrix systems used in composite fabrication and repair because:

(1) They are extremely flexible in terms of their application. More specifically, epoxy resins can be formulated to provide rigid or flexible strength, to perform at high or low temperatures, or to provide a combination of these characteristics.

(2) They exhibit good adhesive characteristics when used with a broad range of cloth reinforcing materials, fillers, and substrates. They exhibit an extraordinary ability to completely wet a wide variety of materials and to adhesively cure together a variety of dissimilar materials.

(3) After being cured, epoxy resins are resistant to deterioration by water, acids, bases, many chemical solvents, and UV light. They are so durable that they present a problem from a disposal perspective. There have been suggestions that discarded epoxy based composite material be ground up and mixed with asphalt to enhance the durability of roadways and at the same time dispose of an almost indestructible material.

(4) Epoxy resins are easily cured at room temperature or at slightly elevated temperatures, and they do not require exotic equipment to process. The cure process emits no volatiles or water and represents a comparatively safe material to work with in terms of toxicity. These characteristics make epoxy material suitable for wet lay-up, pre-preging fabrics or tapes, or wet filament winding.

(5) Epoxy resins are very dimensionally stable—they shrink very little during the curing process and are very acceptable for use as structural parts, mold fabrication material, or tooling fabrication material. Epoxy resins are used in many instances to mold parts in mass production to very close tolerances.

(6) The resins exhibit the strongest adhesive characteristics of any known polymeric material. For this reason alone, epoxy

resins are ideal for the fabrication of lightweight structural materials for aircraft and space vehicles.

(7) Although epoxy resins are initially more expensive than some other matrix material, in the long run, their superior strength, long shelf life, and ease of use make them more economical to use for fabrication and repairs than other matrix materials.

The quality of obtainable bonds is dependent upon the manner in which joints are designed and the surfaces prepared. They may be designed for different uses: high temperature, low temperature, rigidity, flexibility, fast cure, slow cure, or other characteristics. Each system is designed for a specific purpose. For example, a cowling may use an epoxy resin system that withstands high temperatures, while an aileron may use an epoxy resin system made to withstand bending stresses. Both parts are made of advanced composites, but they are used for different purposes—both use epoxy resin systems, but are very different in their chemical makeup, producing structures with different characteristics.

Just because it is an epoxy doesn't mean it will always work. Make sure you are using the type of epoxy resin the application calls for. For example, there are two-part epoxy resins available at hardware stores. This type of epoxy resin is not used on aircraft because it may not exhibit the strength, flexibility, or moisture resistance that is needed.

Resins may be compatible with many different curing agents, depending on the requirements of the component. There are many types of epoxy resins and many curing agents, each with their own advantages. Use the correct catalyst or curing agent as well as the correct resin. The most important rule a technician can follow is to use exactly the type of resin and catalyst specified in the Structural Repair Manual.

CHEMISTRY

One of the reasons for the wide spread use of epoxy resins is that various formulations of the resins and the curing agents allow for most performance characteristics and demands for the cured resin system application to be met. However, there are a few applications that might be somewhat inappropriate such as a combination of room temperature cure for a large, high temperature application. Even in such an apparently contradictory situation, the use of even a moderate amount of heat can dramatically increase the performance characteristics of the cured system.

DILUENTS

The final characteristics of the epoxy resin are determined not only by the characteristics of the curing agent, but also by the molecular structure attached to the basic epoxy group. Diluents are attendant molecular structures attached to the basic epoxy group intended to change the viscosity of the uncured resin system. This is important when it is necessary to have a very fluid matrix. A very fluid matrix can be made by the addition of this product.

FLEXIBILIZERS

The use of a high molecular weight structure attendant to the basic epoxy group makes the final cured system more flexible. These epoxy resins, known as flexibilizers, are added to aromatic epoxy resins to reduce the brittleness of the cured resin. However, the use of flexiblilizers increases the flexibility of the cured epoxy resin at the expense of the tensile strength. In addition, most flexibilizers increase the viscosity of the uncured resin. There are a few curing agents that produce both flexibility and retain good tensile strength. These can be mixed in a wider range of mixing ratios than other curing agents. Thus it is possible to fine-tune the curing agent for the particular application. These are less irritating to skin than some amine curing agents, but they are less resistant to chemical solvents than some other cured epoxy resins.

MECHANICS OF THE CURING PROCESS

To understand how an epoxy resin cures, imagine a two dimensional molecule interacting with similar molecules to form a three dimensional grid. This is, in fact, exactly what happens when the resin is cured. This three dimensional linking between molecules is referred to as crosslinking. This crosslinking effectively forms a single giant molecule that is shaped like and is as large as the finished part. More specifically, the finished part becomes a mollecularly interlinked plastic. The reason the epoxy resin does not crosslink immediately when it is produced, thus making it worthless as a matrix, is due to the inability of the epoxy molecule, by itself, to unlink the chemical bonds between the carbon and oxygen atoms. The crosslinking is made possible when a curing agent is mixed with the epoxy resin. For example, the curing agent can provide nitrogen, which then enables the carbon molecules to interact with large molecules such as the other epoxy resins, thus forming a three dimensional matrix. The nitrogen atom can be made available from a variety of different curing agents. Each agent has its own particular characteristics that it contributes to the final cured material.

AMINE CURING AGENTS

One of the more commonly used curing agents used is referred to as an amine.

The reaction between an amine curing agent and the epoxy resin can usually occur at room temperature. There are other curing agents that require heat and contribute other characteristics to the final cured solid resin. Because these agents add their own characteristics to the cured matrix, it is extremely important to use the correct amount to achieve the correct balance of curing agent and epoxy resin. Chemists determine the correct amount by understanding exactly how the curing agent bonds with the resin at the atomic level. Pay close attention to the mixing ratios as provided by the manufacturer of the epoxy resin and the curing agent or as provided by the manufacturer of the finished composite product.

CATALYSTS

Epoxy resins also crosslink with non-reactive catalysts. Such catalysts are added to the resin in small amounts and initiate a self-perpetuating reaction that causes the epoxy to polymerize. This results in a polyether. Polyethers are not affected by most acids or alkalis and are more stable than the resins cured by amine curing agents.

The epoxy groups are able to cross link without the inclusion of the curing agent. The epoxy is cured alone by using the curing agent to facilitate the crosslinking without actually including additional structures as part of the crosslinked system. This is also referred to as homopolymerization and results in a thermally stable polyether. The resulting matrix is more thermally stable than those created by using amines.

POLYBUTADIENE RESINS

Polybutadiene resins were developed in 1955 by Enjay Laboratories and were introduced into the market under the trade name Buton. Polybutadiene resins are thermosetting resins that offer very good electrical properties, outstanding chemical resistance, very low water absorption, and are stable at relatively high temperatures. They are easy to cure using materials that are relatively low in toxicity such as peroxide catalytic curing agents. The resin formulas are suitable for use in several manufacturing operations including the preparation of pre-preg materials, as well as in wet lay-up operations. Polybutadiene resins are also commonly found in coatings, adhesives, and potting compounds.

One of the most common applications of polybutadiene resin is in the preparation of pre-preg materials for use in radomes. The operation of radar systems in both aircraft and marine environments presents a list of contradictory requirements. The radome structure must be very thin in order to ensure the maximum efficiency of the radar. The radome must at the same time be very strong in order to endure the server impacts that occur, for example, on an aircraft during a hailstorm. The radome must be stable over a wide range of temperatures so it does not expand or contract significantly to cause mechanical problems or cause a distortion of the radar signals. The radome must also be resistant to exposure to ultraviolet light and the corrosive action of water.

Polybutadiene cures in three temperature ranges:

1. Low-temperature cure (room temperature - 200°F)—The resin formula begins to gel or thicken. This is not suitable under most conditions for final structural bonding. Because polybutadiene cures at room temperature to form a gel, the shelf life of the resin is limited. Most resin formulas can be stored at room temperature (68°F) for several months with no noticeable degradation. However, storage at temperatures over 95°F result in increasing gelation of the resin even though no catalytic curing agent is present.

2. High-temperature cure (250°F - 400°F)—This temperature initiates more complete crosslinking so hard resins are formed. It does not provide for complete crosslinking, but is often sufficient for structural applications.

3. Peak thermal cure (450°F - 700°F)—This temperature provides the necessary heat to enable more complete crosslinking. This temperature is required to facilitate the maximum high temperature performance of the resin system. The most common curing agents are catalytic type agents that must be mixed in very carefully measured portions. One of the most common curing agents is a peroxide catalyst marketed under the trade name Lupersol by Lucido Division, Wallace, and Tiernan Incorporated. Lupersol is usually mixed with the base resin in a ratio of 1-2% by weight. Bensoyl peroxide is sometimes added as an additional reactant to the Lupersol at a ratio of 1% by weight to the base resin. Each resin manufacturer specifies proportions.

WORKING WITH RESINS & CATALYSTS

When working with resins and catalysts or curing agents, always follow the procedures specified in the structural repair manual. It is important to mix the resin system properly. Improperly mixed resins do not provide adequate strength. Each part of the resin system is weighed before mixing—weigh resins out, don't mix by volume. Always mix resin and hardener before adding any fillers.

If the resin system requires refrigerated storage, allow each part to warm up to room temperature before weighing and mixing. A cold resin weighs heavier than the same amount of a room temperature resin. Use a calibrated scale or balance to weigh the two parts of the resin to produce the proper mix. The scale surfaces or balance should always be clean. [Figure 3-1]

Mix resins in the proper ratios. The matrix formula for most advanced composites is very exacting. A slight improper mix ratio can make a tremendous amount of difference in the strength of the final composite. This mixing requirement will be found in the aircraft's structural repair manual. [Figure 3-2]

Figure 3-1. Scales are used to accurately measure the mix ratio for a specific resin system

Resin manufacturers will often provide convenient pre-measured packages that are combined by the user. A thorough mixing action will help to achieve maximum strength. Mix resin systems together in a wax free container. If a waxed container is used, the solvents in the resin and curing agents will dissolve any wax on the inside of the container, causing it to be mixed in with the resin. This may cause the repair to cure incorrectly or possibly not cure at all.

BASE RESIN	CURING AGENT	PARTS BY WEIGHT		POT LIFE MINUTES	CURING TIME
		RESIN	CATALYST		
(A) EPON 828	DTA	100	10	15-30	24 HR/RT OR 1 HR/65C
(B) EPON 828	EPICURE 3140	100	33	75	7 days at RT OR 90 min/65C
(C) EPOCAST 50A	EPOCAST 50/9816	100	15	50	24 HR/RT OR 1 HR/65C
(D) REDUX 410-A	REDUX 410-B	100	40	60	5 DAYS RT OR 1 HR/120C

Figure 3-2. This is an example of what might be found in the structural repair manual. The manual gives the type of resin system to be used in a specific repair area such as resin B. In this chart, resin system B is the EPON 828 resin, and the EPICURE 3140 curing agent. The pot life of the mixture is 75 minutes, and can be cured in either 7 days at room temperature or 90 minutes at an elevated temperature of 65°C. This chart is just an example. The correct chart for the type of aircraft you are working on can be found in the Structural Repair Manual provided by the manufacturer.

Mix resins for the proper amount of time. Three to five minutes is usually required to completely mix the components. Resins that are not mixed properly will not cure to the maximum strength obtainable. Do not mix the resins too fast. If they are mixed quickly, small bubbles may rise into the air and could get on your skin or in your hair. Do not be concerned if you have bubbles in the cup because they will be worked out later during the lay-up with a squeegee. Vacuum bagging further ensures that there are no trapped bubbles in the final composite.

Do not mix large amounts together. A large volume of resin and curing agent will cause an acceleration of the chemical reaction. When this happens, it starts to cure in the mixing cup, possibly becoming too thick to work completely into the fabric. The pot life, or amount of time you have to work with the resins, is also reduced. A few smaller quantity mixes will be easier to work with.

All resins cure by chemical reaction, but some generate their own heat, thus accelerating the cure. It is important to consider how long it will take to use the amount of resin that has been prepared. If the work is extensive and takes a long time, the pot life of the resin mixture may be exceeded if too much is initially prepared.

Be sure to know the resin's pot life before starting. This is the amount of time that the mixed resins will be workable. Some resin systems have very short pot life (15 minutes), others have long pot life (4 hours). Pot life is not necessarily the time it is usable in the cup. The resin and fabric should be in place before the actual curing takes place. If a resin with a short pot life is used to impregnate fabric, the patches must be in place on the surface before the resin starts to cure. If the patches are allowed to sit too long they, will start their chemical reaction and become stiffer. Subsequently, when the patches are in place and vacuum bagged to cure, the chemical crosslinking of the resin and the fibers may not take place as it is designed to do. The patches will have cured separately, and may not stick properly to each other or the part. Be sure to follow the mixing procedure correctly and use the mixture before the pot life has expired.

The shelf life is the time the product is good in an unopened container. The shelf life varies from product to product. If the shelf life is exceeded, the resin or catalyst must be discarded because the two components will not produce the desired chemical reaction and the cure of the part may not achieve sufficient strength. The shelf life of pre-preg materials is very important.

If too much resin is used, the part is called resin rich. Unlike traditional fiberglass work, advanced composite work is for structural applications. In this case, excessive resin is not desirable. This affects the strength of the composite by making the part brittle. It also adds extra weight, which is opposite of the reason for using composites in the first place.

A resin starved or resin lean part is one in which too little resin was used, causing the part to be weak because the matrix cannot transfer the stresses to the fibers. Sometimes you can see areas where there is more resin, which may appear as glossy, and resin lean areas that appear to have a whitish effect to the surface.

The correct amount of fiber to resin ratio is important to get the desired strength. In advanced composite work, a 50:50 ratio is good, however a 60:40 fiber to resin ratio is better. Remember, the fibers provide the strength, not the resin.

When working the resin into the fibers, care should be taken not to distort the weave of the fabric. If too much pressure is applied when using a brush or squeegee, the fibers could pull apart, changing the strength characteristic of the fabric.

Curing of the resins must also be accomplished correctly to achieve the maximum strength. Be sure to follow all manufacturer's curing requirements.

Resins and curing agents can be purchased in cans that need to be weighed and thoroughly mixed together. They may also come in convenient prepackaged forms. For technicians, these are very convenient packages that eliminate the weighing process and may eliminate the mess of mixing the two components — a nice safety feature.

The resin and catalyst may be divided into separate plastic packages that are attached on one end. When ready for use, the partition that separates the resin from the catalyst is broken. Still within the package, the resin/catalyst mixture can be mixed together thoroughly. When completely mixed, the corner can be cut with scissors and the resin dispensed. This saves on weighing and handling the resins, and could prevent accidents.

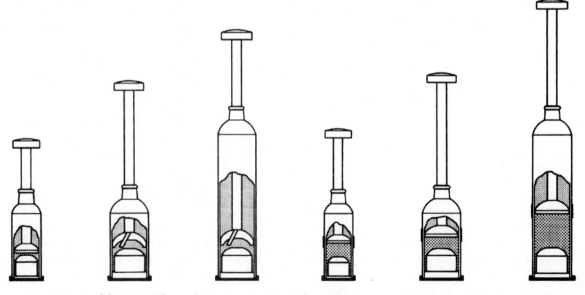

Figure 3-3. Disposable cartridges that store, mix, and apply two-component materials are available. They are frequently specially designed to comply with a specific manufacturer's repair instructions for a certain type of repair. Be sure and check the cartridge part number, expiration date, and any special instructions.

A disposable cartridge that stores, mixes, and applies two component materials is also available and convenient to use. They come in many sizes and can be tailored to a specific use. To use the cartridge, the seal that separates the two components must be broken with a plunger. Then the materials are mixed together by using twisting, up and down motions. The label states how many strokes are required to give a thorough mix. A needle or syringe may be installed onto the end and the resin dispensed through it. [Figure 3-3]

PRE-IMPREGNATED MATERIALS

Pre-impregnated fabrics, or pre-pregs, are fabrics that have the resin system already impregnated into the fabric. Because many epoxy resins have a high viscosity, it is often difficult to mix and work the resin system into the fabric and encapsulate the fibers. Pre-preg fabrics eliminate the need for mixing, so technicians do not have to worry about whether the proper mix ratio was used or if the proper amount of resin was applied. Pre-preg fabrics are manufactured by dipping the woven fabric into a resin solution. The resin solution has the proper amount of resin and curing agent weighed and mixed together. This fabric then goes onto a drying tower that removes any excess resin. Then a parting film may be added to one or both sides to prevent the fabric from sticking when rolled. Pre-preg fabrics come on a roll that is usually refrigerated and ready to use. [Figure 3-4]

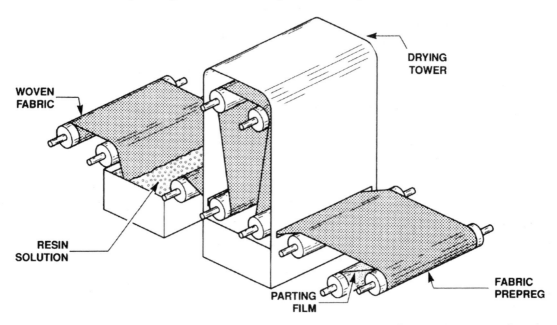

Figure 3-4. Pre-impregnated fabrics require a special manufacturing technique to ensure that not only the resin is mixed correctly, but also applied to the fabric in a manner that will allow complete encapsulation of the fibers. Parting film may be applied to one, or both, sides.

Pre-pregs can also be made in unidirectional material instead of the woven fabric. In this case, the fibers come directly from the spool of thread and are placed in the correct orientation. They are then heated on one surface while a paper with resin on it is applied to the other surface. The heat melts the resin from the paper and impregnates the threads. The paper and the threads are then squeezed together to impregnate the threads more thoroughly. The pre-preg is rolled and is ready to be used. This material should be stored properly, as the two parts of the resin and hardener have already been mixed together. [Figure 3-5]

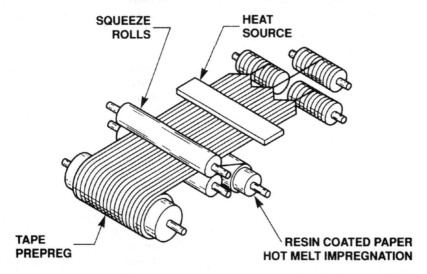

Figure 3-5. Unidirectional pre-preg fabric material is "woven" at the same time it is impregnated. The proper size and number of strands are fed from spools to form the proper width, instead of being "pre-woven" like fabric.

The plastic backing on the pre-preg material typically has a diamond pattern on the back-side. This diamond is longer in one direction than the other. The long direction of the diamond indicates the warp of the fabric. When a piece is cut away from the roll and the selvage edge is not showing, the warp direction can easily be found by looking for the long diamonds on the plastic backing. [Figure 3-6]

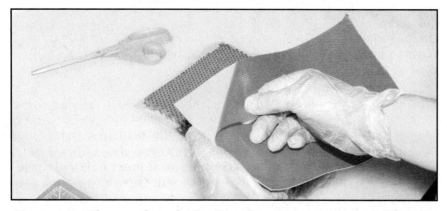

Figure 3-6. When peeling the backing from pre-preg materials, note the direction of the diamond pattern on the backing to determine the warp direction of the fabric.

Pre-preg materials offer a convenience over raw fabrics in many ways.

1. The pre-preg contains the proper amount of matrix. It does not produce a resin rich or resin lean component if cured properly. The pre-preg contains about 50% resin before curing. During the curing process, some of this resin bleeds out of the reinforcing fibers, thus producing a structure that contains about 40% resin and 60% fibers by weight.

2. The reinforcing fibers are completely encapsulated with the matrix. During hand lay-up, if a resin system has a high viscosity, or is very thick, it is sometimes difficult to get the resin into and around each individual fiber to produce the strongest cure. This is not a problem with the pre-preg fabrics. The technician does not have to worry about distorting the fabric weave while working the resin into the fabric.

3. Pre-preg fabrics eliminate the need to manually weigh and mix components. In hand lay-up, the resin and curing agent must be properly weighed. If they are not weighed properly, too much resin or curing agent could result in a part that will not cure properly, causing an unairworthy condition.

4. In many cases, pre-preg materials produce a stronger component or repair. This is because just the right amount of matrix-to-fabric ratio has been applied and it has been mixed properly. However, the strength of a composite repair also varies greatly upon the manner in which the repair is accomplished and the manner in which it is cured.

Pre-pregs were invented for the use of aircraft manufacturers to reduce the problems associated with completely wetting out the fabric with resin. It also saves time and reduces the problems associated with weighing and mixing the resins.

Pre-preg fabrics also have disadvantages when working in a maintenance facility. Some of the disadvantages of working with pre-pregs are:

1. Many pre-pregs must be stored in a freezer. This requirement must be met. If some pre-pregs are allowed to remain at room temperature for even a few hours, the resins/catalysts start their chemical reaction and begin to cure. The term "out-of-freezer life" is the time that the material is actually out of the freezer and is being cut or transported. During this time, the resins are warming up to room temperature and will start to cure. While in the freezer, this chemical reaction is slowed down to allow a longer shelf life. Pre-preg fabrics usually have a limited shelf life even if kept in the freezer. Some

pre-pregs must also be shipped in cold storage overnight, which adds to the expense.

The amount of time out of the freezer should be carefully recorded and kept to a minimum; the allowable out of freezer time may be only a few hours. For example, if a roll of pre-preg fabric is taken out of the freezer in order to cut one yard of fabric, the time that the entire bolt of fabric is exposed to room temperature must be recorded, even if it's only ten minutes. Each time the bolt is out of the freezer, the time must be recorded and added to the rest of the out-of-freezer time. If the manufacturer has designated a five hour out-of-freezer life, once the accumulated time that the material has been out of the freezer totals five hours, the fabric will no longer cure sufficiently in a repair to give the proper strength.

Newly developed pre-pregs allow a room temperature storage temperature. These materials have been available to the aviation maintenance industry for over 15 years, however, this type of material is not recommended by the aircraft manufacturers for repair use.

The shelf life of pre-preg materials is very important. The pre-preg material already has the resin mixed with the curing agent, and if the shelf life is expired, the material has gone through a chemical curing process. If an overtime pre-preg material is used in the repair work, the patches will not stick to the structure or to other patches. The final cured repair could be torn off the part easily. This would be an unairworthy situation.

2. Many companies do not want to sell small quantities of a specific weave and resin system, so a full roll must be purchased. For those shops that do not work with large amounts of these materials, this is not cost effective. For example, a bolt of 100 yards of pre-preg is purchased with a freezer shelf life of one year. Unless a large number of repairs are made, it will only be partially used before it must be discarded at the end of that year. Once the pre-preg material expires at the end of that year, it cannot be used to repair composite aircraft.

3. Pre-preg material is much more expensive than raw fabric that can be impregnated with the same type of resin system. This is especially true if the material exceeds its shelf life and must be discarded.

4. Composite components and materials have not yet been standardized. When working with metal aircraft, any manufacturer can call for 2024-T3, and you would know what type of metal to use. In composites, different manufacturers use different weaves, different types of fibers,

different resins, different core materials, different adhesives, and they use them in different areas of an aircraft. If you are in charge of the composite repairs to two different aircraft with composite components, you may find that the type of materials called for the aileron are completely different from a cowling. To order a whole roll of pre-preg material in one weave with one type of matrix on it would be foolish unless many, many repairs are to be accomplished on the one part that uses that type of fabric and matrix.

RESIN SYSTEMS USED ON SOME PRE-PREG MATERIALS

A curing agent that is very effective as a pre-preging material is dicyandiamide (DICY). The epoxy material is crosslinked using both the amine reaction and the homopolymerization mechanism. The reason for its wide use as a pre-preg material is that it has very little reaction with the epoxy resin at room temperature or at the reduced temperatures at which pre-pregs are normally stored. However, when the material is heated, the cure is very rapid. DICY begins to cure epoxy resins at 293°-309°F. This is why it is common to see a cure temperature of about 350°F for some types of pre-pregs. The cured composite exhibits very good adhesive strength and thermal stability at elevated temperatures. Although this type of curing agent presents several advantages, it also is very irritating to skin. Many people have severe allergic reactions to the uncured material.

A word of caution: the materials stated in the manufacturing manual for a repair may actually be the material that was used in the manufacturing of the aircraft, not the repair pre-preg material. The pre-preg system used in manufacturing may be an autoclave type of pre-preg, which means it produces a very strong, lightweight structure when cured in an autoclave. However, to repair damaged components with the same type of materials as originally used in manufacturing can lead to problems. The autoclave cure is not used very widely in the repair procedure. Hot bond with vacuum bagging techniques are used more commonly. The resin system in these pre-pregs may not produce the same desired strength characteristics when cured with hot bond techniques. They are not getting as much vacuum as an autoclave could produce. The plies of the repair, although they are cured, may be easily peeled from the surface. This could cause dangerous consequences if failure occurred in flight. Always follow the manufactures repair manual, not manufacturing materials.

ADHESIVES

Resins come in different forms. Some resins are made for laminating so they are generally thinner and can be worked into the fibers. Others are used for bonding and are generally known as adhesives because they stick parts together.

Adhesives come in many forms and can be purchased in individual cans that are weighed and mixed together. They may come in the form of a cartridge, or in convenient plastic bags. One of the most unique forms of adhesive is a film form. This type has both the resin and catalyst pre-blended and cast onto a thin film of plastic. Refrigeration of the film is required because if left out at room temperature the two parts would slowly start to cure. In the freezer, the curing process is slowed down, giving the film a longer shelf life. Adhesive films are used many times to help bond a pre-preg patch to a repair area. It is sometimes used when the patch covers an exposed core area and fibers. Adhesive film gives another layer of resin so the resin within the pre-preg patches does not get wicked into the dry surrounding fibers, which could create a resin lean repair. The desired amount of adhesive is cut and positioned in place. Applying heat causes the resin and catalyst mixture to start curing, and the plastic backing may be hard to remove. Simply place them back in the freezer for a short time (15 seconds), then the plastic backing will come off easier. The pre-preg patches are then laid over the adhesive film in the proper places, and cured with heat and pressure. The second part to be bonded is placed over the adhesive and cured with heat and pressure. [Figure 3-7]

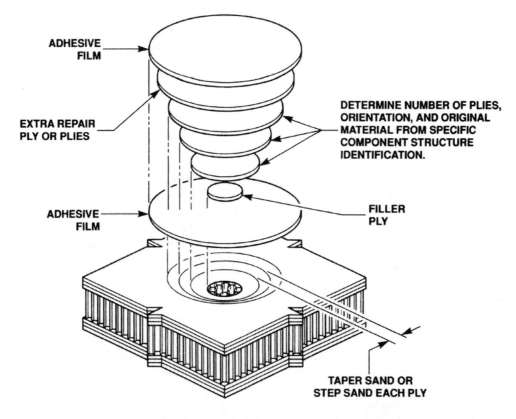

Figure 3-7. When performing a repair to a composite structure, an adhesive film is used in conjunction with the pre-pregs to help bond the patches. When the film is laid into the area, heat is applied with a heat gun to soften the film. The plastic backing is then removed and the repair plies placed over the adhesive layer.

Foaming adhesives are another type of bonding agent used with prepreg materials. When heat is applied to these adhesives, they foam up and expand. These are often used to splice replacement honeycomb core segments to existing honeycomb cores. The foaming adhesive fills up the edges of the honeycomb, creating a larger surface area to bond to. In a similar manner, when installing fasteners, foaming adhesives may be used around the area of the fastener to create more area for bonding. The adhesives come either in a roll or a sheet, and are stored in a freezer. These are primarily used in conjunction with prepreg repairs because they require higher temperatures to cure.

FILLERS

Fillers, a thixotropic agent, are materials that are added to resins to control viscosity and weight, to increase pot life and strength, and to make the application of the resin easier. When filler is used as a thixotropic agent, it increases the volume of the resin, making it less dense and less susceptible to cracking, and lowers the weight of the material.

Fillers are inert and will not chemically react with the resin. Fillers are added to resin systems that have already been properly weighed and mixed together. The fillers are added as a percent of the total weight of the mixed epoxy resin and catalyst. The method by which the resin and fillers should be mixed is outlined in each aircraft's Structural Repair Manual.

Filler material can be in the form of microballoons, chopped fibers, or flox. Microballoons are small spheres of plastic or glass. If plastic spheres are used they must be mixed with a compatible resin system that will not dissolve the plastic from which they are made. Glass microballoons are more common because the solvent action of the matrix does not affect them. Microballoons are used primarily as a thixotropic agent. Microballoons don't add strength the way chopped fibers or flox do.

Chopped fibers and flox can also be used as a filler material. Chopped fibers can be any type of fiber cut to a certain length (1/4- to 1/2-inch are common). Flox is the fuzzy fibers taken from the fabric strands. These are added to the mixed resin system when added strength is desired. For example, if a hole is accidentally drilled in the wrong place in a composite structure, the hole may be repaired by filling it with a mixture of resin and fibers. The mixture gives more strength than pure resin in the final repair. If the hole were to be filled with pure epoxy resin, it might be too brittle and add excess weight. Before filling any holes, the Structural Repair Manual should be consulted to determine the appropriate repair for the type of part being worked on. [Figure 3-8]

GLASS FLOX EPOXIDE MIX

This data sheet gives details of the mixing amounts for glass flox epoxide mixture.

MIXTURE

    Epikote 162 resin   — 100 parts by weight

    Epikure 113 hardener— 38 parts by weight

    Glass flox   — 50 - 70 parts by weight depending on desired thickness.

Do not mix more than 500 gms. at once. Use within 30 minutes of mixing.
Cure time = 24 hours at 70 °F.

Figure 3-8. Example data sheet from a structural repair manual.

METAL MATRIX COMPOSITES

The matrix material does not always have to be in a plastic or resin form—it can be metal. The metal might be aluminum, titanium, or steel. The composite is formed when chopped fibers or fiber strands are mixed into the molten metal. The mixture is then formed, molded, rolled, or extruded in the usual way. The fibers give extra reinforcement to the metal, lending more strength without adding weight. The fibers may dissipate heat more quickly, thus causing less wear in the part, or it may give more flexibility to the part.

Metal matrix composites are still in the experimental stage and are not found on structural airframe parts at this time. Several companies are doing research on metal matrix composites, and these structures will probably be seen in the near future. Some powerplants, however, are being manufactured with ceramic fibers mixed with metals. Turbine engine blades, for example, are fabricated with ceramic fibers and metal to allow heat to dissipate quicker, causing less elongation and distortion to the blade shape. On reciprocating engines, ceramics are being mixed with metals used for cylinder walls, which improves heat dissipation and reduces wear.

Chapter 4
Core Materials

Core material is the central member of an assembly. When bonded between two thin face sheets, it provides a rigid, lightweight component. Composite structures manufactured in this manner are sometimes referred to as a sandwich construction. Two popular core structures are foam and honeycomb.

The core material gives a great deal of compressive strength to a structure. For example, the sheet metal skin on a rotor blade has a tendency to flex in flight as stress is applied. This constant flexing causes metal fatigue. A composite blade with a central foam core, or honeycomb, will eliminate most flexing of the skin because the core is uniformly stiff throughout the blade. [Figure 4-1]

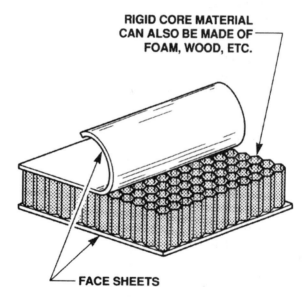

Figure 4-1. The use of a core material can dramatically increase the strength of a structure without adding significant weight.

If made of sheet metal with metal ribs, the skins will twist and flex in the areas where there is no support. The solid core resists the bending and flexing of the skin, greatly increasing its life span. The core could be honeycomb or foam, and the result would be about the same. [Figure 4-2 and 4-3]

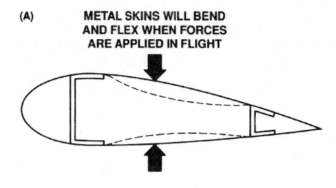

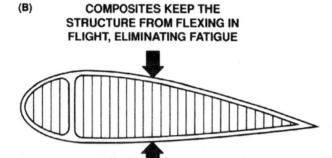

Figure 4-2. Stress comparisons of an aluminum and solid core composite airfoil.

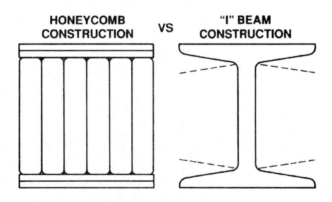

Figure 4-3. Bending and flexing concepts can also be shown using a spar I-beam example. The flanges of the I-beam will bend and flex; however, with a solid core material, the tendency to bend is eliminated.

Core materials may also come in wood. Honeycomb has the greatest strength-to-weight ratio, but foam is usually more forgiving. If a foam core is damaged, its inherent resiliency causes it to have what is commonly referred to as a memory, which returns it to about 80% of its original strength. Most honeycomb cores have little resiliency.

HONEYCOMB

This type of core structure has the shape of natural honeycomb and has a very high strength-to-weight ratio. Characteristics of honeycomb cores, when used in sandwich core construction, have a high strength-to-weight ratio, a high compression strength, a uniform distribution of stress, rigidity, thermal and acoustical insulation, and are fire resistant. Honeycomb cores may be constructed of aluminum, Kevlar®, carbon, fiberglass, paper, Nomex®, or steel. The most common types of honeycomb used in aviation manufacturing are aluminum and Nomex. Nomex, manufactured by DuPont, is widely used as an advanced composite core material. Aluminum honeycomb, which may or may not be considered a composite by the manufacturer, is usually found with aluminum skins. [Figure 4-4]

Figure 4-4. Typically, honeycomb cores used in aircraft construction are made of aluminum or Nomex®.

It is common to find honeycomb cores laminated with either metal or composite skins. [Figure 4-5]

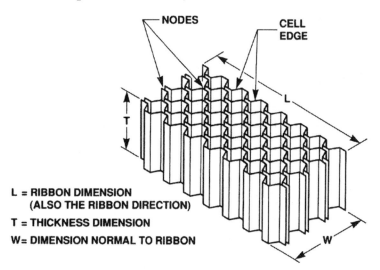

Figure 4-5. Honeycomb comes in a variety of core configurations, thicknesses, and densities.

Honeycomb cores are made by crimping the core material into place. The pattern has what is known as a ribbon direction. The ribbon direction can be found by attempting to tear along one side of the honeycomb. If you are tearing in the ribbon direction, the honeycomb will separate into strands. In this case the direction of the tear is parallel to the direction of the ribbon. The honeycomb will not tear except in the ribbon direction. When doing a repair, it is important to line up the ribbon direction of the replacement honeycomb core with the ribbon direction of the original part.

When using honeycomb for a repair, the same type of honeycomb that was used in the original structure should be used for the replacement material. Identify the honeycomb by the specific type (aluminum, Nomex) in a certain grade (aerospace), cell size in inches (1/16, 1/8), the density in pounds per cubic foot (2.0, 3.0), the thickness in inches (1/2, 1), and the cell shape (hexagon, over expanded). These should be listed in the Structural Repair Manual under the types of materials to be used for a specific repair.

There are different cell shapes in honeycomb, although the hexagon shape is the most common for flat or slightly curved areas. An over expanded cell shape is longer on one side of the cell and is used to bend around single curves. A cell that has a hat shape is used when the material is to be formed around compound curves. To maintain the strength of the component, always use the correct type of honeycomb cell shape in the repair.

Honeycomb can be joined together with a foam adhesive, usually in the form of a tape. The foam adhesive is laid between the parts to be joined and heated to cure. During the curing process, the foam expands into the crevices of the honeycomb core.

FOAMS

There are many different types of foams available depending on the specific application. There are different densities and types of foams for high heat applications, fire resistance, repair foams, structural foams, etc. When using foams in the repair operation it is important to use the proper type and density. [Figure 4-6]

In figure 4-7, the advantages of a sandwich structure can be shown by comparing four layers of solid fiberglass laminate to a foam core sandwich structure that is four times as thick. This part has two layers of fiberglass on top and two layers of fiberglass on the bottom of the foam. The part becomes 37 times stiffer than the laminate and ten times stronger, with only a 6 percent increase in weight. This is not an excessive amount of additional weight in exchange for the amount of strength and stiffness gained by using the foam core.

Figure 4-6. Foam cores for sandwich construction can be styrofoam, urethane, poly vinyl chloride, or strux (cellulose acetate). While easily shaped, foam construction can provide much greater strength and stiffness over plain laminates.

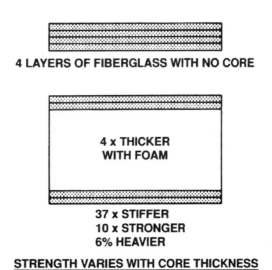

Figure 4-7. Strength-to-weight advantages of sandwich construction.

STYROFOAM

Styrofoam is used commonly on home-built aircraft and should be used only with epoxy resin. Polyester resin will dissolve the Styrofoam. Do not confuse aircraft quality Styrofoam with the type used to make Styrofoam cups. The Styrofoam used in cups has a large cell configuration and cannot be used for structural applications. The type of Styrofoam used to make aircraft components is much stronger. To form the desired shape, Styrofoam can be cut with a hot wire cutter, a tool that uses a heated wire to cut material. The tool is typically homemade and used in constructing home-built aircraft. To make cuts, a template is attached to each end of the foam stock. The wire is then heated and run around the template. Because the wire is held against precut templates, hot wire cutting is ideal for making smooth, curved surfaces. [Figure 4-8]

Figure 4-8. Using a hot wire cutter around templates to shape styrofoam.

URETHANE

This foam can be used with either epoxy or polyester resin. Urethane cannot be cut with a hot wire cutter in the way Styrofoam is cut because a hazardous gas is created when urethane is subjected to high temperatures. Instead of using a hot wire cutter, urethane can be cut with a number of common tools. Knives can be used to get the rough shape, which can then be sanded with another piece of foam to the desired size and shape.

POLY VINYL CHLORIDE (PVC)

Poly Vinyl Chloride foam is used with either polyester or epoxy resins. It is safe to cut this material with a hot wire cutter.

STRUX (ALSO KNOWN AS CELLULAR, CELLULOSE ACETATE)

Strux foam material is used to build up ribs or other structural supports.

WOOD CORES

Balsa wood or laminations of hard wood bonded to laminates of high strength materials are being used for some composite construction.

Chapter 5
Manufacturing

This discussion of composite manufacturing techniques is not intended to be a comprehensive treatment of the subject. There are many books available on the subjects of composite manufacturing and engineering.

The subject of composite manufacturing is addressed herein with the purpose of familiarizing the reader with those methods by which composite structures are manufactured so that when a repair is required, some of the same techniques can be used to restore a good measure of the original structural integrity.

From the manufacturers' perspective, composites represent cost effectiveness. Many case histories show an average 20% cost reduction when composite assemblies are used to replace the metal counterpart. The key word in this comparison is assemblies.

There are three primary factors which are considered in an analysis of manufacturing costs:

1. Materials costs.

2. Fabrication time.

3. Assembly time.

Advanced composite materials cost five to ten times more than aluminum. Fabrication time, i.e. the time required to form the final shape, is about the same for aluminum or composites. In some instances, composites require more fabrication time. The big difference between composites and aluminum lies in the assembly time.

Composite structures can be made in very complicated shapes. Consequently, stiffeners, ribs, lugs, beams, etc. can be molded together as part of the fabrication process. Although this may lengthen the fabrication time, it almost eliminates the assembly time. Since assembly time typically is four to five times greater than fabrication time in aluminum work, the net result is a major savings in time. In addition, an integrated fabrication requires substantially fewer numbers of fasteners, such as rivets, nuts and bolts, than the assembled aluminum counterpart.

The same characteristics that make composites advantageous to use in manufacturing also require a more precise repair procedure once they are damaged. A part that is composed of many metal subassemblies, such as a wing, can be repaired by removing and replacing discrete subassemblies, e.g. skin panels and ribs. Since the composite counterpart may be molded as a single unit, with few or no subassemblies, damage must be corrected with a true repair rather than a replacement of subassemblies.

Composites are becoming increasingly cost effective as the materials and manufacturing technologies mature.

When designing with composite materials, the weight savings are the primary pursuit. However, the composites also lend themselves well to the formation of complex, aerodynamically contoured shapes. The parts do not have to be flat, but can be smooth, sweeping contours, which would be difficult and expensive to fabricate from sheet metal, but not from composite materials.

HEAT & PRESSURE

Most manufacturers of composite structures augment the strength of the finished product by applying heat and pressure to the matrix/fiber mix as it cures. This accomplishes several things:

1. The heat and pressure facilitate the complete saturation of the fiber material.

2. The pressure has a tendency to squeeze out excess resin from the reinforcing fibers so that a more even blend of fiber and matrix is produced. Air pockets between fabric layers or in the matrix are also eliminated when pressure is applied.

3. The heat serves to accelerate the curing process of the matrix. In some instances, a high temperature is required to effect a cure of the matrix formula.

MANUFACTURING METHODS

COMPRESSION MOLDING

Compression molding is a manufacturing process that uses a male and female mold. The reinforcement fabric is wetted with a matrix or a pre-preg material. It is laid into a female mold and a male mold is used to form the shape of the part. If a core material is used, the fabric is wrapped around the core of the desired shape. Again, the two sides of the molds are used to apply pressure and give the part its final shape. The component cures by heating the molds to a specific temperature for a specified amount of time. Two commonly used heating methods with compression molding are accomplished by circulating heated oil through the mold or the use of electric filaments, which are imbedded into the mold. Another option is to place the entire mold assembly into an oven. The objective is to ensure an even, carefully controlled distribution of heat. [Figure 5-1]

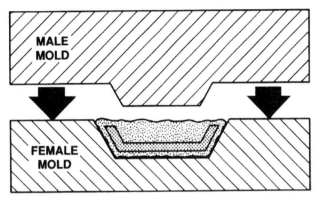

Figure 5-1. Compression molding is normally used to manufacture a large number of precision formed parts.

Because composites start out as reinforcing fibers (cloth) and a liquid (uncured matrix material), the only limitations on the shape of a molded component are those limitations associated with the mold itself. Once a mold has been produced, it can be reused to economically turn out a very large number of precision-formed parts.

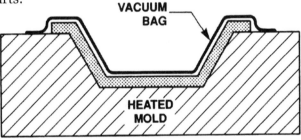

Figure 5-2. Vacuum bag molding can apply pressure to both very large and very complicated shapes. It is used in both manufacturing and repairing composites.

VACUUM BAGGING

With this technique, the object which is to be cured is placed into a plastic bag and the air is then withdrawn by the use of a vacuum source. When the air is evacuated, pressure is applied to the component by the surrounding atmosphere. A good vacuum source for composites will pull about 28 in. Hg at sea level, which results in nearly 14 pounds per square inch pressure being applied to the surface. The vacuum bag technique can be used in combination with molds, wet lay up and autoclave curing. This method applies a very uniform pressure to somewhat complicated shapes and can accommodate moderately large objects. Vacuum bagging is the most commonly used method to apply pressure for composite repairs. [Figure 5-2]

Both compression molding and vacuum molding have the advantage of distributing the matrix evenly throughout the reinforcement. This helps to eliminate air bubbles and results in a seamless structure. It is easier to fabricate and usually stronger than a metallic counterpart.

FILAMENT WINDING

Another manufacturing method that has produced incredibly strong structures is filament winding. Filament winding is widely used because of the manufacturing benefits which include low materials cost, accuracy, automation, and repeatability. In this case, the reinforcing fiber is wound as a continuous thread around a mandrel of the desired shape. In order to provide the precision required in placing this thread, a filament winding machine, or robot, is used. Some filament wound parts use pre-preg threads, while others dip the threads into a resin bath, and use a drying area to dry off extra resin. Once the filament has been wound in the desired pattern, the composite mixture is cured. The part is usually vacuum bagged and cured in an autoclave to further compact the fibers. After the cure the mandrel may stay in place, or washed out using a solvent wash or with a mandrel extractor. Sometimes the fabric is wrapped around the mandrel dry, with no resin on it. It is then used as a base for another form of manufacturing such as resin transfer molding (RTM). [Figure 5-3]

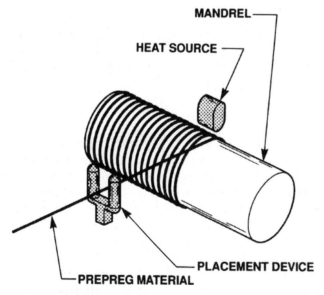

Figure 5-3. Basic filament winding.

This manufacturing method has been used to produce some of the strongest composite structures known. Filament winding is used in the fabrication of helicopter rotor blades, propellers, and even an entire fuselage.

At this time there are very few repairs that have been approved to be used on filament wound parts. This is because if the damage is a dent and has broken a few of the strands, the repair should not be cut out. Sanding the layers out as done on most repairs would cut through more of the continuous fibers, which would weaken the structure more after the repair than it was with the dent or damage.

FIBER PLACEMENT, TAPE LAYING

This is an automated process in which tapes (unidirectional prepregs) are laid over a mandrel and compressed into place. The difference between this and the filament winding process is that the tapes can be cut at the ends and very intricate shapes can be formed. This can be a very expensive manufacturing process.

RESIN TRANSFER MOLDING (RTM)

Resin transfer molding is a manufacturing method that uses a two-part mold with the dry fabric laid into the mold. The two molds are matched together and a system of resin and catalyst is pumped into the mold through injection ports. The resin follows a path throughout the mold. The part inside the mold can be heated and cured. The major advantage to this process is in the timesavings over hand lay-up because of the lay up and vacuum bagging time. It doesn't need to be autoclaved to cure. The major cost of this type of manufacturing technique is in the molds. They can be quite intricate, and unless used many times, they may not be very cost effective.

The resins used in the RTM process must have a very low viscosity. There are new advancements in the resins used in RTM applications. These include the resin and curing agent pre-mixed together and is known as a one-part system.

PULTRUSION

Pultrusion is a relatively simple and low cost automated method of manufacturing composite components. The reinforcing fibers are dipped into a resin bath and pulled into a die, which is the shape of the desired part. The material moves through the die as it is heated and cured. The finished part comes out the end of the die. The parts do not require vacuum bagging or autoclave cure.

WET LAY-UP OR HAND LAY-UP

Hand lay-up is a manufacturing technique that is simply laying prepreg material by hand into a mold. The mold is usually vacuum bagged and placed into an autoclave or oven to cure. If the parts require extra pressure, an autoclave is used. If the parts don't need the extra pressure, an oven can be used.

If prepregs are not used, and the fabric is impregnated with resin by hand, the process is known as a wet lay up. In this case the fabric can be impregnated outside the mold and laid in as with a prepreg, or it can be impregnated in the mold. The parts are then vacuum bagged and cured. Depending on the resin system used, heat may or may not be applied. If the resin is a room temperature cure material, it can be cured with just vacuum pressure at room temperature. If elevated heat is needed, heat lamps or an oven can be used.

In the homebuilt world, many times a core is covered with fabric and then the resin is applied to the fabric. This is also known as wet lay-up. The parts are not vacuum bagged because the resin system cures very quickly, and there is no time to vacuum bag the part. Heat is not used because there is no need to accelerate the cure.

Although this technique is less precise than other manufacturing methods, it is the most flexible procedure available. The simplicity and flexibility of the wet lay-up has made this technique a favorite of home aircraft builders. Furthermore, the materials and methodology associated with wet lay-up are the same as those which are often used to make repairs to composite structures. [Figure 5-4]

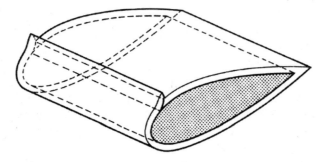

Figure 5-4. Wet lay-up, or hand lay-up, while being the least precise method, is the most flexible and most frequently used in repair procedures.

MOLDS OR TOOLING

Molding means to pull one or more parts from a mold. Each part will be identical.

The molds that are used in the manufacturing of composites are referred to as the "tooling". There is no single material that is considered the material for advanced composite tooling. The major reason for this is the problem of the coefficient of thermal expansion or CTE between the parts and the tool. What this means is that if a tool is made of fiberglass and the part to be made in the tool is made of carbon, the carbon and fiberglass expand at a different rate under heat, causing warpage of the tool, or the part, or both. To reduce warpage, compatible materials and resin system temperature cures should be used.

For higher temperature manufacturing methods, or if the part is to be cured in an autoclave, the materials used to make the mold might include carbon/epoxy, ceramics, hybrids and metals. The steel and aluminum molds are cheaper to make and fabricate and the materials are readily available but the problem of CTE is very high when used with advanced composites. The composite type of tooling has it's own set of problems as well. They sometimes require several stages in their manufacturing and can result in many types of errors. They have the advantage of being able to build in heating elements inside the tool for curing of the composite without the use of an oven. A tool that is manufactured in this way must be used many times for it to be cost effective.

There are simpler methods of manufacturing molds, including building up your own composite mold with either epoxy or polyester resin. Although it is very time consuming, it is a lower cost method, which is used in many facilities. Again, more than one part is usually made from these molds, reducing the unit cost.

BUILDING A PART FROM A SIMPLE MOLD

Molding begins with the creation of a plug that is the same size and shape as the part, which is duplicated. Plugs can be made of an inexpensive material such as foam, fiberglass, and plaster. The plug is then waxed and prepared for the creation of the mold. A mold is constructed to allow numerous parts to be fabricated. The mold itself is typically much heavier and thicker than the part that is fabricated.

For purposes of discussion, assume a part will be made from a mold in an airfoil shape. The materials of the component will be a carbon fiber skin with a lightweight sandwich core, in this case honeycomb, to reduce the weight of the component. We will make the mold so that the part can be vacuum bagged during the curing process. [Figure 5-5]

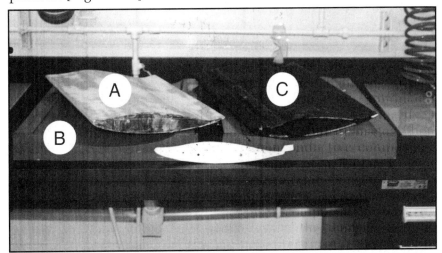

Figure 5-5. This photo shows a sample plug (A), mold (B), and finished component after fabrication (C)

DEVELOP THE PLUG

The plug is a model of the part which is to be duplicated. Sculpt the plug of aircraft Styrofoam and fiberglass to the exact size and shape using the manufacturers blueprint.

a. Construct a template from masonite or other similar material which is the same as a cross section size of the part.

b. Attach the template with small nails to the foam. Using a hot wire cutter, go around the template, cutting the foam. Try not to have lags in the wire which will make indentations in the foam.

c. Lay the raw fiberglass over the foam and brush or squeegee the mixed epoxy resin into the fibers. In this example a layer of course fiberglass weave is put on first, then a layer of fine weave on the outside.

d. When the fiberglass has cured, sand the plug to exactly match the component size.

e. Fillers and primers may be used to build up low areas, and then sand them down to get the exact dimensions desired.

f. The plug needs to have a prepared surface. This is very important because it affects the entire process. The plug is sprayed with a primer coat. When the primer is dry, the surface is sanded with very fine sand paper (first 200 grit, then 400 grit, and finally a wet sanding with 800 grit) to have a perfectly smooth finish.

CONSTRUCT THE PARTING BOARD

A parting board is a tool used to hold the plug on the centerline, which makes it easier for removal from the mold. Mount the plug to expose just half of the component at the centerline.

a. Construct a box using 4 boards (2X4) nailed together to build the base of the box. The box must be taller than half the plug. A piece of masonite is nailed to the top of the box.

b. To make the parting board, outline the plug on a piece of masonite.

c. Cut along the line with a saw. Bigger is better than too small. It is possible to fill in gaps between the plug and the parting board with clay.

d. Wax the plug and the board with a high temp mold release wax.

e. Each coat of wax is allowed to haze, and then it is buffed off, and left to stand for 1 hour before applying the next coat. Apply 4 coats of wax.

f. After waxing, the plug is ready to be mounted in the mounting board.

g. Draw the centerline on the plug with a marker.

h. Build braces for the box so that the plug fits down and rests at the centerline.

i. Next, the gaps around the plug need to be filled in using non-drying, oil based clay. Compatibility of clay and release agent is important.

j. Smooth the clay down into the edges and remove any excess.

k. Wax the mold again including the clay and the board. Don't change the position of the plug on the board. Haze buff.

l. Apply a light mist of liquid PVA release agent. Usually three light mist layers will be enough, allowing 10 minutes between coats. Excess PVA can cause problems; just a light mist per coat. After the third layer of PVA, wait 2-3 hours to dry.

3. LAY UP THE MOLD

For this example, we will be using an epoxy resin, and fiberglass to construct the mold.

a. The first layer to apply is the surface coat. Since this is an epoxy mold, an epoxy surface coat is selected. The surface coat will create the smooth outer surface from which the parts will be pulled. Brush on the surface coat. It will leave brush marks, which will eventually flow out smooth. Surface coat in the corner and all around the edge of the mold. Use a 1" brush to make the lip of the mold. If you want the mold big enough to vacuum bag, use a 3" lip all around the edges. Make sure there are no uncovered areas.

b. After the proper surface coat curing time, (approximately 1 hour) do a brush test to see if a mild impression is left in the surface coat. It should be dry enough that no brush strokes show.

c. A second layer of resin is applied with a fresh batch of surface coat.

d. After drying again (1 hour) the fiberglass can be laid into the resin.

e. While the part is drying, this is a good time to pre-cut the fabric reinforcement to fit the part.

f. Our example is using four layers of 2 oz., and eight layers of 6 oz. fabric. To figure out how much material is needed, use at least enough material to make the mold three times thicker than the part pulled from it.

g. Mix epoxy resin, catalyst and microballoons to make paste. Measure by weight.

h. This paste is used in corners and tight edges where fabric might pull away.

i. Smooth off to even out the edges and corners.

j. The base coat of resin is then mixed by weight. Some types of resin do not allow a very long working time, so you may have to work quickly.

k. Brush a base coat of resin over the entire surface, being careful not to disturb the paste.

l. Lay the fiberglass into the resin, wetting out the fibers. Add additional layers, wetting out as you go. Be sure to add enough fabric to include the lip of the mold.

m. Get out all of the air bubbles with a brush, work out any wrinkles in the fabric with a brush, or your fingers. Cut out any excess fabric and fold over to make the fabric smooth next to the plug.

n. If the type of resin used is a quick cure, you may need to make a fresh batch of resin.

o. Let cure about 30 minutes, to a partially cured state, but soft enough to be cut by a razor knife.

p. Trim the fiberglass all around, leaving about one inch lip to join the halves together. Cut down with the razor knife against the box.

q. After trimming, cure for 24 hours before removing the mold from the parting board.

r. To remove the mold from the parting board, a plastic wedge is used to apply pressure around the edges of the board until it is released.

s. After it has released, wash the mold in warm water and dish soap. Do not use solvents.

t. Inspect the surface for residual clay or surface imperfections. Remove any PVA with soap and water. Trim outside edge to PVA with a Dremel tool.

4. RELEASE THE MOLD FROM THE PLUG

a. Releasing the mold from the plug can be very difficult. If the mold sticks to the plug, the mold surface will need to be repaired before it can be used.

b. Plastic release wedges are available in various sizes, and several wedges may be required to release the mold.

c. Insert the wedge into the crack between the molds. Push the wedge around the edge to get it apart. After one side is off, squeeze gently on the plug, or use a wedge between the plug and mold. Be careful not to damage the mold.

d. Wash the mold again to remove all clay and PVA.

e. Inspect the surface for areas that might need a repair.

f. If a repair is necessary, take care not to alter the geometry of the mold.

g. When a mold is released, there is a small amount of flash around the edges. Flash is the extra extruded resin that needs to be removed. Use a Dremel tool or sander to grind down the edge.

h. The surface is now sanded and polished. A very smooth surface is the best. Use 400 grit, then 600 grit, and then a polish to achieve the smoothest surface possible. The mold is then washed and dried before proceeding.

5. PREPARE THE MOLD FOR FABRICATION OF THE PART

a. The surface of the mold is prepared in the same way as the plug was for release.

b. Apply wax in three layers, buffing out when hazed, allowing 1 hour between coats.

c. PVA is applied in light coats, three coats applied with approximately 10 minutes between coats. Allow it to dry for 2-3 hours on the final coat.

6. LAY UP THE PART

a. Pre-cut the fabric to the correct size and shape, with all material orientation figured out in advance.

b. Mix a small batch of resin and catalyst and brush on a surface coat of resin. If the part is made with prepreg material, a film adhesive could be used.

c. Lay the material into the mold. Allow the material to partially cure, then trim it flush. If prepreg material is used, it can be cut after it is laid into the mold.

d. The part can now be vacuum bagged, using standard vacuum bagging materials and procedures (Chapter 7)

e. Cure the required amount of time before removing the part from the mold.

f. Release the finished part by using wedges. Be careful not to damage the mold or the part.

g. After the part has released from the mold, inspect the surface for imperfections which might require repair, such as air bubbles.

h. Wash off the PVA mold release, sand off excess seam flash, and rim part.

i. The mold should be in good condition and can be used again and again.

MAKING A MOLD FROM AN EXISTING PART (SPLASH)

A two part molding compound can be used against an existing damaged part to make a mold. The damage on the existing part should be removed and the part sanded smooth. The area must be clean of dirt and grease. The area of the existing part should be waxed with mold release. If the damage extends all the way through the skin, a back up can be made with a two part potting compound. The potting compound is mixed and put into the hole, and cured. Sand down the potting compound until it has the same contour as the original part. Seal the area with a coat of resin. Cure the resin, and sand lightly. A mold release should be applied over the entire structure. The two parts of the molding compound are mixed together following manufacturers instructions. It is then applied to the existing part over the damaged area. After the molding compound has cured, remove the part and sand the inside of the mold to create a very smooth surface. Repair materials can be laid into the mold and vacuum bagged and cured. This new piece can then be bonded to the existing component. The manufacturer will give you the type of fabric and resin materials to use when you get an approval to do this type of repair.

LIGHTNING PROTECTION

Frequently, in the manufacturing process, some form of lightning protection must be used. It is important for a technician to be able to identify the type of protection used and able to repair the component with the lightning protection intact. Aircraft require electrical contact between all metallic and composite parts in order to prevent arcing or fiber damage. Aluminum is used to provide a conductive path for the dissipation of the electrical energy. The aluminum may be provided in a number of ways depending on the manufacture of the aircraft. No matter whether an aircraft is aluminum or composite, when lightning hits an aircraft it needs a path for the electricity to flow through [See figure 5-5]. On an aluminum skin, the electricity will flow through the skin and discharge out the static wicks. Since composites do not conduct electricity, lightning protection has to be built into the component. If there is no lightning protection in the composite and the lightning exits through the composite component, the resins in the composite will evaporate, leaving bare cloth.

Carbon/graphite composite was at first believed to conduct enough electricity to dissipate the electrical charge, but this was later found not to be true. Aluminum lightning protection may be found in carbon/graphite parts. A barrier, such as a layer of fiberglass, should be used to prevent a galvanic potential between the carbon/graphite and aluminum. [Figure 5-6]

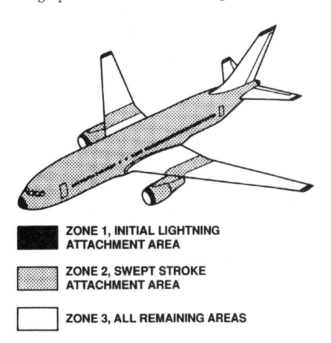

■ ZONE 1, INITIAL LIGHTNING ATTACHMENT AREA

▨ ZONE 2, SWEPT STROKE ATTACHMENT AREA

□ ZONE 3, ALL REMAINING AREAS

Figure 5-6 This figure shows which areas on an aircraft are most susceptible to lightning strikes.

ELECTRICAL BONDING

Different manufacturers use different methods to dissipate the electrical charge on composite structures. These are a few methods:

5-13

1. Aluminum wires may be woven into the top layer of composite fabric. This is usually done with fiberglass or Kevlar® and not with carbon/graphite.

2. A fine aluminum screen may be laminated under the top layer of fabric. If this method is used on a carbon/graphite component, it is usually sandwiched between two layers of fiberglass to prevent a galvanic potential.

3. A thin aluminum foil sheet may be bonded to the outer layer of composite during the manufacturing process.

4. Aluminum may be flame sprayed onto the component. This is molten aluminum that is sprayed on like a paint. Some companies will just paint the component with an aluminized paint.

5. In some structures, a piece of metal is bonded to the composite to allow the dissipation of the electrical charge out to another metal component or static wick.

PAINTING THE COMPOSITE PART

After manufacturing a part, the part is painted to seal the surface from moisture and for cosmetic purposes. For most aircraft, the same type of paint that is used for the metal portions of the aircraft is suitable for use on the composites. Some companies, such as Boeing, use a layer of Tedlar on the composite before painting. Tedlar is a plastic coating which serves as an additional moisture barrier.

GEL COATS

A gel coat is a polyester resin which is used during the manufacturing of the part. The manufacturing mold is coated with a color coat of polyester resin. The plies are laid down into the surface of the colored gel coat, and impregnated with an epoxy resin. After curing, the gel coat is on the outside surface, and provides a smooth finish. The plies of fibers which are embedded with the epoxy matrix are the structural part of the aircraft. The gel coating is not structural; it is more like a paint coat.

Gel coats were used on gliders extensively in the 1970s. The problem with gel coats is that because they are made of polyester resin, they are not as strong or flexible as the epoxy matrix. If the aircraft is stored outside in the sun and weather, the gel coat may crack. The aircraft must be inspected to see if the fibers themselves are cracked, and not just the gel coat. If only the gel coat is cracked, there is no structural damage. However, if the fibers are cracked, the structure will have to be repaired.

Gel coats cannot be rejuvenated as dope and fabric aircraft can. The gel coat must be sanded off and reapplied. Many aircraft owners who have had problems with the gel coat will sand off the gel coat surface and paint the surface with one of the new generation of paints that are very flexible, and can take the weather. Care should be taken when sanding the gel coat off, because the fibers were manufactured into the wet gel coat and will not be perfectly even. Care must be taken not to sand through the fibers.

PAINTS

The new generation epoxy based paints are used on composites just as on aluminum parts. The flexibility and wear resistance of the paint will not deteriorate as some gel coats. The component is primed and painted in the same manner as aluminum.

Fill primers can sometimes be used over a repair, but again, don't add too much weight to the repair, or you will be ruining the whole idea of using composite parts on the aircraft in the first place. Light weight and high strength are the key to doing proper composite repair work.

Chapter 6
Composite Safety

Safety is always of utmost importance around an aircraft. It is no different when working with composite materials. Even if there is no apparent danger, proper safety precautions must be observed at all times to prevent personal injury or aircraft damage. Most accidents dealing with composite materials occur because of improper usage and handling. All employees should not only be aware of the hazards associated with using these materials in a shop, but they should also be taught how to minimize these hazards.

In addition to the safety precautions detailed in this chapter, employees must make sure the materials used for composite repair procedures are confined in a designated work area. Also, eating, drinking, or smoking in the work area should not be allowed.

MATERIAL SAFETY DATA SHEETS

Before working with composite resins, solvents, or fabrics, it is important to know exactly what type of material you will be handling. Prior to any work, obtain the Material Safety Data Sheet (MSDS) for the material. The MSDS contains information on health precautions, flammability of material, ventilation requirements, and information for health professionals in case of an accident. You can get the MSDS through the supplier or the manufacturer of the material, and all employees should know where the sheets are kept in the shop.

As a technician, you may not become directly involved with the MSDS when the material is delivered because they may be kept in the tool crib area, in a notebook, or on the shelf next to the product. Many times the MSDS are kept in the doctor's or nurse's office of the company, or your boss or secretary may have them filed for safe keeping.

By law, the MSDSs for all hazardous materials used in the shop must be available to the people working with the materials.

To maintain the highest level of safety in the shop, you must know where your company keeps the MSDSs. If something should happen to you while working with hazardous chemicals it is important that you take the MSDS to the doctor with you. A doctor cannot be expected to know every chemical, so if you bring an

MSDS with you, the doctor can treat you appropriately, and in many cases, quicker. [Figure 6-1]

NOTE: This is a sample MSDS and is for training purposes only.

MATERIAL SAFETY DATA SHEET

Manufacturers name and address
will be found here.

PHONE: (000) 000-0000

AB9174
REVISION: 01 09/09/90
934 NA
HMIS CODE: H F R P
              2 1 1 C

Information contained herein is believed to be true and accurate. Compliance with applicable Federal, State and local laws and regulations are the responsibility of the user. This data relates only to the specific product designated on the Material Safety Data Sheet, and is not for use in connection with any other material or product.

It is not to be expected that this Material Safety Data Sheet can address all possible individual situations. In order that the Material Safety Data Sheet serve its intended purpose as an effective means of hazard communication, the health and safety information on the form must be provided and its importance emphasized to all those who handle or use the product by developing work practice guidelines and employee instructional programs for the individual operation.

The user has the responsibility to provide a safe workplace by examining all aspects of an individual operation to determine if, or where, precautions, in addition to those described herein, are necessary.

*N.A. = Not Applicable
N.E. = Not Established
0 = Insignificant
1 = Slight
2 = Moderate
3 = High
4 = Extreme

HMIS: Hazardous Materials Identification System, National Paint and Coatings Association Rating applies to product "as packaged" (i.e. ambient temperature)
H = Health   F = Flammability   R = Reactivity   P = Protective Equipment
CARC: Carcinogen or Potential Carcinogen
NTP: National Toxicology Program
IARC: International Agency for Research on Cancer
OSHA: Occupational Safety and Health Administration

SECTION I — NOMENCLATURE

TRADE NAME AND SYNONYMS

943 PART B

SECTION II — HAZARDOUS INGREDIENTS

HAZARDOUS INGREDIENTS	OSHA PEL	ACGIH TLV	CAS NBR	PCT	CARC
Epoxy Resin System	N.A.	N.A.	N.A.	N.A.	NO
Diethylenetriamine	N.A.	N.A.	111-40-0	<15	NO
Triethylenetetramine	N.A.	N.A.	112-24-3	<10	NO

SECTION III — PHYSICAL DATA

BOILING PT (DEG. F)   405   SPECIFIC GRAVITY 0.951
VAPOR PRESSURE (MM HG)   0.37mm   PCT VOLATILE BY VOL N.A.
VAPOR DENSITY (AIR = 1)   3.48   EVAPORATION RATE Nil
SOLUBILITY IN WATER   100%
APPEARANCE AND ODOR — Amber liquid with ammoniacal odor

MFG. NAME   DATE: 10/10/90
PART B   PAGE: 1 OF 3

Figure 6-1. Sample Material Safety Data Sheet.

SECTION IV — FIRE AND EXPLOSION HAZARD DATA			AB9174 .... CONTINUED	
FLASH POINT (DEG. F)	>200	METHOD USED	T.C.C.	
LOWER EXPLOSION LIMIT	N.A.	UPPER LIMIT	N.A.	

EXTINGUISHING MEDIA —
Dry chemical or Halon fire extinguisher, or water spray, foam or fog.

SPECIAL FIRE FIGHTING PRODEDURES —
Use self-contained breathing apparatus when fighting fires in confined areas.

UNUSUAL FIRE AND EXPLOSION HAZARDS —
Dense smoke and toxic gasses may be liberated.

SECTION V — HEALTH HAZARD DATA

HEALTH HAZARDS (ACUTE AND CHRONIC) —
Material is corrosive to skin. May cause chemical burn to eyes and skin. Repeat contact may cause sensitization. Vapors irritating and may cause chest discomfort and bronchitis symptoms.

ROUTE(S) OF ENTRY — Inhalation, Skin, Ingestion

SIGNS AND SYMPTOMS OF EXPOSURE —
Possible burns to eyes and skin; irritation and possible sensitization to skin. Irritation to upper respiratory tract.

MEDICAL CONDITIONS GENERALLY AGGRAVATED BY EXPOSURE — N.A.

EMERGENCY AND FIRST AID PRODEDURES —
Flush skin and eye contact with plenty of water. Wash thoroughly with soap and water, rubbing alcohol or hand cleaner. Do not use solvents. Remove soiled clothing and wash before reuse. If irritation persists, see physician.

NOTES TO PHYSICIANS — N.A.

SECTION VI — REACTIVITY DATA

STABILITY   STABLE

   CONDITIONS TO AVOID — N.A.

INCOMPATIBILITY (MATERIALS TO AVOID) —
Strong oxidizing agents, strong Lewis or mineral acids.

HAZARDOUS DECOMPOSITION PRODUCTS —
CO, NOx, aldehydes, acids and undetermined organics.

HAZARDOUS POLYMERIZATION —
May occur

   CONDITIONS TO AVOID —
   Avoid mixing resin and curing agent in batches greater that 1 pound total. Do not heat mixed adhesive unless curing surfaces to be bonded. Failure to observe caution may result in excessive heat build-up with the release of toxic gasses.

SECTION VII — SPILL OR LEAK PROCEDURES

STEPS TO BE TAKEN IN CASE MATERIAL IS RELEASED OR SPILLED —
Wear protective clothing, gloves and safety glasses. Scrape up and transfer to metal container. Wipe up remaining residue with solvents, observing solvent flammability cautions.

WASTE DISPOSAL METHOD —
Dispose of as hazardous waste according to DOT hazard class. If not regulated by DOT, dispose of as ORM-E.

PRECAUTIONS TO BE TAKEN IN HANDLING —
Keep cool in accordance with label instructions.

MFG. NAME   DATE: 10/10/90
PART B   PAGE: 2 OF 3

Figure 6-1. Sample Material Safety Data Sheet.

SECTION VII — SPILL OR LEAK PROCEDURES AB9174 .... CONTINUED ....

OTHER PRECAUTIONS —
Follow recommended curing schedule.

STORAGE —
Store at room temperature (77 deg. F) for 12 months.

SECTION VIII — SPECIAL PROTECTION INFORMATION

RESPIRATORY PROTECTION (SPECIFY TYPE) —
Not needed with good industrial ventilation.

VENTILATION —
Local exhaust recommended.

PROTECTIVE GLOVES —
Impervious plastic or rubber.

EYE PROTECTION —
Safety glasses or goggles.

OTHER PROTECTIVE EQUIPMENT —
As needed to protect skin and clothing.

SECTION IX — SPECIAL PRECAUTIONS

PRECAUTIONS TO BE TAKEN IN STORAGE AND HANDLING —
Keep cool in accordance with label instructions.

OTHER PRECAUTIONS —
Follow recommended curing schedule.

SECTION X — TRANSPORTATION AND LABELING

DOT PROPER SHIPPING NAME —
Alkaline Liquid, N.O.S.

DOT HAZARD CLASS —
Corrosive Material

UN/NA HAZARD ID NUMBER —
NA 1719

DOT LABEL —
Corrosive

WARNING LABEL —
Danger! May cause severe eye or skin burns. Prolonged or repeated exposure may cause allergic skin reactions. Part B contains Diethylenetriamine. Use only in a well ventilated area. Do not get on skin or clothing. Do not handle or use until the MSDS has been read and understood.

FIRST AID —
In case of contact, immediately flush eyes with plenty of water for at least 15 minutes. Wash skin with soap and water at once. Seek medical attention. Remove contaminated clothing and thoroughly clean before reuse.

IATA PROPER SHIPPING NAME —
Alkylamines, N.O.S. (Diethylenetriamine)

IATA LABEL —
Corrosive

IATA PACKING GROUP —
Group II

MFG. NAME
PART B
DATE: 10/10/90
PAGE: 3 OF 3

Figure 6-1. Sample Material Safety Data Sheet.

PERSONAL SAFETY WITH CHEMICALS AND MATRICES

SKIN PROTECTION

Certain materials can cause allergic reactions when they contact the skin. Some people are more sensitive to these materials than others. Using rubber gloves is the most effective way to provide skin protection with these chemicals. These gloves should be replaced after heavy use.

Shop coats should be worn to prevent clothing contamination and subsequent skin contact. Clothes saturated with epoxy resins should be removed without delay. If contaminated clothing is allowed to stay next to your skin, it can be highly irritating.

Remove any splashed resin from your skin immediately. Wash hands thoroughly before and after work, before eating or smoking, and before putting on gloves.

Always wash your hands before using the restroom. Many of the chemicals are potential carcinogens and may cause serious irritation and possible cancer, not only in the technician, but also with a sex partner. [Figure 6-2]

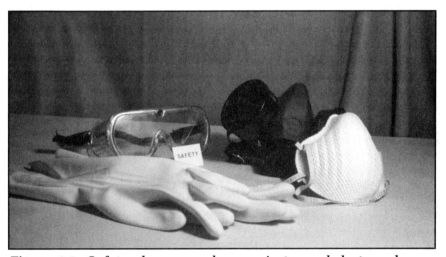

Figure 6-2. Safety gloves, goggles, respirator and dust masks are required when working with composites.

There are special epoxy cleaners available that break down the resins without drying out the skin. Don't use excessively strong solvents to clean your skin because they dry out the natural oils in your skin and cause allergic reactions that may cause your skin to peel (a form of dermatitis).

The proper skin protection required for a specific material can be found in the MSDS for that material.

RESPIRATION AND INGESTION

You must have the proper ventilation when working with any resins or solvents. Additionally, some resins are sufficiently toxic as to require you to wear a respirator when working with them. To alleviate respiratory issues, some shops provide a ventilated mixing booth. However, once the chemicals have been mixed, it is often necessary to apply the resin in an unventilated area or otherwise expose yourself to the chemical fumes. In such instances, it is important that respirators are used once the mixed resins are removed from the mixing booth.

Keep contaminated gloves, clothing, or material away from your hands and mouth. Some of the composite materials are very toxic and have no known antidote. If you drink them, you are as good as dead. So it is imperative that you wash your hands with soap and water before eating, smoking or drinking, and before and after using toilet facilities. There are special soaps and cleansers available that remove epoxies without harming your skin as solvents do.

EYE AND FACE PROTECTION

Some of the solvents and matrix components can cause permanent blindness within a few seconds after contact with the eye. Goggles, which can be worn alone or in combination with prescription glasses, provide complete eye protection against front and side impact hazards, chemical liquid splashes, and dust. If you should splash any epoxy resin or solvents in your eye, rinse the eye out immediately, report the accident to your supervisor, and seek medical help.

Very serious eye accidents have occurred when people did not take the warnings seriously. If you get any substance in your eye, do not wait to seek medical attention. If the substance is left in the eye for a prolonged period of time, or overnight, the damage to the eye can become more severe. Don't take chances. Tell your supervisor and seek medical help immediately. Some resins, hardeners, and solvents may make you go blind.

Face shields also offer good protection when working with resins. However, if you have an up-draft table, face shields should not be used. Up-draft tables, as their name implies, pulls fumes up through an exhaust vent. If a face shield is being worn, the fumes will be pulled up under the shield and have no place to exit. This may cause respiratory problems as well as eye accidents.

CAUTION: Plastic contact lenses may craze from resin fumes. When plastic comes in contact with the fumes of solvents or resins, white lines appear on the surface of the plastic. This is known as crazing. If possible, wear glasses instead of contact lenses, and always wear goggles. [Figure 6-3]

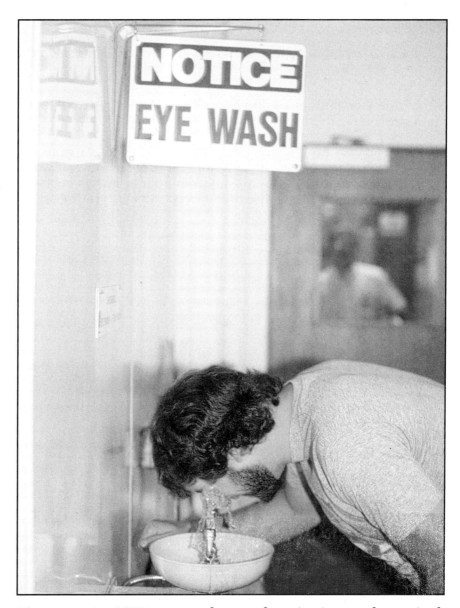

Figure 6-3. An OSHA approved eyewash station is not only required, but extremely important! They should be cleaned and maintained regularly. All approaches to the station should ALWAYS be unobstructed.

SOLVENTS: USAGE AND SAFETY

Many types of solvents are used when working with or repairing composites. Some of the most common solvents used with composites include:

METHYL-ETHYL KEYTONE (MEK) —

Used for cleaning dust, grease, and mold release agents from composite components.

ACETONE —

Used for general cleanup of tools and equipment and used as a prebond prep to clean the composite parts after sanding.

These safety guidelines should be followed with all solvents and matrices:

1. All solvents are flammable so there is a strict no smoking policy in effect when solvents are in use. Do not use solvents in the vicinity of sanding because sparks could create a potential fire hazard. Also, don't have solvents around when bagging films and peel ply materials are unrolled—they may create a static charge.

2. Use solvents neatly. Do not pour any solvent directly onto the part. A soft cloth moistened with the solvent is usually adequate.

3. Use solvents in a well ventilated area and avoid prolonged breathing of the vapors.

4. Wear gloves when applying solvents to protect the skin from drying out.

5. Never use solvents to clean skin. There are more suitable epoxy cleaners that are less dangerous to your health.

6. Wear goggles when pouring solvents.

7. Solvents should be kept in the original containers.

USE & STORAGE OF MATRIX MATERIALS

For safety, read and follow the manufacturer's instructions closely when handling and storing composite materials. Read the labels on containers for all information on handling, storage, and safety precautions. Improperly stored adhesives, resins, or pre-pregs may result in structurally unsafe aircraft components.[Figure 6-4]

1. Follow all manufacturers' instructions for mixing components. If resins are not mixed properly, the maximum cured strength will not be achieved. The two parts of the resin system must be weighed properly to get the proper mixture. Use a scale to mix to the proper ratio desired. Fortunately, some resins and adhesives come prepackaged and already have the proper amounts in the two parts of the package.

2. Always store the matrix materials properly. Some resins and catalysts require special storage temperatures. Three storage temperature ranges are common: room temperature of 75 to 80°F, refrigeration of about 40°F, and freezer temperatures of 0°F or less.

3. Keep records on refrigerated storage to ensure materials that are placed first-in, are the first-out for use.

4. Keep refrigerated materials sealed to prevent entry of moisture. An identification label must accompany the material.

5. Record accumulated time out of refrigerated storage. Some pre-preg fabrics have an "in freezer" storage life and an "out of the freezer" storage life because when the pre-preg is out of the freezer while cutting, the resins are slowly warming up to room temperature, starting their cure cycle. If they are allowed to stay out of the freezer for too long, they will cure too much and won't have adequate strength when you need to use them.

6. Allow components to warm to room temperature before weighing and mixing.

7. Discard all materials that exceed their storage life. Many containers have a "limitation date," which is calculated from the date of manufacture or date of shipment receipt (whichever is applicable). For example, if an item has a manufacturing or shipment date of 1/2001, and a six-month storage life, its "limitation date" may be stamped 7/2001 and should not be used after this date.

To discard the materials properly, consult the MSDS for that material. Many materials can not be thrown away. Instead, they may have to be mixed and cured before disposal because they may be considered as toxic waste if left unmixed. [Figure 6-4]

Figure 6-4. All instructions supplied by the manufacturer of the materials MUST be followed exactly. This includes mixing, as well as safety instructions. Any materials you are not familiar with, you should also consult the MSDS.

8. Handle materials with gloves to maintain cleanliness.

9. Never use brushes contaminated with another type of resin.

10. Store dry fabric and bagging materials in a clean, dry area. Care should be taken not to distort the fabric weave.

11. Do not allow protective hand creams to come in contact with the resins or bond lines. They may create an unbondable surface.

12. Do not remove the backing on pre-preg materials until the material is used.

13. Store honeycomb and foams in the original packing box.

14. Clean rooms are not required for making composite repairs, however, it is nice if you have a separate area for sanding and one for laying up the patches. This helps keep dust particles stirred up during the sanding operation from getting into the repair. If your shop does not have separate areas to do the composite repair work, clean the area thoroughly and vacuum up any dust, then do a solvent wash before attempting to bond patches. [Figure 6-5]

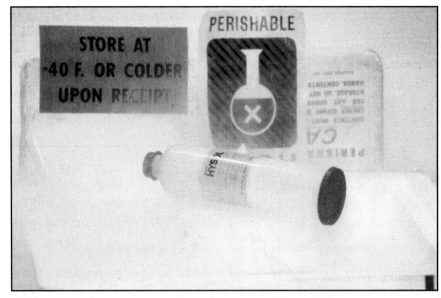

Figure 6-5. Some materials require specific storage temperatures. Again, follow the manufacturer's instructions carefully.

FIRE HAZARD MINIMIZATION

Many of the solvents and resin materials used are flammable so you must keep them away from heat and open flame. To minimize or eliminate the danger of fire, the following requirements should be met:

1. Eliminate all flames, smoking, sparks, and other sources of ignition from areas where solvents are used.

2. Use non-spark producing tools.

3. Ensure that all electrical equipment meets the applicable building and fire codes.

4. Keep flammable solvents in closed containers.

5. Provide adequate ventilation to prevent buildup of vapors.

6. Statically ground the aircraft and any repair carts.

7. Never unroll bagging films or peel ply around solvents. They may produce static electricity.

8. Never have solvents in the area when sanding. The possibility of sparks during the sanding operation is a fire hazard when solvent fumes are present.

PERSONAL SAFETY WHILE MACHINING

While sanding, drilling, or trimming composite structures, very fine dust particles contaminate the air. To help alleviate health risks, respirators must be worn. A dust collector or downdraft table also is very desirable to use while sanding because they pull the fine particles out of the air. However, a dust collector or downdraft table alone should not be solely relied on. Use such equipment in conjunction with a respirator.

Some composites decompose when being trimmed or drilled at high speeds. Because of the friction generated, you are burning away various materials and creating toxic fumes. Composites vary in their toxicity, so you should consider all composites equally hazardous and should observe appropriate safety precautions while working with any of them.

To minimize the possibility of particles entering the pores of the skin, wear protective clothing, such as a shop coat that doesn't have loose fitting sleeves. After working with composites, take a shower at the end of the day to flush particles from the skin and hair.

TOOL SAFETY

Tools should be disconnected from the air supply before changing cutters. Never hold small parts in your hands while drilling.

Always use a backup on the opposite side of the component to help prevent injury or damage.

Because carbon chips may be corrosive to aluminum parts and hazardous to electrical components, carbon composites may have to be removed from the aircraft prior to being worked on.

Always point the exhaust from pneumatic power tools away from other people. And remember, safety goggles are a must when drilling, sanding, routing, or grinding.

Never use compressed air to blow dust from a part that has been sanded. The excessive air pressure could cause an area of the laminate to disbond, causing further damage. To remove the dust, use a vacuum followed by a solvent wash.

WORKING ENVIRONMENT

Good housekeeping is an important aspect of the profession. It directly impacts an individual's safety and general work. Due to the materials used in composite repair, good housekeeping is a must. Here are a few tips on good housekeeping in your working area:

1. Do not block access to any safety equipment.

2. Keep storage areas neat and orderly.

3. Properly dispose of mixing containers.

4. Keep fabric remnants swept up.

5. Wipe up any spills and keep tools clean.

6. Make sure container labeling is legible and that the lids are intact.

7. Empty trash receptacle.

8. Keep bagging materials on rolls with covered storage.

9. Keep sanding away from lay-up area.

10. Down draft or dust collectors should be used while sanding.

11. Ensure there is proper ventilation available while working with resins.

SAFETY TEST QUESTIONS

1. An MSDS should be available to you while working in any shop. What information does it contain?

   _____,

   _____,

   _____.

2. Composite resins and solvents are very corrosive to the skin. What should be worn while working with these materials?

   _____ , _____ .

3. If you should splash any solvents or resin into your eye, what should be done?

   _____ , _____ ,

   _____ , _____ .

4. At the end of the shift when working with composites, what must be done to flush particles from the hair and skin?

   _____ , _____ .

5. When changing cutters or drill bits from power tools, what must be done?

   _____.

6. While sanding, grinding, or drilling, what must be worn?

   _____.

7. If the shelf life of a material is expired, what must be done to the material?

   _____.

8. Why is good housekeeping important while working with composites?

   _____.

9. If proper mixing instructions are not followed, what would be the result of the repair?

   _____.

10. Why should the aircraft and repair cart be statically grounded?

   _____ .

Chapter 7
Applying Pressure

Pressure should be applied to the surface during the curing operation until the component is fully cured. The purpose of applying mechanical pressure is to:

1. Remove excess resin from the components, ensuring the proper ratio of resin to fiber reinforcement. As the resins cure, they start to flow. The pressure will squeeze out some of this excess resin.

2. Remove air trapped between layers.

3. Maintain the contour of the repair relative to the original part.

4. Hold the repair securely, preventing any shifting of the patches during the curing process.

5. Compact the fiber layers together.

METHODS

Various types of tools and equipment are used to apply mechanical pressure. Vacuum bagging is the most widely used and recognized method of applying pressure for use on advanced composites. If vacuum bagging materials and equipment are not available, there are other methods to provide pressure, which can sometimes be used. [Figure 7-1]

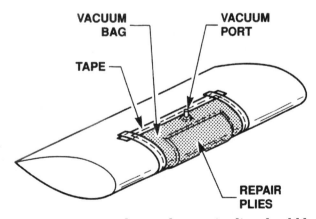

Figure 7-1. On a contoured part, the repair plies should keep the same shape of the part. The pressure should also hold the patches in place during the curing process so they don't shift.

SHOT BAGS

This method is effective when working on large contoured surfaces. A shot bag is a bag filled with shot or other heavy material. The weight of the bag provides the pressure. To prevent the shot bag from sticking to the repair, place a plastic sheet of film between them. Unfortunately, because of the laws of gravity, shot bags cannot apply pressure to the underside of an aircraft part. In this case, the part must be removed from the aircraft and turned upside down to apply this type of pressure.

CLECOS

Clecos are used in conjunction with pre-shaped caul plates to apply pressure to the repair. Holes are drilled around the edges of the repair to accept the clecos. They should be coated with mold release to prevent adhesion. Unfortunately, the holes may cause as much damage to the part as the original damage, so they must be filled. This type of pressure is not recommended.

SPRING CLAMPS

When working with spring clamps, a caul plate should be used to distribute pressure evenly over the area. The idea is that the spring clamps will continue to apply pressure even after the resins flow. This is not a great amount of pressure. The use of "C-clamps" is not recommended because the clamps do not compensate to hold a constant pressure as the resin flows during the cure. Another drawback to C-clamps is that they must be continuously tightened, thus increasing the chance compression damage might occur. [Figure 7-2]

PEEL PLY

Peel ply, a nylon fabric, is primarily used during the vacuum bagging process to facilitate the removal of excess resin into the bleeder material, and to allow for the removal of these materials once the part is cured. However, if other methods of pressure are not available, peel ply can be applied over a patch and resin worked into it, the peel ply removes excess resin and air bubbles, prevents shifting, and creates a "feather-in" of surrounding surfaces. If the part is to be painted, a rough weave of peel ply is desirable. When the peel ply is removed, the surface is also rough, eliminating the need for sanding before painting the repair. Peel ply is used to apply pressure in places that are inaccessible to vacuum bagging or those areas that have varied contour or shape. Peel ply is most commonly used in conjunction with other pressure methods.

VACUUM BAGGING

Vacuum bagging is probably the most effective method of applying pressure to a repair and is recommended for use whenever

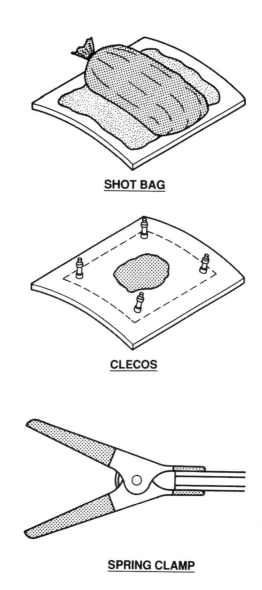

Figure 7-2. Various types of pressure devices.

possible. If you are working in an area with high humidity, vacuum bagging should always be used because high humidity may affect the cure of the resins and the vacuum bag system evacuates the air and the humidity.

Vacuum bagging works by using atmospheric pressure to provide an even pressure over the surface of the repair. Once the air is evacuated inside the bag by the use of a pump, atmospheric pressure pushes down on the part. The pressure of the surrounding atmosphere is greater at lower elevations than it is at higher elevations. Consequently, the amount of pressure a vacuum bag repair creates at sea level is greater than the pressure created during a repair at a high mountain airport. The amount of pressure also varies according to the effectiveness of the vacuum seal and the amount of force drawn by the equipment used.

Surface bagging is used on larger surfaces and for most repair work. On penetration repairs, the backside of the damaged area must be sealed to prevent air from flowing through the repair to the other side. In this case, the puncture is sealed on one side with vacuum bagging material while the repair is vacuum bagged on the other side where the patches are curing. When one side of the puncture has cured, the other side of the repair can be completed. This repair is often done in separate steps.

Self-enclosed bagging material is used on small parts. Self-enclosed bagging material is a plastic tube that can be sealed on the ends. The self-enclosed tube vacuum bag may be used on a repair when the part is removed from the aircraft and is small enough to be placed inside the tube. The process places atmospheric pressure on all surfaces of the part. If the part is hollow, the pressure may cause the part to collapse, especially in the area of the repair since it is not yet cured. In this situation, internal and external bagging should be used. [Figure 7-3]

VACUUM BAGGING PROCESS

Once the repair is made and the patches are in place, the area is covered with a parting film or a parting fabric (peel ply). This allows the excess matrix to flow through to the upper surface and into the bleeder material. Parting film prevents other materials, such as bleeder material, from sticking to the repair and is easily removed after the cure is completed. The parting film or parting fabric also "feathers" in a seam or overlap of fabric to produce a smooth surface. [Figure 7-4]

Some release fabrics, known as peel plies, can be used instead of a parting film to provide a final rough surface that is slightly etched and suitable for painting. Some manufacturers recommend the use of a perforated release film instead of using a peel ply. Like parting film, this plastic is used over the wet repair surface but has small holes in it to allow resins to flow through to the bleeder. A disadvantage to using the perforated release film is that upon completion, there is a resin rich area over the repair area that must be scuff sanded prior to painting. Be careful that sanding does not go through the fibers of the part or the repair plies.

A bleeder material is an absorbent material that is either placed around the edges or on top of the repair to absorb the excess

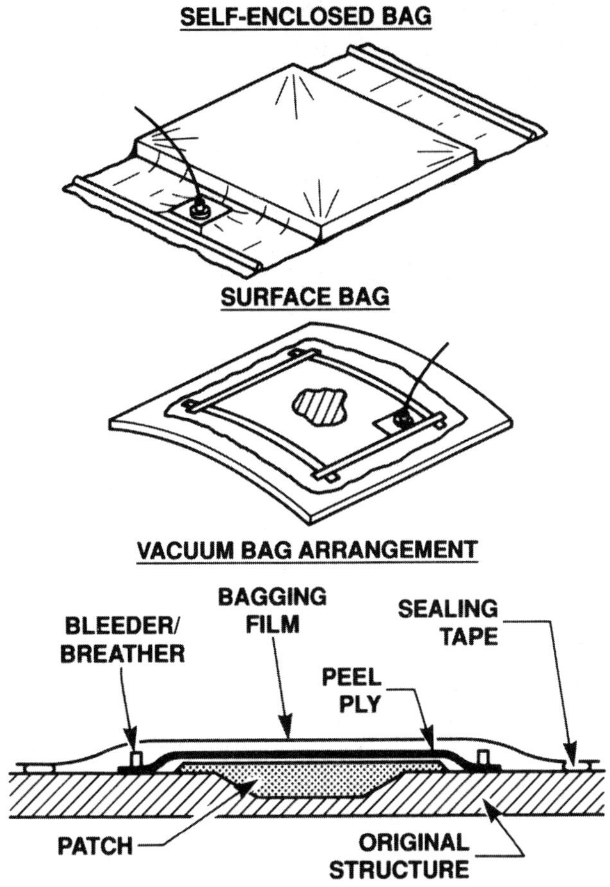

SELF-ENCLOSED BAG

SURFACE BAG

VACUUM BAG ARRANGEMENT

Figure 7-3. Surface bags and self-enclosed bags are basically the same in function. With a surface bag, the part to be repaired serves as one side of the bag.

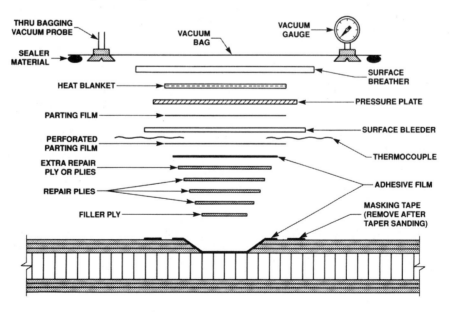

Figure 7-4. Cross sectional view of a complete vacuum bagged surface repair.

7-5

matrix. Different weights of bleeders are used depending on the amount of resin to be bled out of the repair. The most common bleeder materials are 4 oz or 10 oz.

A breather material is placed on one side of the repair to allow air to flow through it and up through the vacuum valve. It is also used over the repair area to ensure vacuum will be pulled throughout the vacuum bag. If a breather is not used, the vacuum bag may seal itself by sticking to an area. Then the rest of the vacuum-bagged area will not receive a correct amount of vacuum pressure. Bleeders and breathers can be made of the same material and can be used interchangeably in many cases. In such a case, the manufacturer may refer to it as a bleeder/breather.

The vacuum valve is placed on top of the breather material to remove the air from inside the vacuum bag. Later, the vacuum valve is attached to a vacuum hose, which connects to the vacuum pump.

A sealant tape is attached around the edges of the repair. When used in conjunction with the vacuum bagging film, sealant tape produces an airtight seal which can be removed from the aircraft surface after the repair is made without taking the paint off. Sealant tape comes on a roll with paper backing on one side. As the tape is laid onto the surface, the paper is left on the tape so that it can be pushed down onto the surface without sticking to your fingers. [Figure 7-5]

Figure 7-5. Sealant tape being applied to the edge of the repair area.

When using a thermocouple or temperature-sensing device to monitor the temperature of the part while curing, it should be laid next to the repair area and sealed into the sealant tape by putting another small strip of tape over the thermocouple wire. This prevents air from leaking around the thermocouple wire.

When using a heat blanket to cure the repair, lay a parting film over the repair to prevent the heat blanket from sticking to it. In this case, the parting film can be a non-perforated release film or a piece of vacuum bagging material. In any case, it should be able to withstand the temperature of the cure since it is directly in contact with the heat blanket. The heat blanket should be placed over the parting film and must also cover the thermocouple wire. If the heat blanket has two wires, they should be split apart, and another strip of sealant tape should be put over them to reduce the chance of air leakage.

Vacuum bagging film is laid over the repair and the edges are worked into the sealant tape to produce an airtight seal. The most commonly used bagging films are made of nylon because they resist tears and punctures, and they are rated at different temperatures. The most effective way to create a seal with the bagging material is to take the paper off the sealant tape on one side and lightly press the bagging film into the sealant tape.

On a contoured part, pleats may be needed to allow extra bagging film to conform to the shape of the part. The pleats are made from small pieces of sealant tape and folded together. These pieces are then positioned in the sealant tape that lies around the edges of the repair. When the bagging film is applied, it is attached to all surfaces of the sealant tape, producing a pleat in the bagging film.

The bagging film should be lightly pressed into the tape until it forms an airtight seal that covers the part. If it is necessary to readjust the bagging film, it can be picked up and repositioned. If the film is stuck to the tape too firmly, however, it is difficult to reposition. Once the film is positioned correctly, it can then be pushed firmly into the tape to produce an airtight seal.

A slit is cut into the bagging film over the vacuum base, then the vacuum valve is inserted into the base and is sealed airtight. Wrinkles should be avoided in the bagging film around the valve because air may leak around it. If any wrinkles form, they should be worked smooth. The valve is then attached to a vacuum hose.

The vacuum source is connected to the vacuum hose and turned on. Check to see if there are any leaks in the bagging film. If there is, the leak produces a hissing sound. These areas of the bagging film that have the hissing sound should be pushed down harder into the sealant tape until there is no hissing. Leaks usually occur where the tapes overlap, at pleats, or where wires pass through the sealant tape. An additional vacuum valve fitted with a vacuum guage can be used at this point to perform a vacuum leak test. [Figure 7-6]

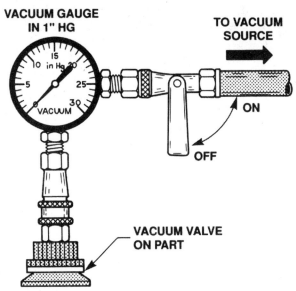

Figure 7-6. The valve with vacuum gauge, ON/OFF valve, and hose attached.

VACUUM LEAK CHECK

A vacuum leak check is done to make sure the bag is sealed properly. After vacuum is drawn on a part, the vacuum hose is disconnected for about two minutes. With a vacuum gauge attached to another vacuum port, the amount of mercury drop is noted. A drop in mercury means there are leaks that haven't been sealed completely. Depending on the manufacturer's instructions, an allowable drop may be one to four inches of mercury.

After the curing process, all the layers of bagging film, sealant tapes, bleeders, breathers, and peel plies or release films are removed from the part are disposed of. The peel ply layer may be kept on the part until it is painted to keep the surface clean.

The rough surface of the peel ply is like a slight etch that allows the paint to adhere to the part better. If a parting film or plastic was used, the surface must be scuff sanded to allow the paint to adhere. Caution should be used while sanding to avoid sanding through the fabric.

Vacuum bagging can be used for parts that are cured in autoclaves, ovens, or with hot bonding units, heat blankets, heat guns, and heat lamps. The vacuum bagging process is used in manufacturing as well as in the repair process.

VACUUM BAGGING MATERIALS

The materials commonly used for vacuum bagging come in a number of types, depending on the manufacturer, and how the repair is to be performed. Vacuum bagging materials are not a permanent part of the repair. They are removed and disposed of after the cure. They are tools used to facilitate the repair. There are many types of vacuum bagging materials, and your decision which ones to use may be based on:

1. The materials ability to withstand the cure temperature. Bagging materials come with different temperature ratings. If a repair is to be made at 350°F, then the vacuum bagging film, bleeders, breathers, peel plies, and sealant tapes should all be able to withstand this temperature.

2. The cleanliness of the material. Foreign materials are not desirable in a repair.

3. The ability to pull the proper amount of vacuum. Pinholes in the plastic, or a moisture content that is too low may cause problems.

4. Will they produce the proper repair? If fiberglass is used in place of the bleeder, will it soak out too much resin, causing a resin dry part?

Although these materials may come with a conformity report, they are not required for the repair. These materials are tools. Only materials that remain on the aircraft need conformity reports. Examples of such materials include repair fabrics and resin systems.

Some of the more commonly used materials for composite repair are listed below.

VACUUM BAGGING FILMS

Vacuum bagging films are used to cover the component and seal out air. They must be made with absolutely no voids or pin holes. If there are small holes in the film, air leaks through and less pressure is applied to the part while curing. Bagging films come in a variety of temperature ranges from room temperature up to 750°F. It is important to use the correct temperature rating for the required cure temperature. The vacuum bagging film should remain flexible at high temperature cures, especially around highly contoured shapes. If the bagging film becomes brittle, it may develop air leaks, which decreases the amount of atmospheric pressure applied to the part.

The selection of the appropriate bagging film depends on the method by which the part is cured and the required temperature of the cure. Bagging film is hydrophilic, or water sensitive material. Moisture acts as a plasticizer. The higher the moisture content of the film, the more flexible and rubbery it becomes. During the vacuum bagging process, it is important that the film is as flexible as possible so the film can be formed around any contoured shape.

It is extremely important to maintain the moisture content when storing this film. When the material is shipped, it should be enclosed in a plastic wrap. Cut only the amount to be used from the roll. The rest of the roll should be stored in the original plastic wrapper. This is especially important in dry climates and during the winter months when the moisture content may dry out and cause the film to become brittle.

SEALANT TAPES

Sealant tapes are used to maintain a positive seal between the surface of the original part and the bagging films. This seal must be leak proof to ensure maximum atmospheric pressure is held against the part. Some sealant tapes have a limited shelf life, so storage and labeling may be required. If the shelf life is exceeded, the seal will not be the standard quality, and the sealant tape might not be easily removed from the surface.

The tape should hold tight even if the bagging film shrinks during the curing process, and it should be able to withstand the temperatures of the cure.

Pleats are made with sealant tape to provide extra bagging film over a part with contours. To make the pleats, a three- to four-inch piece of sealant tape is cut. The middle of the sealant tape is pinched together and the ends are attached to the sealant tape, which has been placed around the part.

When used, a pleat should be placed even with any edge or sharp contour to allow for the extra plastic where it is needed to provide a good seal. No more than half of the backing paper on the sealant tape should be removed prior to attaching the bagging film.

Pleats allow extra room in the bagging film to conform to the shape of the part and achieve a good seal. If extra vacuum bagging material is not available in some places, or if extra material does not conform to the shape of the part, a bridging effect may take place, allowing the excess resin to flow into these areas during the curing process. If enough pleats are added around the vacuum bagging area, the excess material should easily conform to the shape of the part when the vacuum is applied.

RELEASE FABRICS AND FILMS

Release fabrics and films are used when a barrier is needed between the wet patches and the other vacuum bagging materials. Perforated films and release fabrics are also used when the resins are expected to flow up through the material and into a bleeder.

PEEL PLY

A nylon or polyester release fabric may be used next to the wet resin during the curing operation to transfer excess resin to the bleeder material without sticking to the part. After curing, the peel ply is peeled off the part, which causes a slightly rough surface. This is important if the part is to be repainted. Peel ply materials are extremely helpful over seams or where layers of fabric overlap. They will "feather-in" the layers and eliminate the need for sanding.

Teflon release fabric is an excellent material because it releases from the repair area very cleanly. However, there are two types of Teflon release fabric: porous and non-porous. The porous material allows resin to flow through the fabric up into a bleeder material, while the non-porous release does not. The non-porous is used primarily in manufacturing against the side of a mold.

Peel plies come in different finishes; some are very smooth, and others are coarse. Some peel plies may be treated with mold release, corona, or Teflon to release better.

Peel plies are more desirable than release films for repair applications because they allow the resins to flow through more evenly. Peel ply used over a repair eliminates the need for sanding off the gloss or extra resin before painting. If the peel ply is left on over a repair, it keeps the part clean until it is ready to be painted.

RELEASE FILMS

Release films come in two forms. Perforated release film is a plastic with holes that allow excess resin to flow into a bleeder just as a peel ply material would do. This type of film comes with holes in different sizes and spacing depending on how much excess resin needs to be bled away from the repair area. They come in various temperature ratings.

Non-perforated film does not allow the excess resin to flow out, allowing the resin to build up, creating a brittle, heavy repair. The non-perforated release films are used when a barrier is needed between other parts of the vacuum bagging process. They are often used under a heat blanket over the bleeder material. This prevents the bleeder material and resins from coming in contact and damaging the heat blanket.

Before painting a surface that was cured with a release film, the glaze created from the plastic should be removed by hand sanding, otherwise the paint may not adhere to the structure. Carefully sand off the glaze and do not sand into the fiber material.

BLEEDERS

Bleeders are cotton-like absorbent materials used to soak up excess resins. Some companies will use felt or other absorbent material. Do not use the bleeder in contact with the repair. If not used in conjunction with a release fabric, peel ply, or release film, the bleeder material will become a permanent part of the aircraft.

Different bleeder thicknesses and weights are available, depending on the type of lay-up used for the repair. If the patches were impregnated by hand, a heavier bleeder is probably needed to soak up the excess resin. Some technicians, however, use a very dry lay-up and need to use a thinner bleeder. If using a pre-preg, a thinner bleeder material is the best option. Typical weights are 4 oz. and 10 oz. bleeders.

BREATHERS

Breathers are cottony materials that allow air to flow through a valve or over the surface of a part throughout the vacuum-bagged area. This is typically the same material as a bleeder and can be used as a combination material called a bleeder/breather. When the vacuum hose is applied, air must be able to flow to the vacuum port without restrictions. A breather is used over the repair area under the vacuum bagging film.

CALKING PLATE

In some instances, a calking plate or pressure plate is used to add extra pressure that smoothes the contour of the part being cured. This is usually an optional piece made of wood, aluminum, or copper. If there is a slight cure in the part or component, the calking plate must also conform to the shape of the part. If it doesn't, a space between the part and the calking plate may collect resin and not cure properly.

INSULATION LAYERS

Insulation may be added either outside the vacuum film or under the vacuum bagging film and over the heat blanket. It is used to minimize the amount of heat loss during the cure process. The insulation may be a few layers of fiberglass or a sewn blanket with many layers. If the repair work is done in a very cold environment, the heat blanket may lose heat around the edges and cause incomplete curing in some areas. An insulation blanket may prevent this from happening. Insulation is considered optional because if the thermocouple is directly under the heat blanket, the controller will keep adding heat to keep the blanket at the desired temperature. [Figure 7-7]

The vacuum bagging operation can be done around a corner or over an edge, as illustrated in Figure 7-8. Trailing edges can also

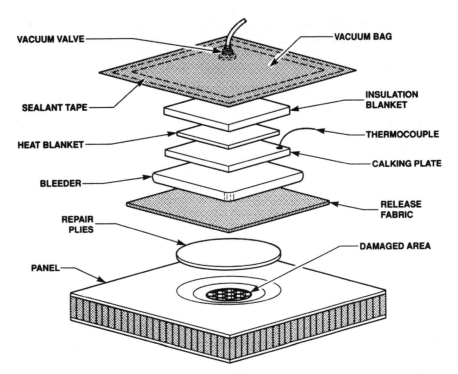

Figure 7-7. A typical stack-up for a heated vacuum bag surface repair.

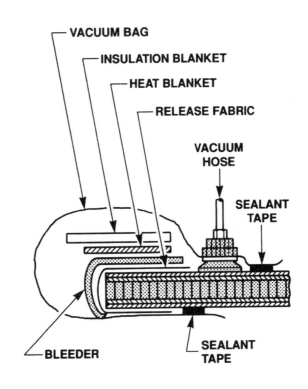

Figure 7-8. Stack-up of heat being applied to the edge of a piece of honeycomb panel.

be vacuum-bagged in this manner. If the repair is done to both sides of the edge, a calking plate should be used in the vacuum bag to prevent the repair plies from bending up or down as the air evacuates the repair.

VACUUM BAGGING EXAMPLES

Below are a few examples that illustrate the vacuum bagging process.

SELF-ENCLOSED BAGGING

When there are multiple repair areas that need vacuum applied to them, instead of vacuum bagging each area separately, one bag can be applied over the entire part. A large bag is made about three times the size of the part, allowing the bagging film to go inside as well as outside the part, thereby preventing the part from collapsing. A large sheet of vacuum bagging material is cut and folded in half. Two of the sides are sealed with sealant tape but the end is left open. On the open end, sealant tape is applied to one side of the bagging film, but the paper backing is left on so the bag does not seal at this time. The part is placed inside the bag with all the proper bagging materials. A breather is very important at this point because it allows air to flow completely throughout the bag. An air valve is connected to the bag, and the bag is sealed on the prepared edge. The vacuum hose is then connected and air removed. It takes time to make sure all of the areas are being covered in pressure and that there are no bridges for resin to build up into. It is best if the bagging film can be smooth over the areas of the repair. This reduces the chance of a resin build up over the repair. If a resin ridge does form, it can be removed by sanding, being careful not to damage the new repair. The part is then cured. [Figure 7-9]

BAGGING ON BOTH SIDES OF A TIGHT RADIUS

Referring to figure 7-10, this leading edge has a very tight radius. The repair requires pressure to be on both sides of the repair, inside and outside the leading edge. To bag this part, a line of sealant tape is placed inside the leading edge and around the repair area, in a square fashion. Another line of sealant tape is placed over the outside of the leading edge and they meet on the edges. A longer piece of sealant tape extends past the edge. A piece of bagging film is placed over the top of the leading edge and pressed into the sealant tape. Another piece of bagging film is placed on the inside and sealed to the sealant tape. The open edge is then sealed with another piece of sealant tape. The air is evacuated and checked for leaks. The most common place for air leaks is on the inside of the curve of the leading edge. A lot of pressure may be needed to press the sealant tape into the part to produce a good seal. A very clean part is a must to get the tape to stick to the surface.

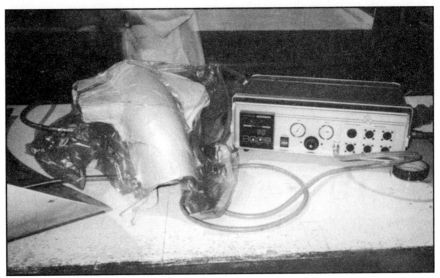

Figure 7-9. This part needs numerous repairs, so the entire part is put into a self-enclosing bag. The bag must be made about three times larger than the part to allow extra bagging film to contour around the part on the inside and outside, giving the proper amount of pressure.

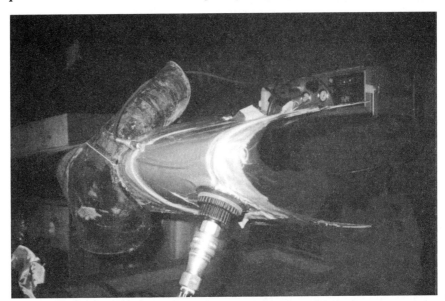

Figure 7-10. The part is bagged on the inside and outside with sealant tape and bagging film. The top bagging film is brought over the top of the repair and sealed to the bagging film attached to the inside of the part.

BAGGING WITH ACCESS TO ONLY ONE SIDE OF THE PART WITH DAMAGE EXTENDING THROUGH THE PART

When damage extends through the skin but there is no access to the other side, a very lightweight potting compound is used. After the damage is removed and step sanded, the hole needs to be filled to seal off the backside. A two-part potting compound is mixed and placed inside the hole, sealing all the edges of the hole, then cured. This fills up any voids from the backside. Once the potting compound has cured, it is sanded to the contour of the hole. The new repair plies are placed over the hole and the part can be vacuum bagged from the topside without drawing air up through the repair. This repair may add weight to the component and must be approved before performing the work. Also, if weight has been added, a weight check or balancing of the component is necessary if it is a control surface.

DOUBLE VACUUM BAGGING

To apply more pressure, which removes more of the resin and air pockets, a double vacuum bagging method can be used. The part is bagged in the normal way, then a steel plate is placed over the area, and a second vacuum bag is put around the first. The second bag takes the pressure off of the first bag, allowing more flow of the resins. This has been used in areas where autoclaving was desired but was not available or feasible. The double bag method produces very good properties almost equivalent to autoclave-repaired parts.

TYPICAL VACUUM BAGGING PROBLEMS

Leaks can be caused by a number of things including:

- Gaps in the sealant tape – The sealant tape is used to give a tight seal to the surface of the part. If there is a gap between the tape and the part, or the tape and the bagging film, it will leak air. Check the most common areas first. Push tightly wherever the sealant tape is attached to the surface. Then check areas such as pleats or areas where the sealant tape overlaps. Areas that have a thermocouple wire or heat blanket wire may leak if not tightly sealed.

- Fabric through the sealant tape – Sometimes in the vacuum bagging process, an edge of peel ply or bleeder material may overlap the sealant tape. The air will flow through this area. Take the vacuum pressure off, and reposition the material. Apply vacuum again to see if the leak is gone.

- Cuts in the bagging material – The use of scissors and razor knives during the bagging operation is common practice. If the vacuum bag is cut accidentally, it could cause a hissing noise. If the cut is small, a piece of sealant tape will seal it. However, if the cut is larger, a smaller vacuum bag may have to be made and placed over the cut area. Line the cut area with more sealant tape and place a piece of bagging film over the area. Apply vacuum pressure again and it will take the air out of the smaller bag at the same time as the original bag.

- Dirty surface – If the area around the repair was not cleaned properly, the sealant tape may not adhere to the surface. It is important to keep the area around the repair clean. Wipe the area with solvent to clean away any grease or dirt that may be on the surface.

Chapter 8
Methods Of Curing

Composite matrix systems cure through chemical reaction between a catalyst and resin. Some matrix systems require heat to cure the composite to achieve maximum strength, while others cure at room temperature but can be accelerated by applying external heat.

Improper curing or handling during the cure has a direct effect on the strength of the repair. Failure to follow the proper curing requirements or improper usage of curing equipment can cause defects, which may in turn cause the repair to be rejected. For example, unless the repair is vacuum bagged during the curing process, humidity may cause a problem.

ROOM TEMPERATURE CURING

Some repairs may be cured at room temperature (65°- 80°F) over a time span of 8-24 hours, depending on the type of resin system used. The curing process can be accelerated by applying low heat (140° - 160°F) to some room temperature resin systems. Check the specific material for the applicable cure time.

Full cure strength usually is not achieved until after five to seven days. If the repair calls for a resin system that can be cured at room temperature, it would be for parts used in areas with no exposure to high operating temperatures (usually above 160°F).

Room temperature cures normally are performed on composite parts that are used on lightly loaded or nonstructural parts.

HEAT CURING

The most widely accepted method of curing structural composites employs resins that cure only at higher temperatures. These adhesives and resins require elevated temperatures in order to develop full strength and to reduce the brittleness of the cured resin. The high heat also reduces the curing time.

When a part is manufactured at a high temperature, the repair patches used in its repair may need to be cured at the same temperature in order to restore the original strength. These resins usually cure at a temperature of 250°F to 750°F. The amount of applied heat should be held constant by monitoring the surface temperature of the repair.

Although curing by applying heat in some instances produces a stronger repair, overheating can cause extensive damage to the component. If too much heat is applied, the vaporization, or gassing, of the matrix may cause bubbles to form on the surface. A dry area is also an indication of excessive heat.

Recently, some aircraft manufacturers have been specifying in the structural repair manual (SRM) that technicians can repair a part using less heat for a longer period of time than was used during the manufacturing of the part. For example, if a part was originally cured at 250°F for 1.5 hours, the repair may use the same materials and cure at 230°F for 2 hours. Repairing a part this way prevents the overheating of the existing area around the repair. If the undamaged area surrounding the repair is placed under high heat a second time, microcracking (tiny cracks in the resin and fibers that are not visible) could develop and weaken the structure. This is why repairs are not cured in an oven or autoclave, but have the heat applied just to the area of the repair.

Although the fibers can withstand higher temperatures than the matrix, exceeding the recommended curing temperature should be avoided to reduce material disintegration or further delamination of the existing structure around the repair. Since the C or F is often eliminated from cure temperature in the repair manual, technicians must know if the proper temperature is in Celsius or Fahrenheit. For example, if a prepreg material comes from Europe, the cure temperatures are stated in Celsius degrees. So if the manual states the material cures at 180°, but a technician uses 180°F, the part will not cure in the proper amount of time. (180°C = 350°F)

When a part needs heat to cure, it is not enough to simply apply heat at the final cure temperature. It is important to allow a slow rate of temperature increase, known as a ramp up, so the resins have enough time to flow out of the fabric and into the bleeder material before going through the curing process. If this doesn't occur, a resin rich area may result.

It is also important to allow a repair to cool at the proper rate. Composites gain much of their cure strength during the cooling down process. A gradual cooling is desirable, but not usually possible unless a controller is available. A controller is a device that regulates the temperature. Hot Bond Equipment includes the controller and a vacuum source for composite repair.

The step cure and ramp and soak heating methods are probably the most used with composite repair because they ensure a slow rate of temperature rise and decline.

STEP CURING

Step curing is used with a manually operated controller and requires the technician to make the adjustments manually at specific time intervals. The simplest thing that a controller will do is maintain a selected temperature. When used in this manner, it is referred to as a setpoint controller. If the technician selects a setpoint above the current temperature, the controller applies heat to change the temperature as rapidly as possible to the new value. If a setpoint is selected below the current temperature, the controller turns off the heat in order to cool down to the setpoint as rapidly as possible.

Step curing is the process of bringing up the temperature slowly by raising the temperature to one point and holding it there, then bringing it up again and holding it there, and repeating this process until the cure temperature is reached. This allows the heat to build slowly, allowing the resins to flow before reaching the cure temperature. The cure temperature is specified in the SRM and held for a period of time which is also specified in the SRM. After the cure time has elapsed, the temperature can be stepped down by reducing the temperature slightly and holding it there, then bringing it down slowly again and holding it there until room temperature is reached. This slow cooling down gives the component a stronger final cure. [Figure 8-1]

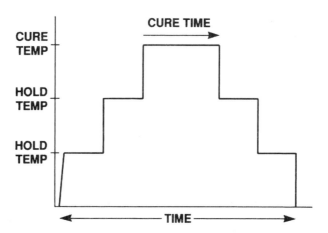

Figure 8-1. Step curing is normally used where a manually operated controller is hand adjusted by the technician. Time and temperature must be watched closely.

RAMP AND SOAK CURING

A programmable controller produces a more sophisticated and accurate curing than the step curing process. For this method, a controller is programmed in a ramp and soak mode, which heats or cools a repair at a specific rate. For example, Figure 8-2 shows a repair that needs to be heated at a slow, constant increase from room temperature to 400°F at eight degrees per minute. If room temperature is 70°, it takes approximately 41 minutes to reach the

400° mark (400° − 70° = 330°; 330° ÷ 8° each minute = 41.25 minutes). This heating process is called the ramp.

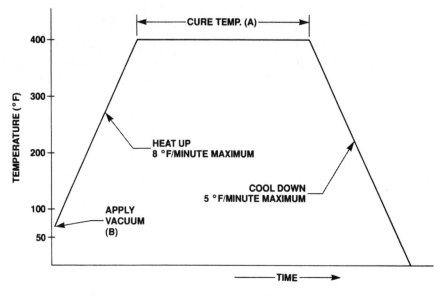

Figure 8-2. *Profile for a ramp and soak cure.*

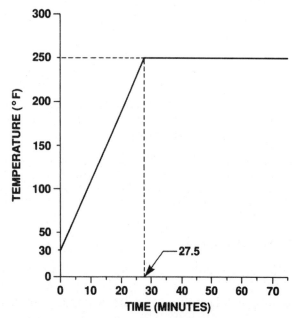

Figure 8-3. *Cold Climate: If the cure is to be done in a cold climate where the temperature outdoors is 30° F, the cure ramp up time is to be 8° F per minute. 250° − 30° = 220° ÷ 8° = 27.5 minutes to climb to the cure temperature of 250° F at a rate of 8° F per minute.*

Once the repair has been heated to 400°F, the SRM may require this temperature to be held for a specific amount of time. In this example, the temperature is held for two hours. When the controller operates during these two hours it is referred to as the soak.

The SRM may specify that the temperature be ramped down to room temperature at a specific rate following the soak. In our example, a five-degree per minute cool down rate takes an hour and six minutes (400° − 70° = 330°, 330° ÷ 5° each minute = 66 minutes). The entire heating and cooling cycle are combined graphically to depict a ramp and soak profile, like the one shown in Figure 8-2.

SRMs typically do not give the ramp up and ramp down times because the starting temperatures may not always be the same. In the example shown in Figure 8-3, the outside temperature is 30°F and the final cure temperature is 250°F. In this scenario, the ramp up is longer than the one shown in Figure 8-4, which starts with a warmer temperature of 105°F.

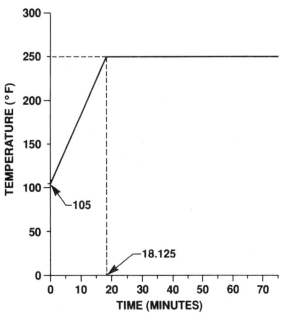

Figure 8-4 Warm Climate: If the cure is to be done in a warm climate where the temperature outdoors is 105° F, the cure ramp up time is to be at 8° F per minute. 250° - 105° = 145° ÷ 8° = 18.125 minutes to climb to the cure temperature of 250° F at a rate of 8° F per minute.

HEATING EQUIPMENT

HOT BOND EQUIPMENT

Simply stated, a hot patch bonding machine performs two functions:

1. It applies atmospheric pressure by means of a vacuum pump.

2. It applies and controls the heat.

Originally, hot bond units were designed for repairing composite components when an oven or autoclave wasn't available. A portable unit was needed to complete the work. Hot bond units are not only portable, it has become apparent that they are also ideal for repairs that do not require remanufacturing, such as those typically called for in the SRM. In addition, the simplicity of these units makes repairs easier and more affordable for maintenance facilities. They are small, portable units that can be carried to the repair site easily. In addition, components do not necessarily have to be removed from the aircraft, which saves time and money.

Hot patch bonding machines make use of heat blankets that have electrical coils bonded into a rubber pad or blanket. You should be aware that these blankets can heat up quickly unless they have a monitoring unit attached to control the temperature and its rise or fall.

A monitor or controller is a device that works with the hot patch bonding equipment to maintain a constant temperature, or changes the temperature at a specific rate. In working with composites, the temperature must be controlled both at a constant and specific rate-of-change. It is critical to perform these functions with minimum effort and maximum efficiency to achieve professional results. The simplest function the controller does is maintain a specified temperature for the repair. The specified temperature is called the "setpoint" of the repair and when the controller is working in this mode it is called a setpoint controller. [Figure 8-5]

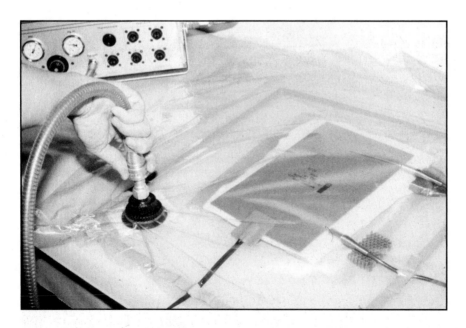

Figure 8-5. Hot patch bonding is accomplished with a heat blanket, and is normally used in conjunction with a vacuum bag. Controller devices are used and the temperatures and times should be recorded.

Another function the controller may be able to perform is the "ramp and soak." The controller allows the temperature to slowly rise at a specific rate, then hold the temperature constant, then allows a slow decline of temperature at a specific rate.

Some airlines require that permanent records of the cure cycle be included in the log of the aircraft repairs. Recording the temperatures of the curing process can be accomplished by using a temperature recording unit. Some hot bond units include a recorder in the unit, while in others it is a separate unit. A note of warning: don't become dependent on the recording record to assure that the part is repaired correctly. There are many aspects of a repair that need close monitoring. Just because the repair was cured at the proper temperature does not mean the repair is airworthy.

Controllers use thermocouples, placed beside the repaired area, under a heat blanket, and under the bagging film, to sense what temperature is being delivered to the part. The thermocouple sends the temperature information to the controller, which then adds heat or stops heating depending on how the controller is set.

In figure 8-6, the controller face set point is 250°F. In this example, if the thermocouple is only sensing 150°F, the controller applies heat to the heat blanket or heat gun until the thermocouple senses 250°F. If the set point during the cooling down process is 150°F and the controller had previously been curing at 250°F, then the controller stops applying heat until the temperature dips slightly below 150°F. [Figure 8-6]

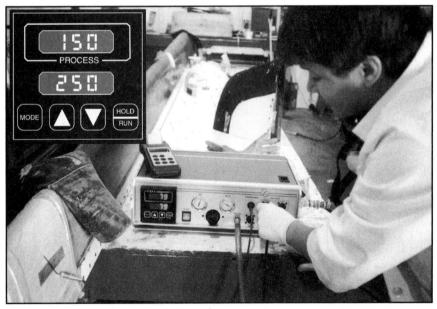

Figure 8-6. Controllers are actually fairly simple in their operation. Settings are straightforward, indicators are clearly represented, and programming is not complicated.

One danger of this process is applying heat at the final cure temperature too quickly, thus not allowing the resins enough time to flow properly before they go through their curing process. This may result in a resin rich area. For example, if 250°F is the final cure temperature and the controller applies heat too soon, it will reach the 250°F mark as soon as it possibly can (usually within 30 seconds). The resin and catalyst mixtures need time to slowly start their chemical reaction before the final cure temperature is reached.

It is also important that the heat be allowed to decrease slowly so the part doesn't cool too quickly. Composites gain much of their strength during the cooling down process, and cooling slowly prevents the part from becoming brittle. A slow rate of temperature rise and decline is desirable, but can usually be achieved only if a monitor or controller is available.

A graph of a technician operating a setpoint controller might look like Figure 8-7. Here, the temperature climbs quickly from room temperature (T1) to a specified temperature (T2). There are many different ways in which a controller can be used.

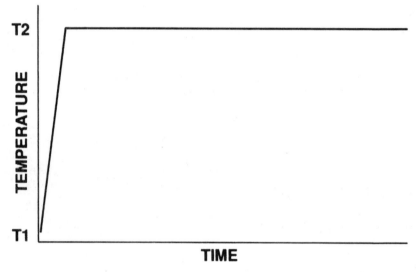

Figure 8-7. The temperature rise from T1 (room temperature) to T2 (set point) would look like this graph.

HEAT BLANKETS

Heat blankets are probably the most widely accepted form of applying heat to a composite component for repair work. They heat the repair area uniformly without heating an area that is larger than necessary. Heat blankets are used with a thermocouple and a controller, or a hot bonding machine to regulate the amount of heat. They can be used with vacuum bagging to hold the heat directly onto the surface.

Heat blankets are made of a flexible silicon and come in a variety of forms and sizes. A thermocouple is used under the blanket to monitor the heat. A controller or regulating unit powers heating coils within the blanket to keep the temperature at the desired setting.

Most manufacturers recommend the use of a heating blanket for curing repairs because of its ability to evenly heat the part. The ramp and soak method of heating is easily accomplished with the heat blanket method, and results in a stronger cure. The heat blanket must cover the repair completely, and usually is an inch or two larger than the largest size patch. However, if the heat blanket is too large, the heat may damage surrounding areas of the part.

The heat blanket is vacuum bagged into the repair area so no matter where the repair is being done, the heat blanket is next to the patches being cured. For example, if the underside of a wing is to be repaired, the vacuum bagging film with vacuum applied will hold the heat blanket tightly to the patches as they cure.

Some heat blankets are very flexible to bend around curved surfaces, such as a leading edge, while others are made for flat use only. A flat heat blanket should not be used on a curved surface because bending it breaks the wires in the heat blanket. Customized heat blankets made to the shape of a specific part can be used if the part is sharply contoured. This would most commonly be used if the same type and size of part were repaired repeatedly.

If the shape of the part to be cured is sharply contoured, a heat gun may be used with a hot bonding machine instead of using a heat blanket. A tent of bagging film is attached to the part to hold the heat in around the component. The heat gun is monitored with a thermocouple and the controller of the hot bonding unit.

Figure 8-8 shows a typical bagging operation with the use of a heat blanket.

SOME LIMITATIONS OF HEAT BLANKETS

1. Using an oversized heat blanket may draw too much current for the machine to handle. Find out what maximum size heat blanket your machine can run. For example, the instructions may say, "Do not use heat blankets that exceed 3000 watts of power." If the heat blanket you have uses 5 watts per square inch, the largest size blankets that could be used would be around 24X24 inches, or 10x60 inches, or 40x15 inches.

2. Some hot bond equipment allows the use of more than one heat blanket on the same ramp and soak. However, the con-

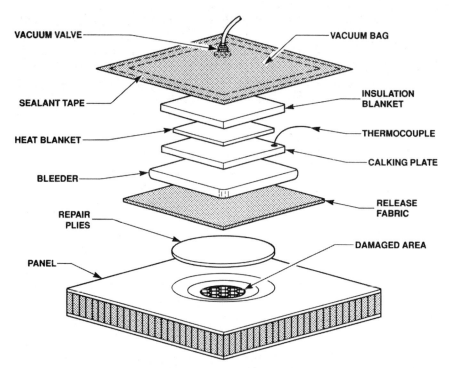

Figure 8-8. A typical bagging operation with the use of a heat blanket.

troller functions are based on only one thermocouple input, so there will be master and slave heat blankets. The position of the thermocouple determines the master. When using more than one heat blanket, the following precautions should be exercised:

a. Use heat blankets that are the same size and use the same amount of wattage per square inch.

b. Always monitor the process temperature of the heat blanket that doesn't have the thermocouple. Accomplish this with a digital thermometer, a solid state recorder, or any other suitable temperature-measuring device. Touch each blanket briefly to determine if one is substantially hotter or cooler than the other.

c. Use all heat blankets with as nearly the same type of materials and environment as possible. Different materials and shapes absorb and dissipate heat at different rates. For example, if a repair is done on a worktable, make sure that all heat blankets are on the same table with the same insulating materials above and below them.

d. Never leave the repair process unattended.

e. Use thermostatically controlled heat blankets for fail-safe temperature limitations. These types of heat blankets open a fuse when the temperature reaches a certain point, stopping the heat from burning a part. For example, for a repair that cures at 350ºF, a blanket with a rating of 400ºF could be used. If the temperature goes beyond 350º, it can only raise to 400ºF before the fuse opens, saving the part.

f. Never use a heat gun and a heat blanket together during the same repair process run.

HEAT GUNS

As previously mentioned, a heat gun is an alternative method for curing repairs when the contour of the part does not allow the use of a heat blanket. On composite components with very contoured shapes, heat blankets sometimes lack enough flexibility to conform to the shape of the part. In this case, a tent can be fabricated around the part to hold the hot air within a confined area. The tent can be made of vacuum bagging film and attached to the part with sealant tape. To prevent excessive curing, be sure the heat gun is not pointed directly at the part. If the cure temperature of the part is 250°F, the bagging film used for the tent should be able to withstand a high heat range.

When using a heat gun to cure a composite part, it must be controlled with a monitor. A typical heat gun can generate temperatures of 500°F to 750°F when it is left on constantly. If the cure temperature is 180°F and a heat gun is used to cure the component, the heat gun should be monitored with a controller to maintain a constant temperature.

To control a heat gun, a thermocouple is used with the controlling unit to keep the temperature constant. The controller allows the heat gun to reach the desired temperature, then the thermocouple senses this and shuts off the heat gun. The heat gun cycles on and off around this temperature to hold the temperature fairly constant.

Problems may occur if the heat gun is focused on one place of the repair. If a heat gun should shift position during the curing cycle, excessive evaporation of the resins in one spot may leave dry areas, which is grounds to reject the repair.

Another alternative to using bagging film as a tent is to use a cardboard box lined with aluminum foil or fiberglass, or anything that holds in the heat.

Heat guns may present a fire hazard and should never be left unattended during the cure process.

HEAT LAMPS

Heat lamps have been used to cure composite parts for many years. However, with the availability of precision heating equipment, heat lamps are generally no longer recommended. On the other hand, if no other heating equipment is available, heat lamps can be used satisfactorily to accelerate the cure of room temperature resins. They should not be used on resins that need to be cured at a very high temperature such as prepregs. They are also not the most reliable heat source because the temperature cannot be accurately controlled and the heat may localize in one spot. Scorching or blistering of the part also may occur if the heat lamp is too close or is left on too long. [Figure 8-9]

Figure 8-9. Heat lamps are NOT recommended. They tend to overheat and heat only localized spots.

Drafts in the work area can also affect the amount of heat when using a heat lamp. The light of the lamp must hit all areas of the part. If there is a shadow on any area, it will not cure at the same rate as a part with the light shining on it.

To help monitor the temperature, use a templestick or other temperature-monitoring device. A templestick is a temperature sensitive crayon that melts at the temperature at which it is rated. Another temperature sensing device is a strip with temperature sensitive ink on it that changes colors when the heat reaches a certain temperature. Both of these temperature-sensing devices must be monitored continuously to avoid an overheating condition.

OVEN CURING

Ovens offer controlled, uniform temperature over all surfaces. Some ovens have vacuum ports installed to provide vacuum pressure while curing. Manufacturers frequently use oven curing. Ovens used to cure composites must be certified for that purpose. When using an oven for repair work, the part must be removed from the aircraft and the part must be small enough to fit into the oven.

When an aircraft part has metal hardware attached, it should not be cured in an oven because the metal heats up at a faster rate than the composite. This uneven heating or high temperature may deteriorate the adhesives under the metal, causing failure of the bond.

Ovens may also present a problem by heating up the whole part, not just the repair area. The areas that are not being repaired are subjected to very high temperatures and may deteriorate the existing structure with microcracking. Again, microcracking is very fine cracks in the resin and the fibers, which cannot be seen with the naked eye. [Figure 8-10]

Figure 8-10. Oven curing is often used in the manufacturing process to cure many parts at the same time.

AUTOCLAVES

If the damage is large and extensive, it may be sent to a remanufacturing facility. Large manufacturing facilities have the molds and capabilities to repair large damaged surfaces. If an extensively damaged component is not cured with molds, high heat, and adequate pressure, the part may not regain its original strength. [Figure 8-11]

Figure 8-11. An autoclave provides both heat and pressure under extremely controlled conditions. They are normally used for manufacturing.

Autoclaves usually are used in the manufacture of composites and are not used in the repair procedures unless the part must be remanufactured. Autoclaves may be used to remanufacture a part if the damage is very large and it is necessary to put the part into the original mold and cure it with high heat and high pressure. In this case, the part is vacuum bagged and heated to the curing temperature at a controlled rate, while additional pressure is applied within the autoclave. Normally, parts that are vacuum bagged are subject to one atmosphere of pressure, but an autoclave can apply substantially more pressure to a part. Two or three atmospheres of additional pressure may be added while the part is being manufactured, or cured, in an autoclave.

Caution should be taken when operating an autoclave. They can be very dangerous if not operated properly. Also, composite parts with metal fasteners or spars should not be cured in an autoclave or oven because the metal heats up at a different rate than the composite, causing the metal to break its bond with the composite structure.

THERMOCOUPLES

A thermocouple senses the temperature of the part and relays the information to the controller or monitor. It should be used under the heat blanket, in close proximity to the repair, between the blanket and a release film. It should be used under the heat blanket, do not place the thermocouple in the repair area or the wet resins will form to the shape of the thermocouple.

Thermocouples are made of two types of wire twisted together to sense the temperature. The older type thermocouples are twisted on the ends. If these are positioned in the wet resin area of the repair, then cured, they can imbed into the resin. In the past, the ends were clipped off and left in the area of the repair. This could cause a stress concentration. Do not leave anything in the repaired area.

The wires of the thermocouples can get tangled and twisted anywhere along it's length. If a break occurs along the wire, it could be sensing the air outside of the repair area, which causes the heat blanket to heat up because the thermocouple is telling the controller there is not enough heat. This could be a very serious situation. The part could burn to the point of destroying it. Make sure your thermocouple wires are in good condition and not kinked.

The newer thermocouples are encased inside a flexible cable, so they are protected against kinking and breaking. The ends do not need to be twisted because they are bonded to a probe. The tip of the probe is the sensing device. Do not place the probe in the wet resin area. It should be placed on top of the release film, under the heat blanket and next to the repair area.

Another common problem associated with thermocouples is that they slip out of place during the vacuum bagging process. During the cure cycle, if the thermocouple doesn't sense the temperature under the blanket, it could cause problems. Make sure that the heat blanket covers the tip of the thermocouple or probe.

Many times a hot bond unit has a number of thermocouples included to monitor the area of the repair. These are used to see if there is a hot spot anywhere in the repair area. A recording needs to be made of the repair and kept with the logs of the aircraft.

TEMPERATURE RECORDING UNITS

A recorder is a unit that records what temperature is on the thermocouple for a period of time. If a ramp and soak profile is being used, it will sense the slight ramping up of the temperature, how long it takes to get to the cure temperature, how long it is held at the cure temperature, and what the temperature is during the ramp down. It also records how long it takes to cool to room temperature. It is very handy to check that you have cured the repair for the required amount of time at the correct temperatures.

Many people, however, see this as a way of checking to see if the repair was completed correctly but it does not do that. Doing so may give the technician a false sense of security.

There are many things that could go wrong with a composite repair: the wrong resin type, incorrect mixing, out of date material, not enough pressure applied, surface contamination, incorrect orientation of the plies , using the wrong type of repair, and not including some lightning protection. The list can go on and on. But if it was cured correctly and had a paper that said it was cured correctly, it could give a false impression. Technicians must know about composites and their repair procedures.

Chapter 9
Machining Composites

Completing an airworthy repair to a composite structure is not any more difficult than conventional repairs, but the techniques, materials, and tools are different, demanding proper training and concentration. For example, composite materials act differently than traditional aluminum when machined. Each different type of fabric machines differently than other types of fabrics. If care is not taken to do a composite repair correctly, the repair will not develop the full strength characteristics that are necessary in a composite structure. The manufacturer's Structural Repair Manual (SRM) should be consulted before attempting a repair to a composite component.

CUTTING UNCURED FABRICS

Before a fiberglass or carbon/graphite fabric is combined with a matrix and cured, it can be cut with conventional fabric scissors. On the other hand, to cut aramid fabric in its raw state, you'll need scissors with special steel or ceramic blades and serrated edges. The serrated edges hold the fabric and cut without fraying the edges. These scissors cut through aramid with ease and last many times longer than conventional fabric scissors. Steel bladed scissors with a diamond cutting edge may also be useful for cutting raw aramid fabric.

Conventional scissors separate the weave and do not cut the fabric properly unless they are very sharp. The scissors' edges also dull quickly and need to be sharpened frequently if used to cut Kevlar® and other aramids.

Scissors that are used to cut aramid should only be used to cut aramid, never fiberglass or carbon/graphite. The same applies to scissors intended to cut fiberglass. They should never be used to cut carbon/graphite, and visa versa. Although fiberglass and carbon/graphite can be cut using the same type of scissors, they should not be used interchangeably. The different fabrics tend to dull the cutting surface in different ways. Keeping your scissors and tools reserved for specific materials will dramatically extend the life of the tool. Make a mark with black, white, and yellow paint on handles of scissors and other tools help identify which material they are for. Yellow for aramid, black for carbon/fiber, and white for fiberglass. This matches the color of the fabric. [Figure 9-1]

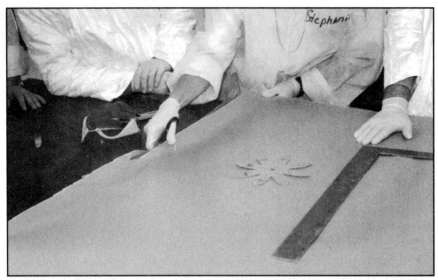

Figure 9-1. Scissors should be marked to identify the materials that they are used on.

Pre-impregnated materials can be cut with a razor blade in a utility knife, and with a template or straight edge. The resin tends to hold the pre-impregnated fibers in place while the razor edge cuts through the fiber.

MACHINING CURED COMPOSITES

The high strength of cured composites requires different machining tools and techniques to be used than those required for metal structures. Aramid fibers may absorb cutting fluids if they are used, and if the wrong type of cutting fluid is used, the area may not bond properly. Typically, water is the only accepted cutting fluid.

Machining characteristics of fiber reinforced plastics or composites vary with the type of reinforcement fiber being used. Again, if a cutting tool is used with aramid, it should only be used on aramid. If that same tool is used on a carbon/graphite or fiberglass structure, it will dull the cutting surface differently than the aramid and will never cut the aramid in the same manner again.

Some composites decompose when being trimmed or drilled at high speeds. The friction generated may burn away various materials, creating toxic fumes. Composites vary in their toxicity, so you should consider all composites equally hazardous and should observe appropriate safety precautions while working with any of them.

DRILLING AND COUNTERSINKING

Drilling holes in composite materials presents different problems than those encountered in drilling metal. Composites are more susceptible than metal to material failures when machined, making hole quality important. The proper selection and application of cutting tools can produce structurally sound holes.

Delamination, fracture, breakout, and separation are types of failures that may occur while drilling composites. Delamination most often occurs as the peeling away of the bottom layer as the force of the drill pushes the layers apart, rather than cutting through the last piece. A fracture occurs when a crack forms along one of the layers due to the force of the drill. Breakout occurs when the bottom layer splinters as the drill completes the hole. Separation occurs when a gap opens between layers as the drill passes through the successive layers.

To combat these problems in drilling, the material being drilled should be backed with wood. When exiting the backside of a hole with a drill, use very light or no pressure. Use a very sharp drill to cut through the laminate, not push through. This prevents the delamination of the last ply.

When a blind fastener is to be used with the composite part and the backside is inaccessible, a wood backup is not possible. In this case, a drill stop is useful to limit how deep the drill goes through the composite structure. By limiting the depth of the drill passage, breaking the fibers on the backside can be eliminated.

Do not use a cutting coolant when drilling holes into bonded honeycomb or foam core structures—the coolant may seep into other areas and may remain in the structure after a patch has been bonded over the repair. In addition, if a coolant is used, the laminate fibers may absorb the cutting fluid and create an unbondable surface.

Solid carbide drill bits work on all types of composites and have a longer life than a standard steel drill. Diamond dust charged cutters perform well on fiberglass and carbon, but they produce excessive fuzzing around the cut if used on an aramid component, so they should be avoided.

Drill motor speed is important. A high speed works best for most types of materials being drilled. However, do not use excessive pressure.

The best included-angle of a conventional drill used on composites is 135°.

DRILLING ARAMID

The physical properties of aramid fibers are unique, so if you are using a conventional sheet metal drill bit, the fabric tends to fuzz around the drilled holes. Due to the flexibility of the aramid fiber, the drill pulls a fiber to the point of breaking instead of cutting it. As each fiber is pulled before it is cut, a fuzzing appearance is produced around the edge of the drilled hole. This fuzzing of the fibers often makes the hole smaller in diameter than the drill that is used.

The fuzzing around the hole may not produce a problem in itself, but if a fastener is to be installed, it may not seat properly in the hole. Consequently, if the fastener doesn't seat properly, mechanical failure may occur when stresses are not properly distributed. [Figure 9-2]

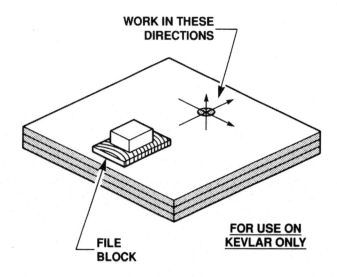

Figure 9-2. Fuzz around a hole drilled in Kevlar can be removed by applying a quick-set epoxy to the fuzzed area, and then filing it off after the epoxy has set.

If the area where the hole is to be drilled has just been cured and the peel ply or release fabric layer has not yet been removed, the hole can be drilled through the peel ply to eliminate the fuzzing around the hole.

Certain manufacturers produce drill bits specifically made for aramid. These bits cut through the fibers without fraying the material. They last longer than conventional drill bits and usually produce a cleaner hole. Carbide bits will extend the life of the bit dramatically. If possible, use a drill made specifically for aramid, and use it only on aramid.

A brad point bit is designed specifically for aramid fabric. It is produced with a C-shape cutting edge to pull the fiber out, then cut through the fiber without stretching. Although they were specifically designed for aramid composites, they also produce good holes in fiberglass and carbon/graphite. [Figure 9-3]

Figure 9-3. Special brad point drills are available for drilling aramid composites.

There are brad point bits available at hardware stores for use on wood. They do not have the C-shape, and they may be used in aramid, but usually don't produce as clean a hole as a brad point made specifically for composite use.

Aramid fiber composites tend to absorb moisture, especially in areas that have been drilled or cut. No cutting fluid should be used except water. If water is used, the fabric should be thoroughly dried before bonding.

Aramid fibers and Kevlar® should be drilled at a high speed. Using a very sharp drill bit produces a much better cut. The pressure on the drill should be light—the weight of the drill motor alone is usually sufficient. When exiting out the backside of the hole with the drill, less pressure should be used in order to prevent breakout. This problem can be eliminated if a drill stop is used that is set so that just the tip of the drill has clearance past the backside of the material.

DRILLING FIBERGLASS OR CARBON/GRAPHITE

Drilling fiberglass or carbon/graphite can be accomplished with most conventional tools; however, the abrasiveness of these composite materials reduce the quality of the cutting edge and drastically shorten the life of the drill.

Carbide, diamond-charged, or carbide coated tools obtain better results and longer tool life. Diamond charged tools are usually steel drills that have a coat of diamond dust to cut through the material. This type of drill works well on carbon/graphite and fiberglass components.

When cutting fiberglass, the fibers in most cases fracture at the cutting edge of the tool. Carbon/graphite fibers are stiffer and stronger and resist the cutting action of the tool. If a dull drill is used to make the hole, the fiber may break inside the composite structure, causing the hole size to be larger than that of the drill.

Holes drilled into carbon/graphite often show larger diameters than the drill used. Dust chips allowed to remain in the holes during the drilling process also can cut, thus enlarging the hole's diameter. This creates a problem in that the excessive hole size causes the fastener to wear in the hole, so it does not offer the required strength. An oversized fastener may have to be used if wear has taken place and the hole is too large.

For fiberglass or carbon/graphite drilling, a dagger or spade bit can be used. The use of these bits reduces the tendency of the fibers to break rather than be cut. This type of bit has a single cutting edge. The best results for drilling and countersinking carbon/graphite materials are obtained when using a carbide dagger bit. [Figure 9-4]

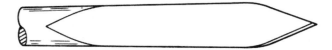

Figure 9-4. A spade bit cuts more with its outer edge; the inner portion mostly removing waste material.

Uni-drills can be used to drill and ream carbon/graphite and fiberglass, but they do not produce an acceptable hole in aramid materials. Uni-drills fuzz the aramid fibers excessively.

COUNTERSINKING COMPOSITES

Countersinking a fastener hole is as important in composites as it is in metal parts. A countersunk hole should be produced to the proper fastener angle, depth, and finish. The tendency of aramid fibers to fuzz around a drilled hole can be eliminated by using very sharp countersinks made for aramid composites. Again, the fastener must seat properly in the hole to produce the greatest strength. All the fuzzing around the hole should be removed to allow all the surfaces of the fastener to be in contact with all the surfaces of the composite.

FASTENERS

The fasteners used on composites are different than those used on sheet metal. Hole filling rivets are not used in composites. If the metal of a rivet were to expand and completely fill a hole in a composite structure, the rivet would expand against the sides of the laminate and possibly delaminate the edges of the hole. The holes drilled into the composite can also cause material failure because each individual strand of the composite carries a load. Many holes drilled for a traditional sheet metal repair patch would severely damage the structural integrity of the composite structure. That is why there are different types of repairs for composite components. The same is true of the fasteners used with composites.

The following general rules should be followed when installing fasteners into a composite structure:

1. When fasteners are used in carbon/graphite structures, they must be made of titanium or corrosion resistant steel. Aluminum fasteners should not be used with carbon/graphite material because of their tendency to corrode the aluminum.

2. If an aluminum fitting is used in a carbon/graphite structure, make sure that the aluminum has a corrosion protection coating.

3. Do not use hole filling fasteners like AN470 rivets in composites because they can damage the hole as they expand, causing the laminate layers to delaminate.

Close tolerance holes and fasteners ensure more equal load distribution.

COMPOSITE FASTENERS

The term "composite fasteners" can be defined in two ways: fasteners made of composite material, or fasteners used to fasten composite materials together. To avoid confusion, a composite fastener in this discussion refers to fasteners used to fasten composite sheets or other composite materials together. The discussion includes fasteners made of both metal and composite materials.

Composite materials in manufacturing reduce the need for fasteners in many applications. The fabrication of complex shapes from composites allows for the creation of molds that produce components in one piece. Another technique known as co-curing allows large or very complicated components to be assembled by curing the materials together, rather than using fasteners to hold the separate components together. This ability to manufacture components without so many mechanical fasteners is one of the great advantages that composite materials offer.

In the production of primary load carrying structures from composite materials, however, the structures to be joined are too large to lend themselves to bonding or co-curing, and require mechanical fasteners. Furthermore, there are instances in which the shape of a component is complex enough to require mechanical fasteners to complete an assembly. Satisfactory fasteners must be found to securely assemble components that are fabricated from advanced composite materials. These new composites seldom work well with traditional fasteners such as aluminum rivets. Consequently, the aviation industry has had to re-evaluate the materials technology and the mechanical engineering associated with aviation fasteners. The problem has been addressed in three ways:

1. Traditional sheet metal fasteners were modified slightly for use with composites.

2. New fasteners were developed specifically for use with composite materials.

3. In reconsidering function, do fasteners need to actually penetrate through materials?

Sheet metal parts are fabricated using a material that constantly exhibits the maximum strength possible. In other words, sheet metal is as stiff on an operating aircraft as it is in the sheet metal fabrication shop. This rigidity substantially affects the formability of the material: if the material is flexed too many times during the fabrication process, the metal is weakened due to work hardening. The sheet metal stretches and subsequently varies in thickness and strength as it is bent into the desired shape. This is why components that are complex in shape or that require multiple strength characteristics must be fabricated as isolated components, and then joined together to form the final design. The best way to join aircraft sheet metal together is to drill holes and install sheet metal rivets.

Composite materials usually start out as preimpregnated (prepreg) fabric. Prior to being cured, the material is very flexible and is stored in rolls. The manufacturer builds a component from this material usually by laying the material into a mold and curing the prepreg material with heat and pressure. The mold can be very complex in shape, as long as the part can be properly cured, and the finished component can be removed from the mold. By the means of fiber science — for example, multiple layers of similar or dissimilar fabric co-bonded together — a very complex and strong component can be engineered.

METALLIC FASTENERS

When the use of advanced composites increased in the design of military and civilian aircraft, the fastener industry was unprepared to meet the mechanical and chemical requirements of advanced composite materials. The most immediate solutions involved fasteners that were slight alterations of those originally designed for metallic structures. At the time, there were no alternatives for aeronautical engineering designers other than to use metallic fasteners on nonmetallic structures.

Results of these short-term solutions offered by metallic fasteners demonstrated the problems associated with the use of incompatible materials.

DISSIMILAR ELECTRICAL POTENTIALS

Most metals are not compatible with carbon composites due to dissimilarity in electrical or galvanic potentials that causes severe galvanic corrosion. This type of corrosion is particularly evident in wet or corrosive environments. There are two ways to prevent this galvanic incompatibility:

1. Fasteners can be fabricated from metals that are compatible with the carbon materials to be used. This includes metals such as titanium alloy, stainless steel, or inconel.

2. A dielectric protective coating can be used to isolate noncompatible metal fasteners from the carbon materials in the composite.

Both of these approaches create new problems.

ELECTRICAL PROBLEMS

Metallic fasteners that are electromotive-compatible add weight to structural designs that offer light weight as a principal advantage. Because these fasteners must be produced using comparatively exotic metals, the cost advantage of using composites is either reduced or eliminated. Finally, metal fasteners compatible in terms of electrical potential are extremely strong mechanically—too strong. The composite structure would fail long before the fasteners that hold it together. The additional strength of these fasteners offers no overall structural or design advantage, and from an engineering perspective this is undesirable. The final result of using traditional metal fasteners in a composite structure might be a structure that is heavier, more expensive, and unbalanced in terms of materials strength.

Applying a protective dielectric coating on a fastener made of an incompatible metal prevents galvanic corrosion. This allows for the use of lighter weight, less expensive metals, and keeps the mechanical aspects of the fastener more in line with those of the composite materials. However, the protective coating must remain completely intact in order to prevent what could be catastrophic failure due to galvanic corrosion. If the dielectric coating cracks, wears off, or otherwise allows for electrolytic action between the fastener and the structure, the structure will ultimately fail. The application or installation of a protective coating adds expense and time to the manufacturing process.

Other problems are created by the use of a dielectric coating, such as reduced lightning strike protection. When lightning strikes traditional sheet metal aircraft, the electricity is conducted through the sheet metal to the static discharge wick. Ordinarily, a lightning strike to a metal aircraft causes very little damage. When lightning strikes an aircraft made of nonconductive composites, however, problems do occur. The presence of an isolated metal conductor in a nonconductive composite aircraft can cause severe damage if struck by lightning. The lightning charges the fastener enough that it either arcs to another metal component, or if arcing is not possible, it explodes. Either way, the damage will be extensive and could be disastrous; these are unacceptable consequences. Although the fastener may be mechanically compatible with a composite structure, the overall design is still susceptible to galvanic corrosion, is more expensive, and is subject to severe problems in the event of lightning strike.

Aircraft structures contain many nut plates and channels, and as with fasteners, these components are often made of titanium or stainless steel to be compatible with the composite structure. Such components are expensive, heavy, and require lightning-strike protection.

MECHANICAL PROBLEMS

Mechanical problems arise when composite parts are assembled using blind or solid metal rivets. Rivets are designed to be used on metal materials. Consequently, the force required to upset the blind side of a rivet is meant for application to metal parts. When this same force is applied in the process of fastening two composite laminar structures, the composite is either crushed, or disbonds occur around the fastener. This problem is exacerbated by the small upset diameter of most metal rivets: their small footprint often causes the laminate to crumble. Also, the fastener may loosen due to the loss of preload as the laminate deforms.

When a composite structure is damaged during the installation of a rivet, the rivet must be drilled out, the damaged portion of the composite must be repaired, and an oversize rivet is usually re-installed. These are costly repairs in terms of time and materials. In an attempt to address this installation problem, a bi-metallic rivet is used in which the upset side of the rivet is made of a softer material, such as columbium. However, one of the advantages of composite structures is the smooth aerodynamic surfaces that are possible, and of particular importance on control surfaces. If a bi-metallic rivet is installed double flush on the trailing edge of a control surface, a shaving operation may be necessary in order to achieve the flush tolerance necessary to avoid turbulence. This tolerance might be between .000 and .010 inches.

Fasteners designed to provide an interference fit were originally designed with metal in mind. An interference fit is of particular value where structural pieces require the longest possible fatigue life. When a traditional interference-fit fastener is installed in an advanced composite laminate, the laminate will separate due to the lateral forces that the fastener exerts. Such separations range from minor cracks to major delaminations.

One way to address this problem is to drill a smooth hole and install a sleeve into which the fastener can be inserted. Although this solves some of the problems of delamination, it adds additional parts and labor to the operation and adds weight to the final design. As with any intrusive process, this also exposes the laminate to environmental degradation if the sleeve is not installed correctly. This is of particular concern when the laminate includes hydrophilic materials such as Kevlar; the sleeve could conceal fluid-damaged or exposed laminate that may occur in the manufacturing process. If the area in question is difficult to inspect, this damage could increase in size as water or other fluids are absorbed into the laminate materials.

NON-METALLIC FASTENERS

Non-metallic fasteners are necessary for composite materials for these reasons, as discussed above:

1. They prevent galvanic corrosion.

2. They provide material strength compatibility.

3. They provide reasonable costs in manufacturing.

4. They enable weight reduction.

5. They provide overall materials compatibility.

COMPOSITE FASTENERS

In addition to offering very good strength-to-weight ratios, advanced composite materials are attractive to airplane manufacturers because of the low costs associated with manufacturing airplane parts. This major improvement in aircraft fabrication technique has eliminated the need to join so many components, as has been the case with sheet metal fabrication. At the time of this writing, however, no one has yet devised a way of making a single piece airplane. Consequently, although composite materials have reduced the number of fasteners needed, there is still a need to fasten composite materials to other composite components and to sheet metal components.

MATERIALS FOR COMPOSITE FASTENERS

Various composite materials have been evaluated for composite fasteners. Some of the considerations for suitable materials are:

Sheer strength

Susceptibility to moisture absorption

Resistance to chemicals

Thermal stability

Fatigue resistance

Vacuum stability (out gassing characteristics)

Compressive strength

Coefficient of thermal expansion

Dielectric strength (conductivity)

Thermal conductivity

The common practice in achieving an acceptable level of these characteristics is to mix a resin/curing agent with fiberglass, aramid, or carbon fibers. Each manufacturer has its own specific resin formulation and fiber specification. Mechanical strength is usually increased using long carbon fibers. Composite fasteners prove to have very high strength-to-weight ratios: one-fifth the weight of steel and one-half the weight of aluminum is typical.

PENETRATING FASTENERS

Penetrating fasteners are used in such applications as lap joints. A hole is drilled through the materials to be joined, and a fastener such as blind rivet is installed. In this way, a unidirectional carbon fiber in a thermoplastic or thermoset resin can achieve a sheer strength of 40,000 psi.

As mentioned earlier, the installation of a blind or a solid rivet can cause the composite material to be crushed or to delaminate when the rivet is upset. This can be successfully addressed by using heat to soften the end of the rivet and then use a minimum amount of pressure to upset the end of the rivet. This design has great advantage over the traditional metal rivet where the rivet is attached to a tapered surface.

The rivet can be formed to the same angle as the surface material because the fastener does not require a rotating mandrel, as does a traditional blind rivet.

Solid composite rivets can be installed flush to the surface of aerodynamic components using a pre-heated anvil in the installation tool. The operator snaps the hot anvil (taken from a portable heating apparatus) into the squeezing tool just prior to installation. The pressure on the installation tool can be adjusted to the clamping requirement of the structure. The rivet fills the rivet hole evenly because it is heated on both ends. The final result is a very even installation, with very good stress distribution.

Where allowed, a metal pin can be installed with an interference fit by using a pin with tapered lobes. The tapered lobes are produced from a straight shank by rolling a negative taper in the valleys of the lobes. The tapered lobes provide an interference fit at the upper or outer part of the skin just under the pinhead. The back-side of the skin is not subjected to an interference fit and does not cause a composite to delaminate.

ADHESIVE BONDED FASTENERS

An alternative to drilling into the skin of the aircraft, is to install adhesive bonded fasteners. Composites carry loads through each individual strand. A hole drilled through an entire structure may cause a weakening to the structure where the fastener is installed. Click Bond is a manufacturer of fasteners designed for adhesive bonding to the structure. They have fasteners that include nut plates, studs, cable tie mounts, standoffs, bushings, and insulation mounting systems. Their systems have been approved for many military and commercial airliners, helicopters, and other vehicles.

The adhesively bonded fastener that seems most impressive is the nut plate. Typically on a metallic installation, the nut plate has three holes drilled in a row. The two on the outer edge are for rivets to attach to the surface, and the middle hole is drilled for the fastener. When three holes are drilled closely together on a composite component, it could severely weaken the surface. With the adhesively bonded nut plate, only one hole is drilled through the component, and the fastener is attached with an adhesive to hold it in place.

FASTNER USE

Common uses of fasteners in composite structures are the removable fasteners, such as those used around door edges. Probably the most common damage to these areas is from wear around the edges of the hole, causing the part to improperly transfer the structural load.

If the composite part fails because of worn holes, one solution is to use an oversize fastener. This solution may be only temporary, as the same loads and wear may re-occur causing the hole to become worn again. A more permanent solution is to use a fastener with a liner to be permanently installed to the composite structure. The fastener can be removed, but the liner stays in place.

Fasteners may pull out of the edges of the composite if placed too close to the edge. Therefore, it is important to place fasteners well enough inside an edge to prevent excessive wear or pull out. The direction of the weave of the fabric is also very important to prevent the fastener from pulling out.

Many times the material around a drilled hole is sealed to prevent the fabric from wicking moisture. One way to seal a hole is to use an insert coated with resin. The resin, in combination with the insert, permanently seals the hole against moisture.

In some instances, aircraft passenger seats are installed using a type of foam adhesive that expands and fills the holes of the honeycomb floor panel to make it possible to permanently attach the seat to the floor. In order to accommodate a removable passenger seat, a fastener can be used with a metal or plastic insert, making it possible to install or remove the passenger seat without causing damage to the honeycomb composite floor panel.

Special composite fasteners that are very similar to a Hi-Lock can be used when a blind fastener is needed. Some of these fasteners have a very small bearing surface with the composite part. This may allow the fastener to puncture through a thin face sheet if too much pressure is imposed on it. If possible, it's best to use a composite fastener that has a large bearing area. These fasteners must be ordered in the proper diameter and length if they are to work properly.

The following general rules should be followed when installing fasteners into a composite structure:

1. When fasteners are used in carbon/graphite structures, they must be made of titanium or corrosion resistant steel. Aluminum fasteners should not be used with carbon/graphite material because of their tendency to corrode the aluminum.

2. If an aluminum fitting is used in a carbon/graphite structure, make sure that the aluminum has a corrosion protection coating.

3. Do not use hole filling fasteners like AN470 rivets in composites because they can damage the hole as they expand, causing the laminate layers to delaminate.

4. Close tolerance holes and fasteners ensure more equal load distribution.

FASTENER REMOVAL

To drill out and remove a fastener, the softer aluminum alloy center should first be drilled out. The outer rim can then be removed using a punch.

COMPOSITE WELDING

Composite welding tools can be used to fasten thermoplastic composites. As you recall, thermoplastic composites may be reformed with the introduction of heat. Composite welders apply heat and pressure, much like a heated rivet gun, to press the thermoplastic down and reform it. This type of tool does not work on thermoset composites because heat that is applied to a cured thermoset part does not cause the resin to reflow.

In manufacturing, composite welders can be used with thermoset resins that have not yet gone through their final curing stage. Once the thermoset has completely cured, it cannot be reformed with the application of heat, and for repair work, composite welding would be ineffective.

SANDING

Sanding is used to remove single layers of fabric during the repair operation. Do not use aluminum oxide for sanding carbon fibers. Small particles of aluminum from the sandpaper may become lodged in the fibers. Silicon-carbide or carbide should be used in order to prevent deterioration due to an electrolytic action.

Hand sanding is used when only one layer, or a very thin coat of paint, is to be removed. Because the fabric layers of composites are very thin, they may sand off very quickly. Be careful not to sand through too many layers of fabric. If sanding a layer of paint, don't sand into the top layer of fabric or an additional repair may have to be performed. Wet sanding is preferred, using a fine grit sandpaper of about 240 grit. [Figure 9-5]

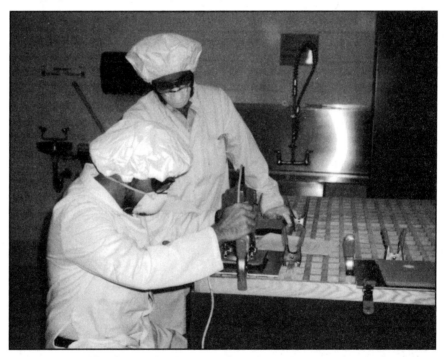

Figure 9-5. The best place to sand any composite material is on a downdraft table. Even there, however, goggles and respirators are a must. Above all, do not use compressed air to blow the residue away. Vacuum it up instead.

MECHANICAL SANDING

When sanding laminates during a repair operation, a right-angle sander or drill motor should be used. The tool should be capable of 20,000 rpm and equipped with a 1", 2", or 3" sanding disc. These come in many different diameters, but a 1" or 2" disc gives you more control when step sanding or scarfing the composite structure.

A right-angle sander is used for scarfing and step cutting the repair. There is much more control with a right-angle sander than with a drill motor because your hand is closer to the work. Some sanders blow exhaust air out the front, others blow the exhaust out the back. If the air is out the front, composite dust blows away from the working area, which is the more desirable of the two.

If sanding carbon/graphite, the dust should not be allowed to blow away, as it may lodge on an aluminum surface causing an electrolytic action. If a dust collector or downdraft table is available, use it. The dust should be vacuumed up and disposed of properly as often as possible. If you are repairing composites frequently, a right-angle sander will help you do a professional job.

Standard composite safety procedures call for a dust mask to be worn when sanding.

All material sands differently, and various techniques should be used with each material. When sanding aramid, for example, expect the material to fuzz. When the sanding is almost through the layer, a lighter color of fuzz will be seen and spots of gloss may appear. During the sanding process, it is important to look carefully for a gloss area. When an area begins to gloss, one layer of laminate has been removed and the sander is just above the following layer.

Carbon/graphite material produces a very fine powder when it is sanded. It is usually easier to see the layers of carbon/graphite than with aramid.

Another way to tell if sanding through one layer has been completed is to look at the weave. Since most composites are made with each layer's weave in different directions, to see a change in weave direction may be an indication of different layers.

The layers of a composite laminate are very thin, and a common problem is to sand with too much pressure, or too quickly, and go through two layers instead of one. This may present a problem if there are only three layers in the laminate over a core structure and the repair calls for sanding down to the core. If the first two layers are sanded down and counted as one layer, then when the next layer is sanded down, the honeycomb core will be exposed, and there will not be enough surface area to laminate a new patch over the plies. [Figure 9-6]

TRIMMING CURED LAMINATES

Standard machining equipment can be used to trim composites, but some modifications to the tooling may be necessary. All cutting surfaces should be carbide coated whenever possible. Diamond edged blades work well on carbon/graphite and fiberglass. [Figure 9-7]

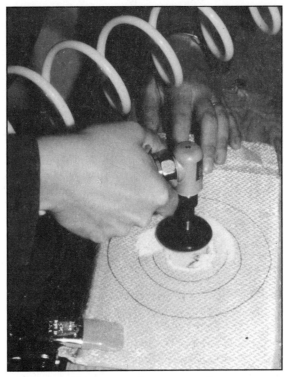

Figure 9-6. Sanding with too much pressure is a common problem. It can be difficult to see where one layer stops and the next starts, resulting in damage to the core.

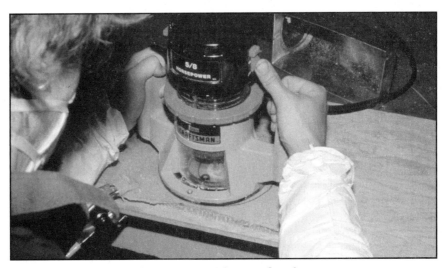

Figure 9-7. Standard routers, with speeds of 25,000 to 30,000 rpm, work well for cutting composites. Using special bits designed for specific materials normally produces good results.

ROUTERS

The most common types of routers operate at 25,000 to 30,000 rpm. They are used to trim composite laminates and to route out damaged core material. For routing nomex honeycomb, carbon/graphite, or fiberglass laminates, a carbide blade diamond cut router bit works best.

A diamond cut router bit does not refer to diamond chips or dust on the cutting surface, but rather to the shape of the cut on the flutes. [Figure 9-8]

Figure 9-8. Diamond cut router bit.

A special router bit has been developed that meets the demands of the physical flexibility of aramid fibers. A herringbone router bit works best on thick laminates of aramid because the flutes change direction. As the bit starts to pull out an aramid fiber, the flute changes direction to cut off the pulled out fiber, giving a clean cut. This works well on thick laminates of aramid without causing excessive fuzzing. [Figure 9-9]

Figure 9-9. Herringbone router bit.

In order to route out damaged core material, a circular or oval area of the top laminate skin over the damaged core must first be routed, using a pointed router bit. If the damage penetrates one skin and the core, care should be taken not to route into the opposite laminate. Adjust the depth of the bit to go through just the top layers of fabric. Hold the router steadily over the area to be routed. The point of the bit will drill down and then can be guided around the hole with the use of a template. A flush bit is then used to clean out the core material. A diamond cut works well to clean out honeycomb core.

Readjust the depth of the bit to clean out the core material. If the damage requires all of the core material to be removed in this area, the depth of the bit should be to the top of the bottom layers of fabric.

To prevent the router from going into the bottom layers, adjust the depth so that some honeycomb can still be seen. This can later be removed by hand sanding.

Some repairs require only a portion of the honeycomb to be removed in the repair area. In this case, adjust the depth of the bit accordingly.

Once the depth has been determined, again use the template to trace around the edges of the cut-out, then using a back and forth motion, remove any remaining honeycomb.

If the area to be routed is tapered, as a trailing edge, then the router template must have shims under it to produce the desired cut.

If the part is curved, the router depth should not go to the bottom skin. This extra precaution is to prevent laminates on the opposite side from being damaged. Any excess honeycomb in this area can be sanded away by hand.

If the damage penetrates both skins as well as the core, the router depth can be set to completely remove the damaged area. [Figure 9-10]

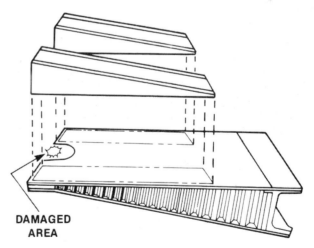

Figure 9-10. Use tapered shims to hold the routing template parallel with the skin when removing the core from a tapered control surface.

HOLE SAWS

Holes may also be cut by using a hole saw. However, the saw will tend to tear out the honeycomb core. A hole saw's teeth usually do not cut through the fibers of an aramid composite, but rather fray the edges, so they are not recommended for that material. For carbon/graphite cutting, the saw may be fitted with a blade that has diamond dust on the cutting edges, which tends to produce a cleaner cut.

WATER JET CUTTING

This cutting system uses a fine stream of water pumped at 30,000 to 50,000 psi through a pin hole nozzle to slice through composites. Water jet cutting doesn't produce dust or fumes, and causes no delamination or fuzzing of aramid laminates.

Water jet cutting is used most often during the manufacturing process and is not commonly used for infield repair applications. A water jet knife uses such a fine spray of water that water wicking into aramid is not a problem. If some water is absorbed on the edges, it can quickly be removed by applying heat from a heat lamp to the part to evaporate any water.

BAND SAWS

A band saw may be used if the blade has a fine tooth with 12 to 14 teeth per inch. Blades made for composite sawing are available in carbide or diamond dust on the cutting edges for use when cutting carbon/graphite material. Band saw cutting produces some fuzzing on aramid, but this can be cleaned up by sanding the edges. A band saw does not produce as clean a cut as a water jet. [Figure 9-11]

Figure 9-11. Special bandsaw blades are available for cutting carbon/graphite material. Some fuzzing is produced when cutting aramid, but can be cleaned up by hand.

COUNTERBORES

When a larger hole is needed, counter bores can be used with all types of composite materials, except aramid. When used with aramid, it may create excessive fuzzing.

HYDRAULIC PRESS CUTTING

During the manufacturing process, raw or pre-preg fabric can be cut using a large hydraulic press. Pattern pieces are made from sharp metal cutting edges that stamp out the fabric piece to be used.

LASER CUTTING

Another manufacturing cutting device is the laser cutter. A laser uses a highly focused light beam to cut through composite materials. Laser cutting can be performed on both uncured and cured composite materials.

Chapter 10
Setting Up Shop

When trying to determine if it's feasible to set up a repair shop, be realistic about the cost effectiveness of composite repairs. Not all companies need state-of-the-art autoclaves and other expensive machinery unless they intend to remanufacture the parts, which would require the original molds and curing equipment. Many companies are hesitant to set up a composite repair shop because they have the following concerns:

1. Lack suitable facilities.

2. Lack proper equipment.

3. Lack experienced technicians.

4. Lack access for on aircraft repairs.

5. Need for short downtime.

Aircraft are only profitable when flying, so the downtime of the aircraft is very important. Repair facilities must figure out when to do the repair, and when it is feasible to set up shop. When determining a repair, the facility needs to ask certain important questions.

1. Can the damage be repaired in a reasonable amount of time?

2. Can the part be fixed at a reasonable cost?

3. What will be the downtime of the aircraft? Would it be faster to do the repair in house or send it to a repair station that specializes in composite work? If the part is sent away, it must be taken off the aircraft and replaced with another part. It can be very expensive to have extra replacement parts on hand. How long will it take the company to fix it? Shipping and crating of the part also adds time and expense factors.

4. Are the proper facilities and equipment available? Suitable facilities for composite work may differ from existing facilities because certain repairs require special equipment specifically created for composite work.

5. Do the technicians have the appropriate skills? Certain skills are required to fix composite parts correctly. Special training needs to be provided for those who are to work on the composite components.

6. Are all the materials available? Some composite materials are not readily available, and many require minimum purchase requirements. Typically, manufactures require shops to purchase full rolls, which could contain anywhere from 100 to 1,000 yards of material. Honeycomb cores are usually purchased in four by eight-foot sheets and, in some cases, several sheets may be the minimum purchase amount. If few or small repairs are accomplished, find a supplier that deals in small quantities.

7. What type of special storage is required for some materials?

8. What safety requirements must be met with composites?

In most instances, it makes sense to repair a composite component vs. scrapping it even if the damage is very large. The damage may be so extensive that it exceeds the limits stated in the Structural Repair Manual, but sending it to a remanufacturing facility saves money compared to purchasing a new component. If you compare the costs of materials and labor involved in fabricating a new component with repairing an existing one, you'll find it usually is more economical to repair it.

Composite repair differs from manufacturing the composite component in that you do not have the molds. Curing also is done differently, usually with hot bonding equipment. Materials for repair may be harder to come by as well. The fabricators of prepreg materials and resin systems are set up to sell very large quantities of materials to the aircraft manufacturers who use it within the 6-12 month shelf life. However, these same material fabricators do not sell small quantities to the repair shops that use only a fraction of the roll. Composite shops must be prepared to meet the requirements of the SRM. Companies that fabricate smaller quantities of prepreg materials used specifically for repairing composites are correcting these problems. These materials are not always stated in the SRM, and engineering approval may be required to use them, but if available, the repair technicians who use them should have the opportunity to get approval for them.

FACILITIES REQUIRED

Good housekeeping is an important aspect of a repair shop because it directly impacts the technician's safety and the equality of work. Due to the materials used in composite repair, good housekeeping is a must on the work floor, as well as in and around the storage areas for the materials.

STORAGE OF MATERIALS

When working with composites, special storage facilities may be required depending on the type of work performed and the materials used. Composite material storage, such as fabrics, resins, foam, and honeycomb, may require special storage temperatures to ensure the quality of the material. Three storage temperature ranges are common: room temperature of 75°F to 80°F, refrigeration of about 40°F, and freezer temperatures of 0°F or less.

Freezer space must be available for most structural grade pre-pregs and adhesives. If improperly stored, the adhesives, resins, or pre-pregs that are used for the repair may result in structurally unsafe aircraft components. Some pre-preg fabrics have both an in-freezer storage life and an out-of-the-freezer storage life because the resins slowly warm up to room temperature and start their cure cycle immediately upon being removed from the freezer. If they are allowed to stay out of the freezer too long, they will cure too much and won't have adequate strength for the repair.

To ensure the materials are being stored properly, every repair shop should:

1. Keep records on refrigerated storage to ensure the first materials in are the first out for use (first in/first out).

2. Seal refrigerated materials properly to prevent entry of moisture.

3. Have an identification label accompany the material.

4. Record accumulated time out of refrigerated storage.

Discarding all materials that exceed their storage life is another important aspect of good housekeeping. Many containers have a limitation date that is calculated from the date of manufacture or date of shipment receipt (whichever is applicable). If an item has a manufacturing or shipment date of 1/02, and a six month storage life, its limitation date may be stamped 7/02, and should not be used after this date.

To discard the materials properly, consult the Material Safety Data Sheet (MSDS). Many resins, catalysts, and pre-preg materials are considered hazardous waste if disposed of without curing, so the two parts may have to be mixed and cured before throwing them away. Prepreg materials can be cured in an oven, or donated to your local A&P school for training purposes. Once the material is cured it is no longer considered toxic.

A chest type freezer is preferred over the upright because the resin system on an upright freezer may tend to slowly flow down because of gravity. That would make some areas of the roll much more resin rich than others. Turning the rolls every week solves this problem, and it is much easier in a chest freezer.

Obviously, the most important factor about a freezer is that it keeps the materials at the required temperature. If power should be lost and the freezer warms, record the fact and label the materials as time out of the freezer. The best way of monitoring the freezer is to use a thermometer that records the high and low temperatures within the freezer. If you notice that the high temperature is outside the range, you should subtract the amount of time it was since someone last checked the freezer temperature. Other recording devices are available, including ones that are similar to those used under the heat blankets to record a cure.

All composite fabrics and vacuum bagging materials should be kept on rolls in a covered, clean, and dry storage area away from contamination. Remember, vacuum bagging materials have a specific moisture content that keeps the material flexible. Vacuum bagging film should be stored in a plastic casing or bag that can be sealed to prevent the film from becoming brittle. Kevlar, on the other hand, wicks in moisture or humidity and therefore should also be protected in plastic. [Figure 10-1]

Store honeycomb and foams in the original packing box away from the working area where dust and other contaminates may damage the material.

WORKING ENVIRONMENT

Safety is vitally important when working with composites because of the danger to the technicians, the repairs, and the machinery. Safety equipment must always be available to the technician working on the composite structure. Dust masks or respirators that filter to five microns are required when sanding, drilling, or trimming some composite structures. When working around a composite sanding environment, it is nice to have a dust mask on even if it isn't required to have one which filters down to fiber microns. Cancer of the sinuses is becoming more common among people who worked with fiberglass in the 1960s.

Clean rooms are desirable when making composite repairs. To maintain cleanliness, separate areas of the shop should be provided for the sanding operations and the lay-up of fabric patches. This eliminates contamination of the repair and provides a cleaner and safer work area. If you do not have separate areas for composite repair, clean the area very well and vacuum up any sanding dust before bonding patches.

Adequate ventilation also must be available while working with any solvents, resins, catalysts, and adhesives. Check the MSDS for each type of chemical used to see what may be required. An updraft table may be used to pull hazardous fumes from the air.

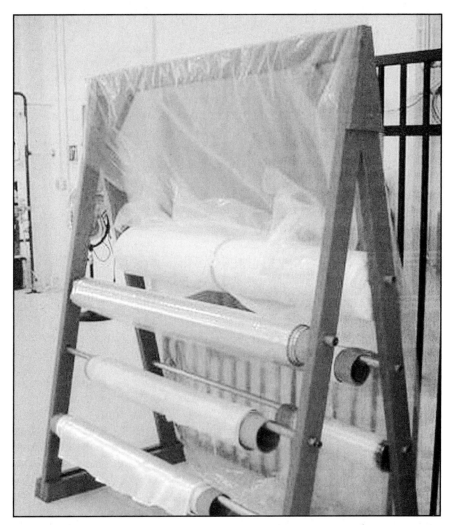

Figure 10-1. Composite fabrics and vacuum bagging materials stored on a rack help maintain cleanliness and safety.

During the sanding and drilling process, use a dust collector or downdraft table to keep the fine sanding particles from contaminating the air.

A downdraft table is a table that pulls air down and pulls small particles away. A dust collector, which should be able to filter down to five microns, is more portable and may be taken to the aircraft if a repair is being made while the part is attached to the aircraft.

Eyewash and first aid station must be available near any repair station and kept unobstructed.

Many of the solvents and resin materials are flammable and must be kept away from heat and open flame when in use. To minimize or eliminate the danger of fire and subsequent destruction of life and property, the following requirements should be met:

1. Eliminate all flames, smoking, sparks, and other sources of ignition from areas where solvents are used.

2. Adequate ventilation is required when working with any resins or solvents.

3. The sanding operation may cause sparks and should not be done in an area where flammable materials are used.

4. Do not have solvents around when bagging films and peel ply materials are unrolled because they may create a static charge.

5. Meet all storage requirements.

COST CONSIDERATIONS

The materials used in composites cost five to ten times more than aluminum. Due to this high cost, repairs must be done correctly in order to maintain a cost productive workshop.

COMPOSITE MATERIALS

The fabric materials used in advanced composite structures come in a variety of weaves and weights. The structural repair manual designates which weave and style to use for various repairs. Typically, fabrics come with a description printed on the paper that details the type of weave and style to show it conforms to a specific requirement. This description may also contain information on what type of fiber was used in the weaving, whether or not there is a finish on the fabric, the roll and lot numbers, and other data that would help track of exactly where and when this particular fabric was woven. If the material is a prepreg, it will also have information of storage temperatures, shelf life, etc. This information is required to be on file for all fabrics. This information may be on the tube the fabric is rolled onto. If the data isn't on the paper or on the tube when you receive the fabric, put this information on the cardboard tube.

The storage of raw, woven fabric (non-prepreg) is usually on storage racks and covered with plastic to prevent dust accumulation. It should also be kept out of the sunlight and protected from high humidity. Some of the fabrics may wick in humidity and be affected by sunlight.

A common problem with these materials is that they cannot be purchased in small quantities. Shops that work exclusively on repairs may not want to buy large quantities and then have their shelf life expire—this could become quite expensive. There are a few companies that supply small quantities of composite materials but as composite materials become more commonly used, more and more may offer these materials in small quantities.

VACUUM BAG MATERIALS

There are many types of bagging materials available for composite work, however, many of them are for high performance use in manufacturing at very high temperatures and pressures. This high performance capability adds to their cost. For most repairs, lower temperatures are used for curing, allowing a wide variety of less costly bagging materials to be used. It may be hard to find small quantities of these materials, but there are some suppliers that break full rolls.

Vacuum bagging materials do not require all the material certification that the composite materials do. These materials are used as tools with the composite repair. They facilitate the vacuum bagging and curing of the repair, and are taken off the repair when completed. Since they are removed, these materials do not become a permanent part of the aircraft, and therefore do not require certification. This is contrary to the belief of some officials that may tell you that the vacuum bagging material does require certification. Although conformity can be verified by contacting the manufacturer of the material, it should not be required. A good argument for this situation is to ask if your ball peen hammer also requires certification.

TOOLS AND EQUIPMENT

Some of the tools and equipment used for composite work are the same as those used with sheet metal. Drills, grinders, and saws, are generally the same. What is different are the parts used with some of these tools. For example, special drills and sanding discs of various grits are required to complete fabrication and repair work. Vacuum bagging and hot bonding equipment are also special tools needed with composites. There are many hot bond equipment models that range from simple to operate to very complex. The following information provides an idea of what may be appropriate for different size shops.

MACHINING EQUIPMENT

When working with machining tools, use non-spark producing tools designed for use with composite materials. Traditional drills can be used but special drill bits should be used to produce cleaner holes in aramid and carbon/graphite. Brad point and dagger drill bits are common (Refer to additional machining information in Chapter 9).

Band saws equipped with fine tooth blades work on all types of composite materials, however, they may produce a slight fuzzing on aramid fabrics. These edges must then be cleaned up by wet sanding with a fine grit sandpaper to smooth the rough edges produced by the band saw.

When sanding, a right-angle sander is a good choice because it offers more control because the disc is close to the area being sanded. Drills fitted with a small sanding disk also could be used, but there won't be as much control for very fine work.

Other machining tools that may be desirable, but not necessarily required, are routers, water jet cutters, counter bores, hole saws, and hot wire cutters (See Machining Chapter 9).

VACUUM BAGGING EQUIPMENT

Vacuum equipment is available separately with a hot patch bonding system that also includes a heat source. Vacuum pumps are available in various configurations. Many conventional vacuum pumps are driven by electricity, but the noise level is very high and they may generate heat, which may make them less acceptable in certain shops.

Other vacuum systems work with compressed air. Since the vacuum equipment is driven by compressed air, it is quiet, does not generate heat, and therefore the working environment is improved.

VACUUM HOSES

Depending on if you are curing in an oven or an autoclave, or with heat blankets, heat guns, or heat lamps, there are different types of hoses to be used. If the hose is enclosed in the heating environment such as with ovens or autoclaves, the hose must be able to withstand the high heat.

If your application of heat is by another method, plastic hoses can be used as long as they are equipped with an internal wire to keep them from collapsing.

Vacuum hoses are usually included in the hot bonding system.

VACUUM VALVES

The valves used within the vacuum bagging operation must be able to withstand the temperatures and the vacuum being pulled. Again, if the part is to be cured in an oven or autoclave, the valve must be made of metal to withstand the heat.

If repair heat is to be applied by a heat blanket, the valve can not be in direct contact with the heat, and a less expensive plastic valve may be used. Most vacuum valves incorporate a channel in the base to allow easier air-flow through it and prevent the valve from sealing to the part when a vacuum is drawn on it. The vacuum valves usually come as a part of the hot bonding equipment

ACOUSTICAL LEAK TESTER

To check for leaks around the vacuum bagging seal and to locate any pinholes in the plastic, an acoustical leak tester may be used. A probe is pointed anywhere a leak is suspected, the hissing sound is amplified and heard through earphones. A funnel is a simpler version that may be used. The large end is pointed at the areas suspected of leaking, as your ear is next to the small end. This will also magnify the hissing sound somewhat.

LAY-UP TOOLS

Use a balance or scale to mix the two parts of the resin system to the desired weight. A digital scale is the most accurate. Do not mix by volume; always mix by weight. Homebuilt aircraft designers have made a quick and easy apparatus for measuring the resins used for building a homebuilt aircraft. This device is not used in the repair field because there are many types of resins with different ratios for mixing.

Scissors to cut various materials are required. Carbon/graphite and fiberglass can be cut with conventional fabric scissors. Aramid fabric should be cut with special scissors which cut the fibers without fraying. If a lot of aramid cutting is to be done, these special scissors are very desirable.

Squeegees come in various types depending on what is preferred by the user. Some are soft and flexible, while others are a hard plastic. This is just a matter of preference.

CURING EQUIPMENT

Structural repairs require equipment to heat the repair. There are a number of ways to cure the composite with heat. Failure to follow the proper curing requirements, or improper usage of curing equipment could be reason to reject the repair

As previously mentioned, some resin systems may be cured at room temperature (65°F -80°F) in a time span of 8-24 hours depending on the type of resin system used. Using heat with some room temperature curing matrix systems may accelerate the curing process. However, most structural composite parts are manufactured at a high heat, and the repair must also be cured at high heat.

The most widely accepted method of curing structural composites is by using resins that cure at high temperatures. The adhesives and matrix systems used for repairs require elevated temperatures during their cure to develop full strength. This heat also reduces the brittleness of the resins. The cure temperature may range anywhere from 150°F to 750°F. The amount of heat applied should be held constant by monitoring the surface temperature of the repair.

HEAT LAMPS

The use of heat lamps to cure advanced composite parts is not recommended. Temperature cannot be accurately controlled and heat lamps may localize the heat in one spot.

HEAT GUNS

When a heat gun is used to cure a composite part, it must be controlled with a temperature monitor. This is necessary because a typical heat gun can generate temperatures of up to 750°F when it is left on continuously. If, for example, the cure temperature is 350°F, the heat gun should be monitored with a controller. Problems may occur if the heat gun is pointed to one place on the repair; the excessive curing in that spot may evaporate the resins, leaving dry areas which are cause to reject the repair.

OVEN CURING

Ovens offer controlled and uniform heating of all repair surfaces. Some ovens have vacuum ports to provide vacuum pressure while curing. One problem associated with using an oven to cure repairs is that the part must be removed from the aircraft, and must be small enough to fit into the oven. Oven curing is frequently used by manufacturers to produce a part. Ovens used to cure composites must be certified for that purpose.

AUTOCLAVES

Autoclaves are customarily used in the manufacturing of composites rather than in the repair procedures. An exception to this is when the damage is very extensive; the part must be put into the original mold and cured with heat and extra pressure. A composite part repaired to this extent is more accurately referred to as a remanufactured part.

In remanufacturing, the part is placed back into its original mold used during manufacturing, then vacuum bagged and heated up to the curing temperature at a controlled rate while more pressure is applied.

HEAT BLANKETS

Flexible silicon heating blankets come in a variety of forms and sizes. This is the preferred method of curing repairs for most composites because of the controlled even heating of the part. Most hot bond equipment comes with all of the vacuum valves, vacuum hoses, thermocouples, and heat blankets required to start working with the unit. Other sizes of heat blankets can be ordered later as the technician sees the need for various sizes.

HOT PATCH BONDING EQUIPMENT

Composite hot patch bonding machines are most often used to repair composite components in the field or when the damage is small enough not to require remanufacturing of the part. They offer many advantages over autoclave and oven curing. They include both the controller for heat application by a heat blanket or heat gun, and the vacuum pump for applying pressure. [Figure 10-2]

Composite Educational Services, a commercial firm, offers a composite hot patch bonding system that incorporates a heat control unit and a vacuum source to complete composite repairs. This portable unit is very lightweight and ideal for use in shop repairs.

The 100 percent solid state heat control unit works as a setpoint controller as well as a ramp and soak controller, depending on the type of repairs being performed. The digital display panel is easy to read and can be programmed up to 99 hours long with a maximum of eight steps. The vacuum unit provides up to 27 in. Hg at 58 psi. It converts standard shop air into vacuum pressure.

This machine also comes complete with all heat blankets, vacuum hoses and valves, thermocouples, gauges, and instructions. A solid state recorder or a strip chart recorder is also available which can be used with this controller.

Other companies that offer composite hot patch bonding machines include Wichitek and Heatcon.

TRAINING

The use of composite materials is gaining rapidly in the aviation industry because of its high strength and light weight structures.

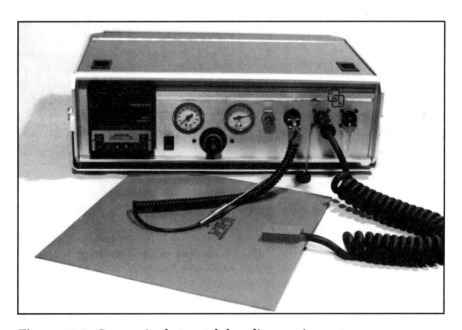

Figure 10-2. Composite hot patch bonding equipment.

Presently, one of the most significant drawbacks to the use of composites is the lack of trained technicians who are able to perform acceptable repairs to damaged composite structures. Such repairs must be accomplished properly in order to restore the structural integrity of the damaged part. The techniques required to properly complete composite repairs are not commonly known.

Technicians, inspectors, maintenance managers, and critical maintenance personnel need to achieve a level of technical expertise to work on the advanced composite components. The emphasis of training should provide practical information that will familiarize the technician with common field repairs, tools, materials, and techniques. Upon completion of the training course, a technician should be able to easily translate the manufacturer's instructions into airworthy repairs using skills and knowledge gained.

Chapter 11
Assessment & Repair

The task of repair begins when a technician determines the structure has been damaged to the extent that it requires a repair. It is important to evaluate the damage to determine the type, depth, size, and location of the defect. Some defects may be more serious to the performance of the part, and this information needs to be considered seriously to determine the best method of repair.

CLASSIFICATION OF DAMAGE

Classification of damage is placed in one of three categories: negligible, repairable, or non-repairable. Although all manufacturer definitions vary slightly, negligible damage is described as any damage that may be corrected by a simple procedure with no restrictions on flight operation. Repairable damage is damage to the skin, bond, or core that places restrictions on the aircraft or part. All permanent repairs must be structural load carrying repairs that meet aerodynamic smoothness requirements. A non-repairable part is one that is damaged beyond established repair limits.

If a composite part has been damaged beyond the specified repairable limitations, it should be removed and replaced. In some cases, however, the part may be remanufactured if the manufacturer approves. The part should be crated and sent to the original manufacturer, or an authorized repair station equipped to perform the necessary remanufacturing operations.

There are definite engineering reasons for establishing repair limits for critical airframe components. Standard repair procedures cannot always replace 100 percent of the damaged composite part's strength. Therefore, it is imperative that the manufacturer's specified repair limits not be exceeded during field repairs.

Many times the damage is a combination of two different types of damage. For example, a part may be delaminated and also have a crack. For a particular component, the delamination may be within the repairable limits, and the crack may be within the repairable limits. However, a delamination with a crack may not be within limits. Read the entire section of the SRM when determining the repairability of a component.

Repair methods and the classification of damage have not yet been standardized in the aviation industry. Each manufacturer has developed a method of classifying damage with an appropriate repair procedure. Figure 11-1 is an example of a damage classification chart, which may be found in the structural repair manual for the

NOTES: EXAMPLE DAMAGE CLASSIFICATION

1. Any dent damage causing delamination, breaking and/or creasing of the skin must be considered as a fracture and must be repaired accordingly.

2. The repair adhesives do not adhere well if are not properly bonded initially.

3. It is permissible to straighten out dents in the .008 gauge vee edge that are confined to within .25" of edge. Use three-ounce hammer and backup bar. Care must be taken to avoid debonding.

4. Surface damage is defined as cuts, deep scratches, abrasions, and dents with broken fibers that do not penetrate the skin.

5. Surface damages such as scratches and abrasions that damage paint and/or protective fiberglass outer ply but do not scratch or abrade the carbon laminate fibers underneath are classified as negligible damages.

6. Dents in skin that are stable and are not accompanied with delaminations or broken fibers are classified as negligible damage.

7. Sum of void dimensions in any direction shall not exceed 20% of maximum dimensions in that direction.

8. There are no restrictions on size, locations, or number of negligible repairs.

9. Repairable holes in vertical stabilizer box skin are limited to holes that do not extend into the internal structure before or after cleanup.

10. This table is taken from Structural Repair Manual. It is not to be used while making a repair.

Figure 11-1 (A). Typical example of a Damage Classification Chart.

Repair Area A — Laminated Carbon/Epoxy Structural Skins		
Type of Damage	Negligible Damage (Note 8)	Repairable Damage
Scratches	Glass Ply Damage (Note 5)	0.010 to 0.030 inch in depth and less than 3.25 inches in diameter or length without Carbon failure. (Note 1)
Dents (Note 1)	Less than 0.010 inch in depth (Note 6)	
Panel Edge Damage	Less than 0.125 inch wide by 6.0 inches in length and less than depth of skin. (Note 1)	None
Surface Damage	Not defined	Less than 1.0 inch diameter and less that 0.085 inch deep.
		Greater than 1.0 inch diameter but less than 3.25 inch diameter and less than 0.035 inch deep.
		Greater than 1.0 inch diameter and .035 inch deep but less than 3.25 inch diameter and .085 inch deep.
Surface Damage and Holes	Not Defined	Greater than hole limits set in Fig. 3-15 (55-32-01) but less than 6.0 inches in diameter.
Holes (Note 9)	None	Holes through skin after clean-up that are within limits set forth in Fig. 3-15 (55-32-01)

Figure 11-1 (B). Typical example of a Damage Classification Chart.

Repair Area A & B			
Laminate to Laminate Voids	Skin Thickness (in.)	Length (in.)	
	.016	Zero	Greater than allowable but less than 10 times allowable in length.
	.016-.020	.25	
	.021-.032	.50	
	.033-.051	.60	
	.051-.064	.84	
	.065	.93	

Figure 11-1 (C). Typical example of a Damage Classification Chart.

Repair Area B —Bonded Carbon/Epoxy Skins to Honeycomb Sandwich Structure		
Type of Damage	Negligible Damage (Note 8)	Repairable Damage
Scratches	Does not penetrate beyond protective glass ply into Carbon composite	Penetrates one or more Carbon plies but not through more than 1.0 inch.
		Penetrates one or more Carbon plies but through skin and not longer than 3.25 inches.
Dents (Notes 1 and 3)	Less than .010 inch in depth (Note 6)	.010 to .030 inch in depth and less than 1.0 inch in diameter. (Note 1)
Panel Edge Member Damage	Less than .125 inch wide and 6.0 inches in length and less than depth of skin (Note 1)	None
Holes and/or cracks through one skin	Not Defined	1.0 inch diameter hole or less (Note 1)
		1.0 inch to 3.0 inch diameter hole (Note 1)
Holes and/or cracks through both skins	Not Defined	1.0 inch diameter hole or less on either side (Note 1)
		1.0 inch to 3.0 inch diameter hole on either side (Note 1)
Skin to core voids	Less than .50 inch diameter in area	Greater than .50 inch but less than 2.50 inches in diameter or no greater than .70 inch wide by 4.0 inches long.
Leading or Trailing Edge Damage	Less than .25 inch deep (Note 3)	Greater than .25 inch deep but less than .380 inch beyond .008 inch stainless steel leading edge and 3.0 inches in length (Note 1)

Figure 11-1 (D). Typical example of a Damage Classification Chart.

specific aircraft. The repair procedures, which are presented in this book, are intended to give the technician some background as to the most commonly used procedures.

TYPES OF DAMAGE

COSMETIC DEFECTS

A cosmetic defect is a defect on the outer surface that does not involve damage to the structural reinforcing fibers. Cosmetic damage is often caused by chipping or scratching during handling. Since it does not affect the strength of the part, and usually is repaired for esthetic reasons. If there is damage to the top fiberglass layer of structural components made of either aramid or carbon/graphite, it may be considered negligible or cosmetic damage.

IMPACT DAMAGE

Impact damage occurs when a foreign object strikes the part. The degree of damage may range from slight to severe. The most common cause of impact damage is careless handling during transportation or storage, or standing parts on their edge without adequate protection.

The thin face sheets on a sandwich panel are very susceptible to impact damage. An area that has been subjected to impact damage should also be inspected for delamination around the impacted area.

Nicking, chipping, cracking, or breaking away pieces of the edge or corner can also be caused from improper handling.

DELAMINATION

Delamination is the separation of fabric layers of material in a laminate. Delamination can occur with no visible indications from the outer skin. To compound the problem, delamination often accompanies other types of damage, particularly impact damage. This damage occurs as the result of several causes, including impact, moisture in the fabric, or lightning strikes. Another type of delamination is an unbond, or as it is sometimes called, a disbond. A disbond occurs when the skin of a sandwich structure becomes separated from the core. [Figure 11-2]

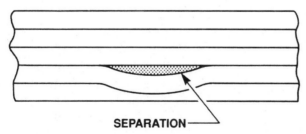

Figure 11-2. Delamination of fabric layers.

In those instances in which damage is visible, it is best to assume the damage has radiated into areas that exhibit no visual damage.

An air pocket between layers of fabric may also be the result of improper bonding of the composite. This may occur during manufacturing or during a repair operation. If this is the case, it may have been caused by any of the following:

1. Improper resin/catalyst

2. Improper mixing or weighing of the two matrix components

3. Inadequate amount of pressure or heat during the cure cycle

4. Improper cleaning of dirt, grease, or foreign materials on the surface to be bonded

CRACKS

Cracks can occur in advanced composite structures just as in metallic ones. Sometimes they can be detected visually, other times they may require more advanced methods of nondestructive inspection (NDI). A crack may be just in the top paint or matrix layer, and not penetrate into the fiber material at all. A crack may also extend into the fiber material and into the core yet appear to be just in the top surface. A thorough inspection should be made to determine the extent of each crack.

HOLE DAMAGE

Holes may occur from impact damage, over-torquing fasteners, or as a result of fastener pull-through. Holes drilled in the wrong location, wrong size, or wrong number of holes drilled can also be classified as hole damage.

Holes caused by a lightning strike may burn off resins, leaving bare cloth.

Tiny holes, known as pin holes, in the skin surface are not easily detected, however, they could lead to more extensive damage. If moisture is allowed to get into the core structure, along with the airflow over the part, it could cause a small delamination, which could grow into a very large delamination.

INSPECTION METHODOLOGY

Areas on the aircraft that are susceptible to damage, such as leading edges made of thin face sheets over a honeycomb panel, should be inspected more often than areas that are more protected, such as the vertical stabilizer. Visual inspection to these areas should be accomplished periodically, while more in depth inspection should be done at regular overhaul intervals.

Many times the inspection method requires that the component be removed from the aircraft in order to be inspected correctly. This type of inspection is usually accomplished at the time of the aircraft's overhaul. Between overhaul inspections, visual inspection usually is adequate. Each manufacturer calls out a specific test method depending on the location and type of structure.

VISUAL INSPECTION

Visual inspection is used to detect cracks, surface irregularities (from an internal flaw), and surface defects such as delamination and blistering. A good visual inspection usually detects surface flaws. A light and a magnifying glass are useful in detecting cracked or broken fibers. A small microscope also is helpful in determining whether the fibers in a cracked surface are broken or if the crack affects only the resin.

Delaminations may sometimes be found by visual inspection if the area is examined at an angle with a bright light shown on the surface. The delaminated area may appear to be a bubble, or an indentation in the surface. Use a coin tap test if you suspect an area of delamination.

COIN TAP TEST

One of the most important tools used to detect internal flaws or delaminations is a coin tap test. Use a coin or rounded edge steel washer, as shown in Figure 11-3, to tap lightly along a bond line or area suspected of having the flaws. Listen for variations in the tapping sound. A sharp solid sound indicates a good bond, but a dull thud indicates bond separation. However, changes in the thickness of the part, reinforcements, fasteners, and previous repairs may give false readings. Whenever damage is found visually, coin tap around the area to find damage such as a delamination that cannot be seen visually. Much of the time if there is a hole, crack, or other damage, there is also delamination around the area. This type of test only works on one side of the component at a time. The opposite side of the component must also be coin tapped to find delaminations.

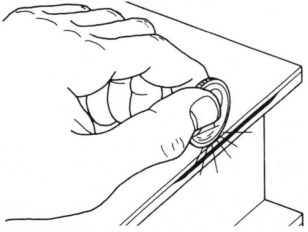

Figure 11-3. Coin tap test.

ULTRASONIC INSPECTION

For internal damage inspection an ultrasonic tester may be used. Ultrasonic testing uses a high frequency sound wave as a means of detecting flaws in a part by beaming a high frequency wave through the part and viewing the echo pattern (pip) on an oscilloscope. By examining the variations of a given response, delaminations, flaws, or other conditions are detected. Some ultrasonic equipment cannot differentiate between a honeycomb cell and a void, resulting in an unreliable reading. A new type of ultrasonic machine has been recently developed to detect flaws in skins over honeycomb cores. This equipment only works on one kind of material, carbon/graphite, and does not work on others such as Aramid. Ultrasonic equipment may be ineffective for detecting some types of damage on some composite structures, so make sure the equipment you are using can be used on the type of component you are testing. [Figure 11-4]

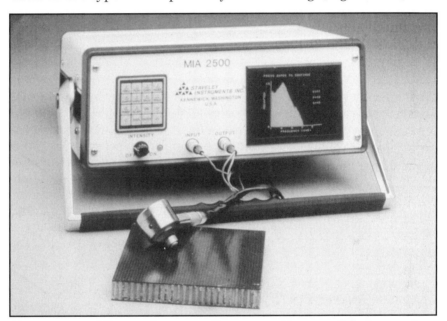

Figure 11-4. Ultrasonic tester for composite use. (Photo courtesy Staveley Instruments)

There are three types of commonly used ultrasonic testers: A-SCAN, B-SCAN, and C-SCAN. An A-SCAN is a time versus amplitude display read from left to right. A known reference must be scanned first. Then the height of the specimen pip is compared to the height of the pip on the reference. A B-SCAN takes a cross-sectional view of the material being tested and uses an oscilloscope screen to compare the sample. A C-SCAN imaging shows the shape, size, and location of the damage, but does not show the depth.

Ultrasonic inspection methods require specialized training to provide reliable results.

THERMOGRAPHY

Thermography locates flaws by temperature variations at the surface of a damaged part. Heat is applied to the part then the temperature gradients are measured using an infrared camera or film. On the film, a material's thickness varies and shows up as different colors because of the heat build up in different areas of the material. Thermography requires knowledge of the thermal conductivity of the test specimen and a reference standard for comparison purposes.

LASER HOLOGRAPHY

Laser holography calls for the suspect part to be heated and then photographed using a laser light source and a special infrared camera film system. It is used to detect disbonds or water in honeycomb and impact damage. Laser holography is quite expensive to use so at this time only manufacturers and very large airline maintenance facilities use the process.

RADIOGRAPHY

Radiography can be used to detect cracks that cannot be visually detected, both internally and externally. Radiography also detects water inside the honeycomb core cells. It is useful in detecting the extent of the damage that cannot be visually detected. Again, this type of testing is used only by manufacturers and large airlines. These facilities test the manufactured components to see if the ply orientation is correct, and that matrix cracks, delaminations, subsurface damage, resin content (resin rich or starved), and porosity can all be seen. This is helpful to the manufacturers so they can adjust their methods of manufacturing to get the perfect part.

HARDNESS TESTING

After a repair has cured, a hardness tester, such as a Barcol tester, can be used to determine whether the resins have reached their proper strength. A special chart is used to interpret the results for different types of resins and pre-pregs. Hardness testing does not test the strength of the composite, only the matrix strength.

DYE PENETRANT

Dye penetrant is used successfully for detecting cracks in metallic surfaces, however, it should not be used with advanced composites because if it is allowed to sit on the surface, the wicking action of the fibers may take in the dye penetrant and would no longer bond to new material. The entire effected area would have to be removed before new patches could be applied. This, in effect, could extend the damage to the size that would make the part non-repairable.

Figure 11-5 shows defects that can be inspected by various types of inspection equipment.

INSPECTION	SERVICE-INCURRED DEFECTS						
	IMPACT	DELAMINATIONS/ (DISBONDS)	CRACKS	HOLE DAMAGE	WATER	LIGHTNING STRIKE	BURNS/ OVERHEATING
VISUAL	X		X	X		X	X
X-RAY	X		X	X	X	X	
ULTRASONIC		X	X				

Figure 11-5. Defects that can be located by various types of inspection equipment.

REPAIR OPERATION

It is not necessarily difficult to complete an airworthy repair to a composite structure. However, the techniques, materials, and tools that are used are different than those used on conventional repairs. If care is not taken to do a composite repair correctly, the repair will not develop the full strength characteristics that are desirable in a composite structure.

The question within the aviation industry is no longer one of, "Will the composite work?" The most relevant question that is now facing the aviation industry in regard to composites is, "How do you fix it?"

Aeronautical and materials engineers have designed composites to perform in the air, but the most common types of damage to composite structures occur during ground handling. Aircraft damage most commonly occurs during the servicing of the aircraft, storage, and maintenance, or during landing and takeoff.

Composites that use very thin laminates over cores are susceptible to impact damage which might occur from a dropped tool, mishandling by tugs or other ground support equipment, or in the case of a component part, simply by being dropped on a hard surface.

If the part is subject to continuous loading and unloading of stress, the resins may develop very tiny cracks. These cracks may eventually cause failure of the resins to transfer the stress loads to the fibers. The fibers themselves will probably not crack and fail, but the damage to the resin could seriously weaken the structural integrity of the part.

Aviation composites are designed to be strong, lightweight, and durable. These components are usually very expensive parts because they are made in one piece, often including stiffeners and internal components on one part. A composite repair must be made correctly because the alternative cost of replacing the part is often not feasible. The responsibility of the technician then is to be able to complete the repair with sufficient expertise so as to restore the original structural strength. Engineers and manufacturers are testing many new repair techniques to help technicians achieve these goals.

This is a new technology and new repairs are expected to be introduced periodically. The FAA guidelines for structural repair state that the design strength and remaining service life of the part must be restored. All the repair procedures found in this book, although not specific, are typical found in Structural Repair Manuals.

TRADITIONAL FIBERGLASS REPAIRS VS. ADVANCED COMPOSITE REPAIRS

The older type of fiberglass repairs cannot be used on the advanced composite structures of today because the advanced composites are often used for structural applications. The fiberglass structures of the past were typically used for nonstructural applications. Consequently, the old style fiberglass repair methods were not necessarily intended to restore full structural strength.

Many fiberglass repairs were done with polyester resins and cured at room temperature. The resins were often applied very thick and were not bled out of the fabric during the cure process. Fabric weaves and ply direction were not considered, and many times the patches were bonded on without removing the damaged area. When a part is used structurally, it must deliver the same characteristics in flight as the original part.

A very dangerous temptation in the industry has been to relegate composite repairs to the fiberglass shop. Fiberglass, in the past, has been used mostly for nonstructural components. To repair an advanced composite part using the materials and techniques that have traditionally been used for fiberglass repairs results in an unairworthy repair. Such traditional repairs allow for excessive weight, increased susceptibility to material fatigue, and decreasing flexibility.

With this understanding of the difference between the old style of fiberglass repairs and the more advanced structural composite materials, let's look at a typical repair problem. A classic example of the consequences of using fiberglass repair techniques to repair a composite structure was recently demonstrated in a repair facility.

An aircraft with a damaged engine cowling made of a composite of fiberglass, Kevlar®, and carbon/graphite fiber was under repair. An A&P technician who had been trained in composite repairs was assigned to the task. He began the repair in the proper fashion by isolating the damaged area and scarfing the area in accordance with the structural repair manual. However, shortly after completing the scarfing operation, he was called away from the project and the damaged part was taken to the fiberglass shop for completion of the repair.

The technicians in the fiberglass shop were seasoned professionals and masters of traditional fiberglass repair. The problem was that they didn't know the first thing about composites. Engine cowlings typically use the higher temperature matrix materials to withstand the high operating temperatures around a cowling. The patches used to repair the cowling were of fiberglass, not of the advanced composite materials that should have been used. The weave and proper orientation of the plies were also ignored, and the type of resin used was not compatible with the existing structure. They used a room temperature cure, and did not vacuum bag the repair.

The patch was primed, painted, inspected, and approved, then the cowling was installed on the aircraft. However, the original composite technician doubted that the fiberglass shop had made a proper repair. Along with his supervisor, he found the repaired cowling on an aircraft waiting on the flight line. The technician hit the repair squarely in the center of the patch, causing the edges of the patch to pop up and separate from the surface skin. He peeled the patch off with a quick snap and handed it to his supervisor.

Obviously, the repair was not airworthy. In addition, the routed-out area now exceeded the repairable limits of the engine cowling. Thus a very expensive component was ruined. Those in the aviation maintenance industry cannot be so arrogant that we don't recognize that composites are different and require sufficient training to repair properly. Had this engine cowling failed in flight, it could have jeopardized the safety of the aircraft.

The engine cowling in question was a hybrid structure made of fiberglass, Kevlar®, and carbon/graphite. Each of the five layers of the cowling was composed of a different fiber (an inter-ply hybrid). When the fiberglass shop used only fiberglass to fill the hole, they failed to restore a uniform strength to the reinforcing elements of the composite. The resulting patch, using polyester resin, did not allow the matrix to disperse the imposed stress to the full reinforcing fiber network, only to the fibers in the localized patch area. This could have been corrected by using the proper repair techniques with the same composite resin as the original structure and by installing the correct reinforcing fibers in the same orientation of the existing fiber network. Since this was not done, even the slight stress of a human hand striking the patch caused it to separate from the engine cowling.

FLIGHT 587 ACCIDENT INVESTIGATION RAISES QUESTIONS ABOUT THE SAFETY OF COMPOSITE COMPONENTS AND THEIR REPAIR.

At the time of this printing, the NTSB has not yet determined the cause of the Flight 587 accident. However, there is evidence that a composite component with a major repair might be involved. Advanced composite materials were extensively used to fabricate primary and secondary structural components of the Airbus A300 because of the manufacturability of composite materials and their ability to withstand stresses. This tragic accident has brought to question the safety of using composite materials for primary structural components. Some people feel that there are, in fact, some problems within the aviation industry relating to standard industry practices for composite repair. As a maintenance technician, you can take an active role to correct some of these problems and improve the level of professionalism within our industry.

REPAIR PROCEDURES

This section describes procedures that are common to many types of advanced composite repair. This section is only intended to present typical repair situations. In an actual repair situation, the manufacturer's structural repair manual must be consulted regarding such information as operating environment, damage size limits, repair proximity limits, and other information pertaining to a specific repair.

NOTE: The information contained in this book is for training purposes only. Consult the appropriate Structural Repair Manual.

DETERMINE DAMAGE

To determine the damage of a part:

1. Visually examine the part for the extent of the damage.

2. Check in the vicinity of damaged area for entry of water, oil, fuel, dirt, or other foreign matter.

3. Check for delamination around the damage by coin tapping or other technique.

4. Check in the applicable section of the manufacturer's structural repair manual to determine whether the damage is within the repairable damage limits.

SURFACE PREPARATION

To prepare the surface for the repair process, remove surface contaminants such as exhaust residue, hydraulic fluid, and surface film by using a suitable soap and water solution, followed by a solvent wash of MEK or acetone.

The paint also must be removed from around the repair area in order to promote adhesion of the repair materials. Paint strippers, however, should not be used on composite structures. The problem is that since paint strippers are designed to remove epoxy-based paint, and because the resin systems used on most composites are epoxy based, the paint stripper deteriorates the resins within the component.

NOTE: Paint strippers of any type should never be used on any composite structure. Strippers can remove surface layers of resin and expose fabric. Some fabrics may absorb the stripper and create a surface that will not bond to another surface or paint.

Care must be taken when using a power sander to remove paint. Most power sanders are not recommended for paint removal because they do not provide sufficient operator control. If the top layer of composite fibers is sanded through, more extensive repairs may be required. Composite plies may not be perfectly even. In this instance, the sanding of the top layer in one area would be fine, but in another area the same depth of sanding could result in sanding through to the core material. This is especially prevalent in composites that were manufactured using a gel coating on the outside.

Care must be taken not to damage the plies that surround the repair area. If surrounding plies are damaged during the paint removal operation, the repair may have to be enlarged. If this happens, it may not fall within the repair limits, and some manufacturers limit the number of repairs within a certain area. If two repairs are being made, they may be too close together and the part may become non-repairable.

Once the paint has been removed from the area surrounding the damage, the repair zone should be masked off. This portion of the repair procedure defines the area that will be cut and stepped to accommodate the patch. The proper amount of space for each cut can be marked by using the following procedures:

1. Outline the entire damaged area that must be cut out and removed.

2. Expand the repair radius (assuming the repair is a circle) by one-half inch for each ply that must be repaired.

3. If an overlap patch is used, the extended radius is typically an additional inch. Place the masking tape along the lines where the repair is to be made.

For example, if the damage to the skin and core is three inches in diameter, and there are five surface plies, the three-inch diameter will be routed out. Then one-half inch per ply will be sanded around with an overlap layer of one inch, so the total size of the repair will be:

$$3 + (8 \times 1/2) + 1 + 1 = 9 \text{ inches diameter.}$$

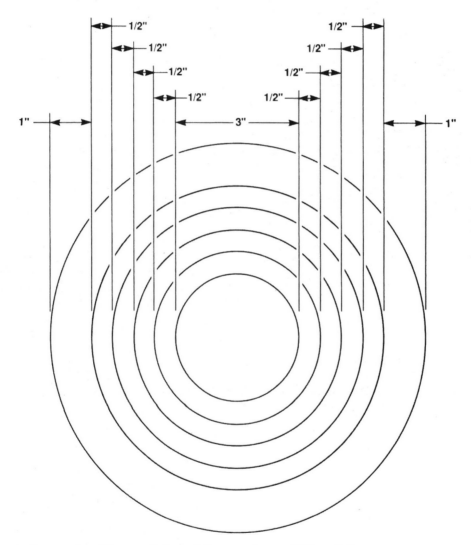

Figure 11-6. Example repair – The total size of the repair would be 9" diameter.

WORKING AROUND DEICER BOOTS

When a repair takes place near a deicer boot, carefully remove the boot to produce a good working area around the repair. Be sure to allow enough room for the vacuum bagging materials to fit around the repair. If the boot needs to be partially taken off, be careful not to damage it, or the underlying structure. When deice boots are over a composite structure, the boot is removed by using a solvent soaked rag (usually MEK or Toluene) and slightly pulling up on the boot, then spraying or wiping underneath with the solvent. This may take some time, but in the long run it is well worth it. Using a razor blade is common practice when removing a boot that is over a metal leading edge. Do not use a razor blade when removing a boot over a composite leading edge because it could damage the composite surface if the glue or cement isn't softened up enough. This could cause some of the composite material to peel up with the boot. This area would then need to be repaired.

Remember, do not use any kind of paint stripper with the composites or in the removal of the boot because the chemicals will damage the composite structure.

Once the boot is pulled back but before a repair is done, all the glue from the deice boot must be removed in the area of the repair. This can be done by soaking rags in solvent and laying them over the glue area. The rags may have to be resoaked a few times before the glue will wipe off cleanly. Once the glue is removed and the surface is clean, the repair to the composite material can take place. After the repair is cured, the boot can be replaced with the appropriate cement.

An exception to the above rule is when working around propeller de-ice boots. Because many propellers are made with foam cores, the solvent used to remove the adhesive on the boot may deteriorate the foam core. If your propeller has a foam core, the only way to remove the boot is to use mechanical means such as a knife. If you follow this process, be careful not to etch or cut into the surface of the composite material.

REMOVAL OF CORE DAMAGE

If damage has occurred to the core material of a sandwich structure, the damaged area must be removed first, prior to sanding the laminate.

For this example of core removal, the top fiber layers may show some damage that penetrates to the core. However, the bottom sandwich layers for this discussion are undamaged.

Use a suitable marking device to outline the area where the core must be removed. A router is usually used to remove the damaged core material. The first cut should be made with a pointed router bit to outline the plug in the damaged core. This top laminate layer plug should then be removed with a pair of pliers. If the surface to be routed is flat, simply set and lock the depth of the cut on the router base. Determine the depth by referring to the structural repair manual. When routing to a partial depth, the router should be supported on a flat template so the core surface is flat. Remember, it is better to route to a partial depth than it is to route through the opposite layer of laminate. [Figure 11-7]

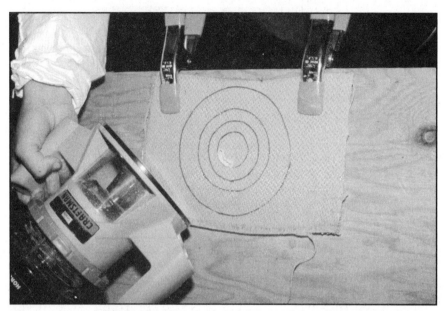

Figure 11-7. A high-speed router can be used to cut through the top layer. The bit used should be pointed.

The second cut is made by a flush bit to route out the entire honeycomb area. Again, be cautious to route only to the surface of the opposing laminate. As a precaution, leave about 1/16-inch of the honeycomb showing—this can then be hand sanded down to the opposite layer. Route the honeycomb out to the top of the opposite face sheet. If the router damages the opposing laminate, it will have to be sanded and have repair plies added to repair it.

If the repair surface is sloped (such as on a trailing edge) or curved (such as on a leading edge), it may be necessary to use a wedged template to ensure the router is held at the correct relative depth of cut.

LAMINATE STEP CUTTING AND SCARFING

To accomplish the proper step cuts in the laminate, each successive layer of fiber and matrix must be removed without damaging the underlying layer. Great care must be taken during this portion of the repair procedure to avoid damaging the fibers surrounding the area being removed. Sanding is the best method of removing the plies because it offers the most control.

Manual sanding offers a great deal of control, but is tedious and time consuming. Mechanical sanding is faster and easier, but it's also more likely to cause additional damage by sanding away too much material. One of the best tools for mechanically sanding composites is a small pneumatic right angle sander. If this is not available, a drill with a sanding disc attachment can be used. Patience and experience are the best ways to achieve adequate control of the sanding operation. [Figure 11-8]

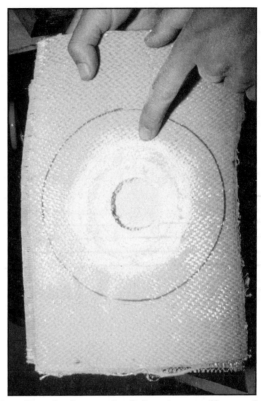

Figure 11-8. Sanding is the method that is usually used to remove the plies with the most control.

Each layer will be sanded down about one-half inch all the way around the damaged area. The idea is to sand one-half inch wide concentric circles (assuming a round repair) that taper down to the core material. Start sanding at the outermost mark and work down, toward the center, removing one layer at a time.

If using an overlap patch, do not taper or step sand into the top ply in this area, as this weakens the repair. Structural strength loss of the component occurs if sanding on the top layer exposes or damages the fibers in the unsanded area. The more accurately the sanding cuts are made, the more easily it is to shape the replacement plies and accurately place them into the repair. The sanding operation may be accomplished by step cutting or by scarfing.

WARNING: Sanding of composite structures produces dust that may cause skin irritations. Breathing excessive amounts of this dust may be irritating to your lungs. Observe proper safety precautions.

NOTE: Finer grit sandpaper usually keeps the fuzzing down

when sanding aramid fabric. The finer grit also removes the material slowly, giving more time to find the individual plies.

STEP CUTTING

The step effect is accomplished by sanding away approximately one-half inch of each layer as you taper down to the center of the repair. Initially, the aramid will fuzz and the carbon/graphite will produce a fine powder as each layer is being sanded through. Eventually, the materials will show a gloss area for each removed ply. As the fiber/matrix is being sanded, watch for a slight glossing of the work area. The glossing indicates that one layer of material has been removed and the top of the next layer has been exposed. [Figure 11-9]

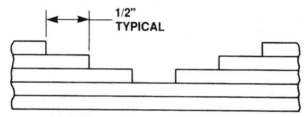

Figure 11-9. Step cut sanding.

When the glossing effect is seen, be cautious to stop sanding in that area or the next layer of material may be damaged. The layers are very thin and the inexperienced technician may sand through into the next layer. However, with practice, this portion of the repair technique can be mastered.

Another way to detect if one layer has been sanded is to look for a change in major fiber direction. This is possible only when the warp direction of each layer has been manufactured in alternating positions. As the top ply is sanded, the next layer produces the weave in a different orientation, signaling that one layer has been removed, exposing the top of the next layer.

The most difficult layer to sand is probably the second to the last layer, especially if it's located over a core structure. Be careful not to sand through the last layer and expose the core during this sanding operation. Don't use excessive pressure on the sander, or excessive speed. These rings will make the replacement plies easier to cut and easier to place them into the repair area more accurately.

SCARFING

Use scarf cutting to remove damaged material with a tapered cutout. Dimensions of the scarf are based on the ratio of the total height of the plies to a given length. The scarf should be an even taper down to the center of the repair. By shining a light on the surface of a scarf cut, you can identify the layer transitions. [Figure 11-10]

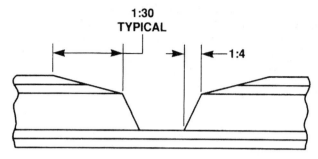

Figure 11-10. Scarf sanding.

A 1:30 ratio means the thickness of the skin is 1, the taper is 30. Cores may be scarfed at a different ratio than the laminates, 1:4 for example. It is important to read the repair manual carefully and fully understand how to make the appropriate cuts. It should be noted that in some structural repair manuals the text may call for a scarf cut, however, the illustration may be of a step cut. As long as the patches have enough bonding area, either sanding operation may be correct. [Figure 11-11]

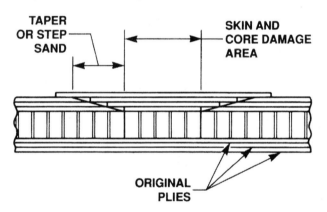

Figure 11-11. Stack-up of sanded scarf skin repair.

Because the composite repair science is still relatively new, there is much controversy as to which type of sanding operation is better, the step cut or the scarf. Not only is the type of sanding controversial, but the order and the way the patches are laid into a sanded area are also controversial. You should follow what is presented in the structural repair manual as closely as possible. Direct any questions you have to the manufacturer or a designated engineering representative.

CLEANING

All repairs must be cleaned after the sanding in order to create a suitable surface for the structural adhesion of the repair plies. The strength of a bond is directly related to the condition of the surfaces involved in the adhesion process. Many times during the sanding operations, the technician might touch the surface of the repair to see how the sanding is preceding and to see if the next ply has been exposed. The oils from a person's hands can contaminate the surface and must be removed before bonding any patches. To avoid the problem of oils seeping from the hands to the repair surface, many companies require the use of thin cotton gloves that allow the hands to feel the surface without leaving residue on the surface. If the surface is not properly cleaned, the patches may not bond adequately.

To develop a strong bond between the patch and the existing part, the adhesive or resin must be in complete contact with both parts. The dust from sanding can be removed by using a vacuum cleaner. A solvent wash of MEK, acetone, or butyl alcohol with a lint-free cloth, such as cheesecloth, cleans away any residual oils. Always allow the cleaning solvent to dry before proceeding with the repair. Aramid may require a longer drying time because of its wicking characteristic.

Once the part has been cleaned, it is important not to touch the surface or any of the repair materials with bare hands or the entire cleaning process must be repeated.

Do not use compressed air to blow away dust because this may cause delamination of the layers or cause the skin to delaminate from the bottom core.

WATER BREAK TEST

Prior to bonding, some manufacturers may require a water break test to detect oil or grease contamination. This test ensures there are no contaminating surface oils on the part. To accomplish the water break test, flush the repair surface with room temperature water. If the surface is not clean, the water film breaks into beads. If this occurs, the solvent cleaning process should be repeated until the water sheets off rather than beads.

Water sprayed on a freshly waxed aircraft will bead. If it has been a while since the aircraft was waxed, the water will flow off and not bead up. This is what you will look for. If the composite surface is clean, the water will not bead up, but rather flow off of the surface. The water introduced should be evaporated off by applying a heat lamp for a few minutes. If the part is not completely dry before bonding the patches, they will not adhere properly, and be cause for rejection of the repair.

REMOVAL OF WATER FROM DAMAGED AREA

Moisture in the composite component can be very dangerous if it is allowed to remain within the structure during the repair, and subsequently, after the repair is accomplished. Water that is trapped within a structure expands when heated, building up pressure which could cause delamination. If the trapped water is allowed to freeze, it will expand, also causing delamination. The water may also act as a plasticizer, reducing the composite structures' strength characteristics.

If water is not removed before bonding the patches, blisters may form, or the patches will not bond at all.

Water or moisture can enter edges that are not properly sealed or around holes drilled to accept hardware that also has not been properly sealed. The part may gather moisture from humidity or from rain and snow that soaks into the edges.

When the part has been damaged, it is important to bring the part into a dry area to avoid excessive moisture from wicking into the part. If the part has been properly sealed with paint or sealant after manufacturing or repairing, moisture should not be a problem.

Radiography and laser holography are good methods of detecting moisture within a composite structure. An ohmmeter is another way to detect moisture; if the ohmmeter indicates continuity when the two probes are placed on the suspect surface, there is probably moisture present in the material.

Once moisture has been detected, it must be removed. The following steps should be observed when removing water from a composite component.

1. Remove any standing water with a wet/dry vacuum cleaner.

2. Vacuum bag the surface using a vacuum unit to pullout water. The bleeder helps soak up water, too. Use a screen with a heat blanket to evaporate the water. As the vacuum unit is connected, the reduced pressure pulls out most of the water, the bleeder helps absorb the water, and the heat blanket with the screen evaporates any remaining water. [Figure 11-12]

3. An alternative method is to apply heat with a heat lamp to dry the component out.

4. During the repair process when curing patches, a slower temperature rise reduces the probability of blisters and voids forming, but this is true only if a small quantity of moisture is present.

5. If all the contaminant cannot satisfactorily be removed by using the above methods, the affected part must be removed and replaced.

After a repair is finished, it must be protected from moisture. Paint and edge sealant can be used to help prevent moisture from entering the structure. Some manufacturers recommend the use of a layer of plastic known as Tedlar to prevent moisture from entering through the fibers. [Figure 11-12]

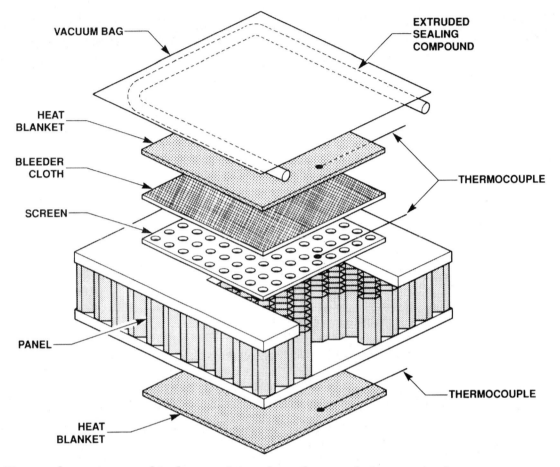

Figure 11-12. Vacuum bag set-up used to draw moisture from the area being repaired.

MATERIALS PREPARATION

Gather together the materials needed for the repair. The structural repair manual lists the materials you need.

1. Cross-reference the area on the aircraft where the damaged occurred with the manufacturer's description of the composite that was used to fabricate the part. The materials used should be identified by:

    a. Material type, class, and style.

    b. Number of plies, orientation, and stacking sequence.

    c. Adhesive and matrix system.

    d. Type of core, ribbon direction, core splicing adhesive, and potting compound.

2. Be sure all resins, adhesives, and pre-pregs are within their usable life.

3. Identify and understand all deviations from the original manufacturing materials. For example, in some cases, repairs to aramid material will use fiberglass patches to prevent the blistering problems that are more apparent with aramid. Also, availability of materials and storage facilities may be considered. (See note below on Pre-preg patches)

4. Identify the manufacturer's recommended cure system and ensure the proper tools are available. For example, a hot patch bonding machine, heat blankets of the proper size, and vacuum bagging equipment and materials. Be sure to check if the material cure temperatures are in Celsius or Fahrenheit.

5. Use the proper resins. Weigh and mix resins properly. [Figure 11-13]

Some manufacturers recommend the use of Semkits, prepackaged two-part resins systems. Often the two-part resins are packaged so the chemicals can be mixed together in a plastic bag without weighing or handling. This type of packaging usually provides the resin and the activator in two colors. The idea is to mix both colors together well enough that neither original color can be identified in the mixture. This visual check ensures a complete blending of the two chemicals. When the resin and activator are thoroughly mixed, the corner of the plastic bag can simply be cut off to remove the matrix mixture.

Another type of packaging has the two parts of resin in a plastic tube with a foil separator to prevent the two parts from mixing accidentally. A stem is used to break the foil, then mixed with an up and down motion while turning the stem. The package informs the technician as to how many strokes are required to mix the resin system properly.

Pot life is not necessarily the time it is usable in the cup. The resin and fabric should be in place before the actual curing takes place. If a resin with a short pot life is used to impregnate fabric, and the patches are cut to size, the patches must be in place on the sanded surface before the resin starts to cure. If the patches are allowed to sit too long within the plastic backing, they will start their chemical reaction and become stiffer. Subsequently, when the patches are in place and vacuum bagged to cure, the chemical cross-linking of the resin and the fibers may not take place as it is designed to do. The patches will have cured separately, and may not stick respectively to each other or the part properly. Be sure to follow the mixing procedure correctly and use the mixture before the pot life has expired.

Use caution when using the same pre-pregs as those used in the manufacture of the aircraft. This may or may not be the correct repair pre-preg material to use because the pre-preg system used

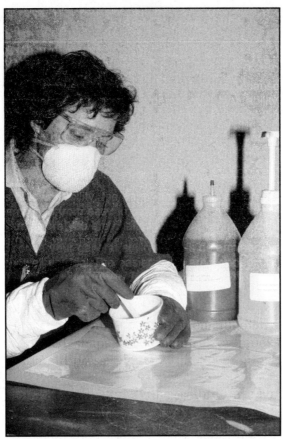

Figure 11-13. Follow the manufacturer's instructions carefully to ensure resins are mixed properly.

in manufacturing may be an autoclave type of pre-preg, which means it produces a very strong, lightweight structure when cured in an autoclave. However, to repair damaged components with the same type of materials as originally used in manufacturing can lead to problems. The autoclave cure is not used very widely in the repair procedure; hot bond with vacuum bagging techniques are used more commonly. The resin system in these pre-pregs may not produce the same desired strength characteristics when cured with hot bond techniques. They are not getting as much vacuum as an autoclave could produce. The plies of the repair, although they are cured, may be easily peeled from the surface. This could cause dangerous consequences if failure occurred in flight. Always follow the manufactures repair manual, not manufacturing materials.

HONEYCOMB RIBBON DIRECTION

As fabric has a warp direction, honeycomb also has a specific way it should be inserted into the repair. The ribbon of the honeycomb is the direction the honeycomb can be pulled apart. The ribbon of the repair plug must be oriented in the same direction as the ribbon of the original part.

When installing the honeycomb or foam plug into the cutout area, some manufacturers recommend using a film adhesive. If this is used, it is important that the plastic backing be removed from the adhesive before the repair core is inserted. If not removed, it acts as a barrier and prevents the materials from bonding, providing a repair that's not airworthy. To use a film adhesive, the diameter of adhesive is cut to the same diameter of the replacement plug. It is inserted in the hole with the plastic backing still intact.

Use a heat gun to soften the adhesive. Lightly apply pressure with a squeegee, then remove the plastic and insert the core.

An expanding foam adhesive is another method of installing the core. The new core's edges are wrapped with the adhesive and inserted into the routed-out hole. The part is typically vacuum bagged then heated. The foam adhesive around the edges of the core expands to fill the edges of the honeycomb plug and secures it to the internal edges of the part.

Another manufacturer may call for the use of a resin and micro balloon mixture. If using this method, a light coat of the mixture is all that is needed. Remember that excessive resin makes the part heavier and more susceptible to cracking. The micro balloon mixture may be spread over the bottom and on the sides of the core to hold a plug into place. This mixture may also be used when repairing foam core structures.

FIBER ORIENTATION

The patches made from the reinforcing material for the repair must carry the stress loads originally carried by the fibers that were manufactured into the part. Structural composite parts are engineered and manufactured to endure specific stress loads. Their ability to endure these stress loads is dependent in great measure to the way in which the fibers are oriented. [Figure 11-14]

There should be one fabric bonding patch ply of the same thickness and ply orientation for each damaged ply removed.

The fiber orientation of the new patches must be in the same direction as those of the original structure so any stress imposed on the part can flex through the repair as well as it does throughout the entire structure. If the fiber orientation is not correctly applied during a repair operation, the strength of the part is dramatically reduced, which may cause failure of the component.

A warp compass is a tool used to reference the orientation of the warp of the fiber. The warp fibers are a reference for properly aligning the fabric of a patch with the original part. If a fabric weave is to have a stronger direction, it is usually on the warp threads.

ITEM	DESCRIPTION	GAUGE	MATERIAL	EFFECTIVITY
1	ELEVATOR PANEL SKIN CORE		GRAPHITE/EPOXY HONEYCOMB SANDWICH SEE DETAIL I NON-METALLIC HONEYCOMB CORE	

LIST OF MATERIALS

ITEM	PLY NO.	MATERIAL	PLY ORIENTATION [A]
1	P1	[B]	+45°
	P2	[C]	90°
	P3	[C]	90°
	P4	[B]	+45°
	P16	[B]	+45°
	P17	[C]	90°
	P18	[C]	90°
	P19	[B]	+45°

MATERIAL AND PLY ORIENTATION SHOWN FOR FIELD AREAS ONLY.
SEE DRAWINGS FOR EDGE BANDS AND AREAS WITH DOUBLERS.

TABLE 1

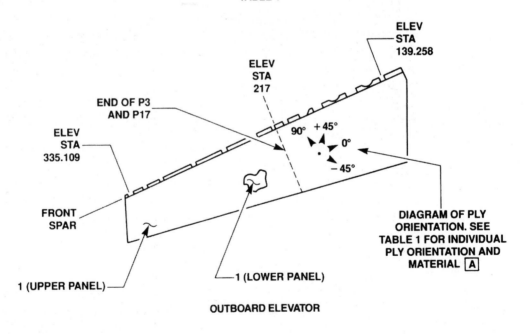

OUTBOARD ELEVATOR

Figure 11-14. The structural repair manual will list the materials you need, identify each ply, and give the ply orientation.

For most composite repairs, the surface layer of the original part is considered the reference, or the zero warp angles, that corresponds with the warp of the fabric. The structural repair manual supplies information on the ply direction of each layer of the part.

On a bolt of fabric, it is easy to determine the warp direction by simply looking at the direction of the selvage edge. On a finished part, the selvage edge is removed, making it more difficult to identify 0° or the direction of the warp. The structural repair manual should define the 0° reference direction in relation to the part being repaired (longitudinally, chord wise, etc.). [Figure 11-15]

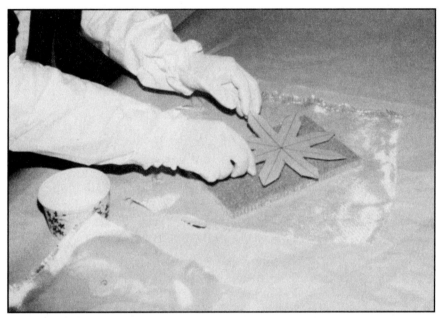

Figure 11-15. A warp compass is a tool that can be used to reference the orientation of the warp of the fiber.

The warp compass is used by placing the compass on the repair and aligning the warp direction of each successive patch in the same orientation as the corresponding laminate layer. An easy way to cut the replacement patches to the correct size and shape is to proceed as follows:

1. Lay the warp compass onto the repair.

2. Orient the 0° reference mark on the compass with the 0° reference of the part.

3. Lay a clear piece of plastic material on top of the repair area.

4. Trace the shape of the repair cutout onto the plastic, starting with the bottom cut.

5. Note the warp orientation on the plastic for the particular layer being traced.

6. Remove the plastic from the repair and place it over the replacement fabric, being careful to orient the warp in the correct direction.

7. After the fabric is impregnated with resin, cut the fabric to the correct shape using a sharp razor knife to cut along the shape outlined on the plastic.

8. As the patches are cut out, keep the plastic stuck onto the patch so the fiber direction can be easily recognized and the patches can be laid into the repair in the proper sequence.

9. Once the patches are cut out, lay the patches into the sanded area with the fiber direction in the correct direction.

BONDING PATCHES

When replacing laminate plies over a repaired core in a sandwich structure, some manufacturers call for the installation of an extra ply of the same size as the core plug. This extra patch is placed on top of the core plug at either 0° or 90°. The purpose of the extra patch is to minimize the possibility of a surface depression forming in the finished repair.

To develop a strong bond between the new patch and the existing part, the adhesive or resin must be in complete contact with both parts. To ensure this contact, the surface of the existing part must be cleaned of grease or foreign material. The raw repair patch material should be clean and free of oil such as the natural oils that occur on a person's hands. For this reason, a technician should wear plastic or cotton gloves when handling the repair fabric. This applies to both pre-pregs and raw fabric.

IMPREGNATING RAW FABRIC

Some manufacturers call for the use of pre-preg materials in certain repairs, however, other repairs can be accomplished by allowing the technician to fabricate and impregnate resin into raw fabric. Since pre-pregs may not be available for a repair, it is often necessary to impregnate the fabric at the time of the repair.

Once the shape of the bonding patches has been determined using a sheet of plastic and a warp compass, the repair fabric should be placed on a suitably clean work surface, such as another sheet of plastic, so the resin can be worked into the fabric. Be sure to weigh and mix the resins properly. Follow all manufacturers' instructions. Exercise the correct safety precautions.

The liquid resin should be poured onto the fabric and worked in using a squeegee. Keep in mind that the resins must fully permeate the fabric so that after curing the resin and the fabric form a single solid structure. Caution must be exercised when working with the squeegee not to damage the fiber orientation or fray the fabric. The fabric/resin mixture should be about 60/40. A resin rich repair is more susceptible to cracking due to a lack of adequate fiber support. A resin starved repair is weak in those areas where sufficient resin does not provide stiffness or because the fibers are not held together and supported as in a completely impregnated repair. Mix only enough resin to complete the repair. [Figure 11-16]

Figure 11-16. Impregnating the fabric with catalyzed resin.

Once the fabric has been impregnated with the resin, place the plastic sheet, with the repair patch shapes marked on them, over the fabric. Be sure to line up the selvage edge with the correct position on the plastic. Cut out the patches using a utility knife. [Figure 11-17]

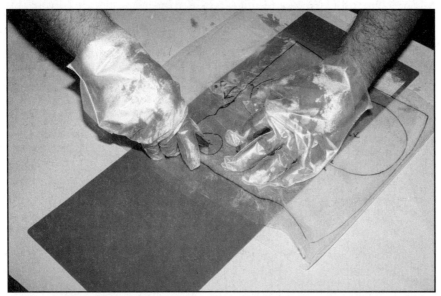

Figure 11-17. Once the fabric is impregnated with resin and the marked plastic sheet placed over it, the patches can be cut out with a utility knife.

Find out how long the pot life, or working life, of the resin is. As previously discussed, some resin systems have very short pot life (15 minutes), others have long pot life (4 hours). One of the misconceptions of pot life is that it is the time that it is usable in the cup. Although this is true to a point, the resin and fabric should be in place before the curing takes place. If a resin with a short pot life is used to impregnate fabric, and the patches are cut to size, the patches must be in place on the sanded and cleaned surface before the resin starts to cure. If the patches are allowed to sit too long within the plastic backing, they will start their chemical reaction and become stiffer. Subsequently when the patches are in place and vacuum bagged to cure, the chemical cross-linking of the resin and the fibers may not take place as it is designed to do. The patches have cured separately and may not stick respectively to each other properly. Be sure to follow the mixing procedure correctly, and use the mixture before the pot life has expired.

INSTALLATION OF THE PATCH

Once the repair patches have been impregnated with resin and cut to shape, the repair area can be prepared for the lay-up patch. The plies of fabric can then be laid into the step cuts. Lay the patches over the sanded area and remove all plastic backing. Be sure to place them with the correct ply orientation and in the right sequence following your structural repair manual.

Do not squeegee each layer. Doing so could work the resin down into the core or disorient the fibers. Place a layer of peel ply or perforated release film over the final patch and then work out any air pockets using a squeegee. The peel ply will hold the fibers in place and keep the fibers from fraying.

PRE-PREG PATCHES

Some repairs may require cure temperatures that are the same as those used during the manufacturing process. In those cases, pre-preg materials are often used. Pre-impregnated materials, or prepregs are remarkably easy to use.

Pre-pregs are removed from the freezer and a sufficient amount cut off. Remember to store the bolt of fabric in the freezer as quickly as possible. The plastic used to outline the patches and identify the warp can be placed over the pre-preg material and cut out with a razor knife.

A word of caution: The materials stated in the manufacturing manual for a repair may actually be the material that was used in the manufacturing of the aircraft, not for the pre-preg repair material. The pre-preg system used in manufacturing may be an autoclave type, which means it produces a very strong, lightweight structure when cured in an autoclave. However, to repair damaged components with the same type of materials as originally used in manufacturing can lead to problems. The autoclave cure is not used very widely in the repair procedure. Hot bond with vacuum bagging techniques are more commonly used. The resin system in these pre-pregs may not produce the same desired strength characteristics when cured with hot bond techniques. They are not getting as much vacuum as an autoclave could produce. The plies of the repair, although they are cured, may be easily peeled from the surface. This could cause dangerous consequences if failure occurred in flight. Always follow the manufactures repair manual instructions and not those provided with the manufacturing materials.

Some manufacturers call for an adhesive to be used over the sanded surface before the patches are applied. A thin layer of adhesive film or tape, is sometimes used. In this case, the adhesive is taken from the freezer storage and cut to size. The adhesive is cast onto a thin plastic film that needs to be removed before applying the patches.

The adhesive film with the plastic backing is applied to the sanded area with the adhesive side down. Heat is used to soften the adhesive from the film. With light strokes from a squeegee, the plastic should soon separate from the adhesive. Then the fiber patches can be laid into the repair area.

The pre-cut pre-preg patches can be laid into the repair area at this time. Be sure to remove any plastic backing from the patches. If the plastic is allowed to remain, the patches will not bond to the surface, causing a repair that is not airworthy. Pre-pregs may be squeegeed after each patch is applied. There is no danger of wet resin dripping into the core area. A perforated release film, or peel ply, may be added at this time to prevent any shifting of the patches during the vacuum bagging operation.

Once the repair patches are in place, the vacuum bagging materials are placed around and over the repair area. Heat should also be applied to produce a proper cure. Follow all manufacturer's instructions when vacuum bagging and curing a composite repair.

METAL-TO-METAL BONDING

Metal honeycomb cores with metal skins have been in use for years. The older type of repairs done to the skin may have been to rivet a new metal patch into place or to use fiberglass patches. The rivets would crush some of the honeycomb core and make a weak area in the repair. These metal honeycombs with metal skins are sometimes considered composite components and have newer types of repair procedures that use hot bonding equipment. The newer types of repairs bond metal patches in place using adhesive and can be made without using rivets or fiberglass.

Metal to metal bonding is done by taping off the area to be repaired and removing the paint. Use caution when using a paint stripper that it only comes in contact with those areas to be repaired and bonded. Remove the damaged skin area with a router or hole saw. If the honeycomb is not damaged, be very careful not to route into the honeycomb under the skin. The pilot bit in a hole saw should be a very small diameter to prevent too much damage to the core. Once the skin is removed, check for internal corrosion, vacuum out any cutting debris, and use a solvent to clean the area. If there is damage or internal corrosion in the core, this area should also be removed. If there is moisture within the area, this should be removed by vacuum bagging the area just as drying out the fiber composites is done. If the core is removed, make a new core using the same type, weight, and ribbon direction as the original honeycomb.

A skin plug that fits the removed area must be fabricated from the same alloy and at the same thickness of metal as the damaged skin. A doubler may also be fabricated from the same alloy as the damaged skin. The doubler should cover and overlap the repair area. The most important factor in achieving a sound repair is to clean the surface and properly prepare the metal for bonding. If the metal surfaces are not prepared properly, the metal may not adhere to the honeycomb or the metal. Surface preparation is critical. Use a phosphoric acid anodizing etch to prepare the surface. Alternative methods may include chromic acid anodize or an alodine. The bond may also be affected if clad aluminum is used for the plug and doubler. A non-clad aluminum surface is best.

Thoroughly clean the area with the appropriate solvent and do not touch the metal surfaces with bare hands or the oils in the skin will contaminate the surface. A very fine Scotch Brite pad can be used to scrub the surface. Perform a water break test to ensure the surface is oil free. Once the area has been cleaned, it should be bonded within 24 hours to prevent contamination of the surfaces. An adhesive primer may be used on all the metal areas to help bond the components.

If a new core is to be inserted into the repair, use a foaming type of adhesive. Remove the foaming adhesive from the freezer and cut it so it fits around the core. Place the core plug into the routed out area. This should be cured first to prevent the foaming adhesive from expanding up into the sheet metal skin plug area and creating a gap. Cure the foaming adhesive at the proper cure temperature. Once it has cured, any excess foaming adhesive is sanded out and the area cleaned thoroughly again.

Use a film adhesive over the core to bond the new skin plug into place, then use another layer of film adhesive to bond the doubler in place. When all materials are placed properly into the repair area, a high temp or flash tape is used to hold the materials in place while the part is prepared for vacuum bagging. A parting film, bleeders, heat blankets, and breathers are all vacuum bagged over the repair. Vacuum pressure is applied and the part is cured using a heat blanket at the proper cure temperature. During the cure, the metal acts a little differently than when curing an all-composite structure. The metal dissipates the heat much more quickly, which means an insulation blanket of fiberglass should be used over all the repair area and surrounding metal. [Figure 11-18]

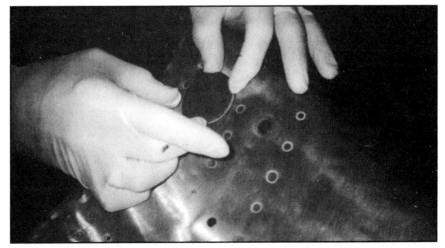

Figure 11-18. Use an adhesive film over the core to bond in the new skin plug.

After the repair has cooled completely, remove all bagging material. Place masking tape around the metal that surrounds the doubler and expose about 1/8 inch at the metal bond line. Apply sealant around the doubler edge. For a smooth bead, use a mixing stick on its edge around the area. Cure the sealant as per the instructions. Take off the masking tape and inspect the repair. [Figure 11-19]

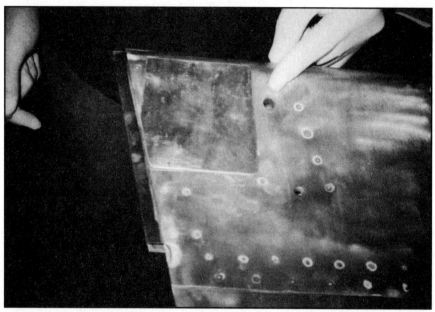

Figure 11-19. Once the doubler plate has cured and the edges have been sealed, the repair area can be painted to match the surrounding area.

BORON PATCHING TO ALUMINUM SKINS

The cracks and fatigue stresses in aluminum aircraft structures, known as the aging aircraft syndrome, are currently being tested with boron patching. This procedure is effective in reducing the fatigue of the aluminum panels. The procedure may vary depending on the type of metal or aluminum, and the area of damage.

Similar to the metal-to-metal bonding, the boron patches eliminate the use of fasteners, which could cause additional stress concentrations and cracks. Many times, the component does not need to be dissembled from the aircraft, which reduces the time and labor involved in making these repairs.

The metal surface preparation is extremely important to establish a good bond to the patch. All paint, grease, and dirt must be removed from the surface. Then the metal is prepared by acid etching the surface. Pre-preg unidirectional patches are used for the bonding, with the direction of the fibers at a 0° to a 45° orientation. The patches are vacuum bagged to the surface, usually with peel ply over the patches, and cured at an elevated temperature. The patching is relatively simple since the orientation does not necessarily have to match up with any existing orientation of the fibers—the orientation is more for direct strength between the two plies themselves.

The boron patches will take the bending and flexing of the aluminum part and prevent the micro cracks of the aluminum from becoming larger.

LIGHTNING PROTECTION

Whether an aircraft is aluminum or composite, when lightning hits it, the aircraft needs a path for the electricity to flow through. Aircraft require electrical contact between all metallic and composite parts in order to prevent arcing or fiber damage. Aluminum is used to provide a conductive path for the dissipation of the electrical energy. This path is usually provided to static wicks.

Since composites do not conduct electricity, lightning protection has to be built into the component. If there is no lightning protection in the composite and the lightning exits through the composite component, the resins in the composite will evaporate, leaving bare cloth. Another indication of lightning damage is dark brown or black spots or smudges that appear to be heated. When doing a repair, it is important to replace any lightning protection that may have been removed during the repair operation.

The type of lightning protection needed may be one of the following:

1. A top layer of material that has fiberglass and aluminum wires woven together.

2. A top layer of very thin aluminum that is either bonded or flame sprayed onto the composite surface.

3. A very fine screen or mesh made of either aluminum or copper and bonded under the top layer. Many times a fine layer of fiberglass is used over this mesh. In the case of carbon/graphite composites, the mesh may be protected by a layer of fiberglass against the carbon/graphite surface, then the mesh is placed down, followed by another layer of fiberglass. This is used to prevent dissimilar metal corrosion.

4. A bonding strap from the composite component to an aluminum structure.

Regardless of what type of lightning protection was used originally in manufacturing the aircraft, when the repair is made, the part must be restored to provide a path for the dissipation of an electrical charge.

If the aluminum wires are woven into the top layer or if there is a fine aluminum screen or mesh under the top layer, repair the part by laying all repair plies into the sanded area until the ply with the aluminum protection is reached. A fine screen of aluminum is then placed on top of the repair plies. Care should be taken to line up the wires so the new aluminum wires contact the wires in the original part. If the wires do not contact each other, there will not be a path for the electrical charge to follow and the charge will exit out the repair. Once the aluminum screen patch is installed, the fiber patch is put into the repair, and cured into place.

After curing, test to see if there is continuity by scratching the surface of the original part and inserting an ohmmeter probe. The repair area is also scratched and the other probe of the ohmmeter is placed on it. There should be a good conductance between these areas. If there is good continuity between these areas, the lightning charge will be able to flow through the structure and out to a static port.

If a thin aluminum foil is used for lightning protection, there may be a problem in attempting to bond to the repair area. The resins cannot flow through the aluminum sheet and the bottom repair plies may be resin rich. This type of aluminum should be installed after the part has completely cured and is bonded on with an adhesive. If the part was originally flame sprayed with aluminum or painted with aluminized paint, it should be applied following manufacturer's instructions.

INSPECTION OF THE REPAIR

Quality control inspection is exercised to ensure that the proper steps are followed during the repair process and that the final repair meets the requirements of the manufacturer.

1. Remove and discard all peel ply, release film, bleeder, breather, sealant tape, and bagging film from the repair area once it has been cured.

2. Check to see if the repair has cured properly (hardness testing).

3. Check for delamination. Any delamination of the skin to core is cause for rejection of the repair.

4. Ensure there are no voids. Voids may be cause for rejection.

5. Check for any white areas that would indicate excessive heat might have caused the resins to bleed out, leaving only fabric.

6. Check to make sure there is no excessive foreign material in the repair. Many manufacturers give a maximum amount of foreign material that can be included and still be an airworthy repair.

7. Check for excessive resin on the edges. This is usually not allowed.

8. Look for blisters or white areas because they could be an indication of moisture in the composite during cure.

9. If lightning protection was installed during the lay-up, there should be good electrical continuity (check with ohmmeter).

10. Check for brown spots on the part, which would indicate oil or grease contamination.

11. All repairs should be inspected to the requirements of the manufacturer, which may or may not include nondestructive inspections.

12. Lightly sand the edges to produce a feathered edge before painting.

13. Clean the part and prepare the surface for painting.

14. Paint the structure with the original type of paint in accordance with manufacturer's specification.

15. If this is a control surface, it must be rebalanced.

PAINTING THE COMPOSITE PART

After completing a repair, the part should be painted. For most aircraft, the same type of paint used for the metal portions of the aircraft is suitable for use on the composites. Some companies, such as Boeing, use a layer of Tedlar® on the composite before painting. Tedlar is a plastic coating that serves as a moisture barrier. [Figure 11-19]

Figure 11-20. The painting equipment and application techniques used on composite parts are similar to those used for metallic parts.

GEL COATS

A gel coat is a polyester resin used during the manufacturing of the part. The manufacturing mold is coated with a color coat of polyester resin. The plies are laid down onto the surface of the colored gel coat and impregnated with an epoxy resin.

After curing, the gel coat on the outside surface provides a smooth finish. The plies of fibers that are embedded with the epoxy are the structural part of the aircraft. The gel coating is not structural; it is more like a paint coat. Gel coats were used on gliders extensively in the 1970s.

The problem with gel coats is that they are made of polyester resin, so they are not very strong or flexible. If the aircraft is parked outside in the sun and weather, the gel coat may crack. The aircraft must be inspected to see if the fibers themselves are cracked, and not just the gel coat. If only the gel coat is cracked, there is no structural damage. However, if the fibers are cracked, the structure will have to be repaired.

Gel coats cannot be rejuvenated as dope on fabric can. The gel coat must be sanded off and reapplied. Many aircraft owners who have had problems with the gel coat will sand off the gel coat surface and paint the surface with one of the new generation of paints that are very flexible and can take the weather. Care should be taken when sanding the coat off because the fibers were manufactured into the wet gel coat and the gel coat thickness will not be perfectly even. Do not sand through the fibers.

Fill primers can sometimes be used over the repair, but don't add too much weight to the repair or you will ruin the whole idea of using composite parts on the aircraft in the first place. Lightweight and high strength are the keys to doing proper composite repair work.

RECORDING YOUR WORK

A log entry or FAA Form 337 must be prepared to show conformance to the recommended repair procedure. These items should be included in your records:

1. Part and serial number

2. Steps taken to restore the item to a serviceable condition

3. Cross-reference to the manufacturing record

4. Time, temperature, and pressure used in the repair cure cycle (This may or may not require a recording of the cure cycle)

5. Type of fabric material, matrix and adhesives, and core material used. Traceability of materials, such as a certification of conformity, or certification of materials, must be included.

Chapter 12
Types Of Repairs

There are many composite repair methods for various parts of an aircraft that are detailed in the appropriate Structural Repair Manual. The repairs discussed in this chapter are only a sampling of the most common repairs, and many repairs are simplified for training purposes. A repair procedure described in this book may resemble a repair in an SRM, but depending on the aircraft, and the manufacturer, different materials and resin systems may be used. If you understand the basics, and can apply the different materials called for in the Structural Repair Manual, you can master composite repairs. In any repair situation, the SRM for the aircraft should be consulted before performing any repair procedures.

Repairs may fall into one of four types:

1. Bolted on metal or cured composite patches

2. Bonded on metal or cured composite patches

3. Resin injection

4. Laminating on new repair plies

The bolted and bonded on surface patches are not preferred because the repair may not restore the part's original strength. A patch that is bolted or bonded above the surface of an external part will also cause aerodynamic changes. If the part is a rotor blade, a surface repair could cause an undesirable flutter and concentrated load stresses. These induced stress loads may prematurely pull out the blind fasteners that attach the repair.

Bolted and bonded on surface repairs may be useful for emergency field repairs where the proper equipment, tools, and materials are not available. Such repairs are many times considered to be only temporary.

Resin injection is used to fill holes or voids. This type of repair is accomplished simply by using a needle and syringe to inject resin into the void of a damaged area. Most manufacturers use this type of repair only on nonstructural parts or parts that are not subject to a great deal of stress. The injected resin repair does not restore very much strength and in some cases may actually cause the delamination or damage to expand.

The most reliable type of repair is laminating on new repair plies. This involves removing the damaged plies and laminating on new plies of the correct material.

REPAIR FAILURES

All repairs should be performed correctly based on the type of damage and the function of the part on the aircraft. Some of the most common reasons for a repair to fail are:

1. Poor surface preparation.

2. Contamination of fabric or other materials.

3. Incorrect measuring and mixing of the resin system.

4. Incorrect cure time, incorrect temperature, or inappropriate temperature rise and drop.

5. Inadequate pressure.

TYPICAL REPAIR PROCEDURES

The following repair procedures are outlined to illustrate some of the various techniques and procedures commonly used for repairing composite structures.

NOTE: All repair procedures in this book are for training purposes only. Before any repair is made to an aircraft, consult the Structural Repair Manual for the type of aircraft involved. The following repairs are only example repairs and are provided for training purposes only.

MECHANICALLY-FASTENED REPAIRS WITH PRE-CURED PATCHES

When the proper facilities, or curing and bagging equipment are not available for on-line work, a pre-cured patch inserted with blind fasteners may be used. This type of repair usually does not give the maximum strength. Because it is not a flush repair, it may cause vibration when performed on critical parts. This type of repair may be considered a temporary repair until the damage can be scarfed down and the patches correctly laminated on with heat and pressure.

Many times these repairs are performed with common repair materials such as sheet metal plates and rivets. If composite patches are required, kits with pre-cured patches may be available.

Pre-cured patches come in several sizes: two-inch, three-inch, and four-inch. These patches were produced to have the fibers of each layer in the correct orientation. Such a patch may have a peel ply layer that indicates the orientation in which it should be laid into the routed out repair.

Some manufacturers offer various sizes of core material that is bonded to pre-cured laminates. These pre-made patches are available so the technician can simply route out the damaged area and insert the core and laminate patch. This type of repair may have a type of adhesive pre-applied to help it bond.

Usually the patch uses some type of mechanical blind fastener that is drilled through the patch into the surface of the original part to hold the patch in place while it is further stabilized with blind fasteners. The problem with using blind fasteners in a core structure is that they have a tendency to crush the core structure. This may cause the core to delaminate from the plies. Again, this type of repair may be considered a good temporary repair. [Figure 12-1]

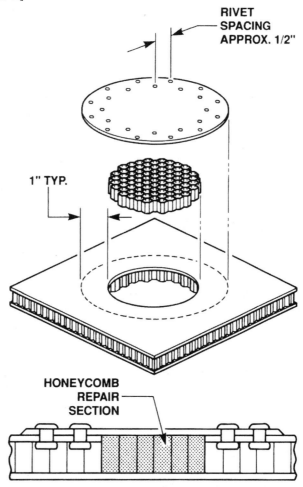

Figure 12-1. *Patches using blind fasteners and a sheet metal plate are normally considered a temporary repair.*

COMPOSITE SKIN REPAIR AT RIB LOCATIONS

This repair uses an aluminum doubler fastened with blind rivets to a composite skin for reinforcement over a damaged rib area. This is an interesting example of fastener use in composites.

1. Remove surface finish.

2. Remove as much of the damaged skin as possible, without causing further damage to the skin or rib.

3. Clean area with solvent.

4. Fill in removed skin areas with a potting compound.

5. Use an aluminum doubler extending two inches past the edges of the damage. Form the aluminum doubler to conform to the shape of the part.

6. Drill rivet holes in aluminum sheet and countersink on one side. Rivet holes should be spaced evenly at approximately one-inch spacing and close to the rib.

7. Abrade the surface of aluminum with a Scotchbrite® pad for bonding to the composite.

8. Prepare adhesive and apply to composite skin and aluminum doubler.

9. Position doubler over damaged area and insert fastener.

10. Clean up excess adhesive that squeezes out around doubler.

11. Cure adhesive following manufacturer's instructions.

12. Finish per manufacturer's instructions. [Figure 12-2]

POTTED REPAIR

Potted repairs do not give as much strength to the composite structure as refitting the hole with a new core. Filling the hole with a resin/microballoon mixture adds weight to the part and decreases the flexibility. Further flexing of the part might cause the potted plug to dislodge, but many structural repair manuals still list this type of repair for advanced composite structures.

For this repair:

    1. Clean the damaged area.

    2. Sand out the delaminated area.

    3. Fill the core area with a resin/microballoon mixture.

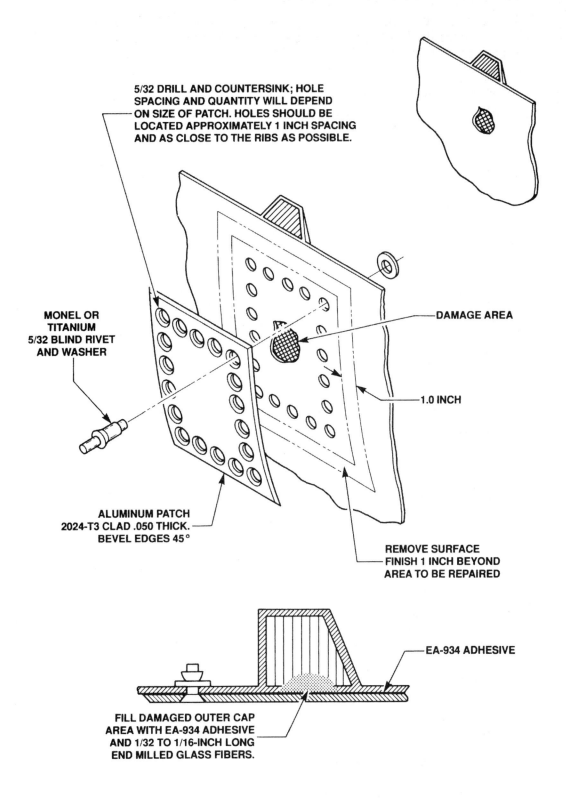

Figure 12-2. An aluminum patch installed, bonded and fastened to the surface with a composite stiffener on the inside of the structure.

4. Prepare patches.

5. Apply pressure and cure.

6. Refinish.

Most potted repairs are appropriate for foam core sandwich structures. However, in some cases, it may be permissible to drill a small hole into the delaminated area and inject resin into a honeycomb disbonded area.

DAMAGE TO ONE FACE AND CORE (POTTED REPAIR)

The following type of repair is similar to an older type of fiberglass repair that calls for the damaged core to be routed at a vertical angle. This is a problem because the plug can pop out if the repaired part flexes during flight.

This is no problem if the repair is done to nonstructural parts. New advanced composites, however, are commonly used for structural applications. For example, if a plug repair should pop out of a control surface, it could cause aerodynamic flutter and a subsequent loss of control. Consequently, to prevent a catastrophic failure, it is critical that any structurally repaired part be performed correctly.

One of the primary differences between the composite repair and the fiberglass repair is in the way the repair plug is retained in the routed hole in the core. The composite repair calls for the damaged core material to be undercut with respect to the surface laminate. In this way the original laminate skin helps to retain the repair plug during the flexing of the surface. In addition, the composite repair utilizes an overlap patch to further increase the strength of the repair. [Figure 12-3]

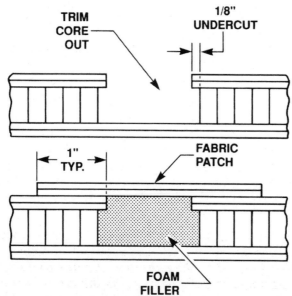

Figure 12-3. An undercut potted repair with the repair plies bonded to the surface.

1. Open up the puncture with a drill or router to remove the ragged edges and broken fibers.

2. Clean out crushed core and undercut core approximately .125 inch. Mark the outline of the overlap plies on the part.

3. Prepare the surface.

4. Clean out sanding dust and vacuum the hole.

5. Apply a foam filler by pouring or by using a spatula to fill up the hole . Agitate the foam to displace air pockets and fill the cavity. Allow the foam to cure.

6. Cut the repair patches to size, allowing an overlap in all directions beyond the edge of the hole.

7. Prepare the bonding patches.

8. Apply pressure and cure.

9. Refinish.

DELAMINATIONS

Delamination occurs when the laminate layers become separated or when the plies separate from the core material. Delamination is sometimes referred to as unbonding, or disbonding, of the plies. Sometimes a delamination can be detected by shining a light over the part and looking at the damaged area at an angle. The damage can be recognized as a bubble or an indentation.

Internal delamination is the separation of plies that do not extend to the edge or a drilled hole area.

It is important to properly assess the extent of an internal delamination using the appropriate NDI method. If the delamination is over a core area, the resin might fill up the core and not help in the sealing of the skin. In excessive cases, the skin might be delaminated even further because of resin injection. If you perform a resin injection, use a low viscosity resin and apply pressure to the area so the skin attaches to the core.

NOTE: This type of repair may be considered a temporary repair until a more permanent repair can be made to the structure. If this repair is not approved by the manufacturer due to the type of part, the size of damage, or the type of stress the part endures, a repair should be accomplished by removing the damaged plies by step cutting or scarf sanding and laying in new repair plies.

DELAMINATION INJECTION REPAIR

If the internal delamination is sufficiently minor, it can sometimes be repaired by simply injecting resin into the cavity formed by the ply separation. Injecting resin fills the area and reattaches the skin.

1. Clean both surfaces of the part.

2. Drill a .060-inch diameter hole from one surface down to the delamination at each end of the delamination. Be careful not to drill through the part.

3. Clean the part again with acetone or MEK.

4. Select and mix resin and curing agent as required.

5. Load the mixed resin into a clean syringe with a needle attached. Inject the resin into one drilled hole until resin comes out the other drilled hole.

6. Apply pressure and cure.

7. After the cure, remove clamps and vacuum bagging materials, then sand and refinish [Figure 12-4].

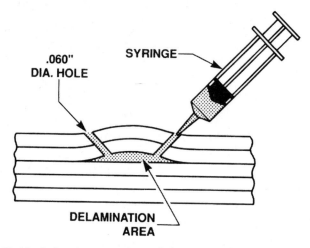

Figure 12-4. Resin injection repair to delaminated area.

This repair may not be approved by the manufacturer because the delamination cavity is filled with resin, which adds extra weight. This would be of major significance if the damaged part were a primary control surface. Furthermore, the resin alone could be ineffective in restoring the strength and could cause brittleness. In flight, the extra resin in this area would not be as flexible and may cause further delamination in the damaged area.

DELAMINATION AT HONEYCOMB CORE EDGEBAND

This simple repair does not need vacuum bagging, and rarely is cured with heat.

1. Clean surface with solvent.

2. Outline void area and mark injection hole locations.

3. Using a .060-inch diameter drill, slowly drill into disbonded area. Do not drill through the part.

4. Use a syringe to inject mixed resin into one hole, allowing air to escape through the other.

5. Clean excess resin from the surface of the part.

6. Cure according to manufacturer's instructions. [Figure 12-5]

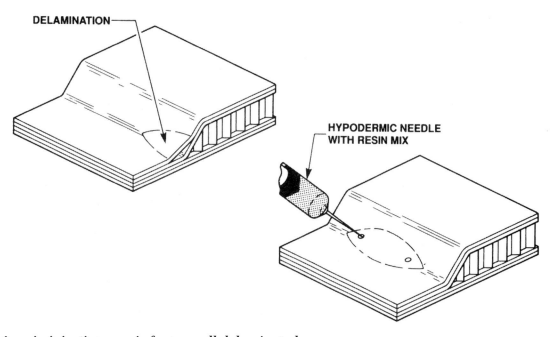

Figure 12-5. A resin injection repair for a small delaminated area.

MISLOCATED POTTING COMPOUND WITHIN A HONEYCOMB STRUCTURE

In some cases, the manufacturer supplies a component with potting compound installed to accommodate a fastener. If this is not correctly positioned, it may need to be repositioned.

1. Locate the correct location of the fastener that requires the additional potting compound.

2. Drill a 1/8-inch hole at the correction through one skin only.

3. Insert a small Allen wrench through the hole and rotate 360° to break the honeycomb cell walls to a one-inch radius around the drilled holes.

4. Vacuum out debris.

5. Using a sealant gun, or syringe, force the potting compound through the drilled hole.

6. Cure in accordance with the manufacturer's instructions.

7. Re-drill the hole and install the fitting in accordance with the manufacturer's requirements.

If the part failed because the fastener pulled out, filling the damaged hole and re-drilling it may not be a good repair; it may pull out because the resin/filler mix may not provide adequate strength. An insert or grommet may be installed permanently with an adhesive. The fastener can then be used without causing further damage to the composite structure. [Figure 12-6]

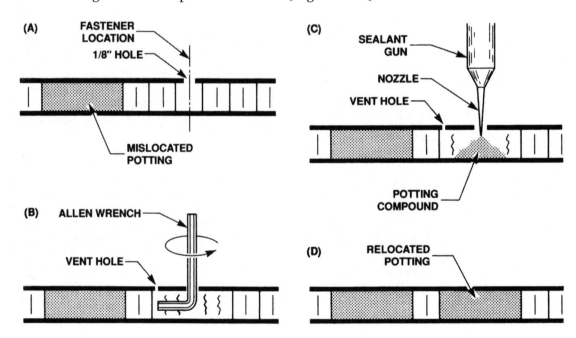

Figure 12-6. When the potting compound for a fastener location is mislocated, these steps are necessary to relocate the fastener.

DAMAGE TO LAMINATE STRUCTURES

Solid laminates are those structures that do not have a core. They require different repairs depending on how badly they are damaged, where the damage is, and how thick the laminate is. Here are a few types of repairs for solid laminate structures.

COSMETIC DEFECT

A cosmetic defect is a surface resin scratch that does not penetrate the first structural ply (negligible damage).

1. Clean area with MEK or acetone.

2. Sand painted area around damage and feather the edges.

3. Scuff sand damage, then clean with solvent.

4. Mix resin with filler or approved surfacing putty.

5. Fill damaged area with resin-filler mixture. It may be applied with a squeegee, brush, or fairing tool.

6. Cure repair.

7. Sand and refinish.

DAMAGE REMOVAL AND PLY REPLACEMENT

This type of repair calls for the removal of the damaged laminate plies and the subsequent replacement of the removed plies with new ones. The replacement plies are cured with heat and pressure to restore the original composite strength. The new impregnated and pre-cut patches are laid into the sanded-out area with the weave of the new patches in the same orientation as those of the original part.

An overlap patch usually is one inch larger than the last repair ply. It is used as a bridge between the repair and the original part. It may not be required. The overlap patch initially sits on top of the part, but with the heat and pressure that are applied during the cure cycle, it compresses it to be level with the surface.

DAMAGE TO ONE SURFACE

Fiber damage to one side of the surface that does not completely penetrate the part may be repaired as follows:

1. Prepare the surface by cleaning and removing paint.

2. Remove damage by scarfing or step-cutting the plies.

3. Select and mix the proper resin and repair material.

4. Prepare the bonding patches.

5. Vacuum bag or apply pressure and cure.

6. Remove vacuum bag materials, blend edges, refinish (Figure 12-7).

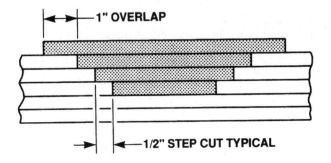

Figure 12-7. Step cut repair in which the damaged material is removed, and new reinforcing patches are applied.

GLIDER STEP CUT REPAIR

The step cut repair is probably the most common type of step cut repair, however, there are differing opinions as to how the plies should be laid into the repair. Figure 12-8 shows the plies being laid in a different fashion.

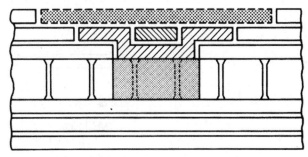

Figure 12-8. This variation of the step cut repair uses alternating plies.

Some glider repair manuals call for this type of repair. The purpose for using this type of repair as opposed to the more traditional step cut repairs is to prevent the surface plies of the repair from delaminating and peeling off the surface of the skin in case of high impact. Too often the repair patch does not conform to the shape of the step cut area. This creates an air gap around the edges of the patch. If such an air gap occurs, the repair should not be considered airworthy.

FIBER DAMAGE THROUGH THE PART

Damage that affects all of the laminate layers of a structure can be addressed in several ways depending on:

1. The number of plies in the part.

2. The location of the damage.

3. The size of the damage.

To perform this repair:

1. Prepare the surface.

2. Remove the damage by scarfing or step cutting the plies.

3. Select and mix the proper resin and repair material.

4. Prepare the bonding patches.

5. Use a backing plate, if desired, to support the structure from the backside.

6. Vacuum bag or apply pressure and cure.

7. Remove vacuum bagging materials, blend edges, and refinish. [Figure 12-9]

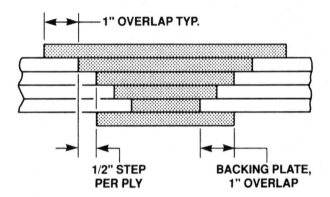

Figure 12-9. Repair to fiber damage which extends through the part on a thin laminate uses a step cut with a backing plate.

When the laminate is very thick, instead of starting out to sand one-half inch per ply, which would make the repair very large, the repair can be sanded down from one side and up from the other. This makes the repair smaller but can only be used if access to the opposite side is available. [Figure 12-10]

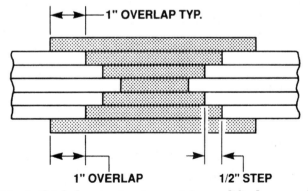

Figure 12-10. A thick laminate step cut is modified somewhat. The step goes in both directions.

LAMINATE REPAIR WITH ACCESS TO ONE SIDE

If the damage extends through the laminate, but access to the opposite side is not available, a pre-cured patch is attached to the inside of the repair and repair plies built on it.

1. Clean area to be repaired.

2. Cut out damaged area in a rectangular shape with rounded corners. This permits passage of a backup plate that extends at least one inch beyond all edges of the cutout.

3. Working through the cutout area, lightly abrade interior skin surface in a one-inch area around the cutout.

4. Clean sanded area with solvent.

5. Prepare a backup plate with the proper materials as described by the manufacturer. These may be made by impregnating the materials yourself or by using pre-pregs.

6. Cut out the plies to make up the backup plate, and lay out a flat surface prepared with parting film.

7. Vacuum bag the patch and cure with heat.

8. Drill two holes at each end of the cutout in the backup plates. These holes are used to retain the backup plate in place during installation.

9. Pass a short loop of lockwire through each pair of holes in the backup plate. Twist the wires together one turn to hold in place.

10. Mix the proper adhesive and coat one side of the backup plate.

11. Pass the backup plate through the cutout and position them against the interior skin.

12. Place a wood or steel rod through the wire loops to bridge the cutout. Twist wires against rod until backup plate is held firmly against the interior skin.

13. Cure with heat per manufacturer's instructions [Figure 12-11].

14. After cure, remove lockwire and fill holes with adhesive.

15. Prepare patches by impregnating the fabric or using pre-pregs as per manufacturer's instructions.

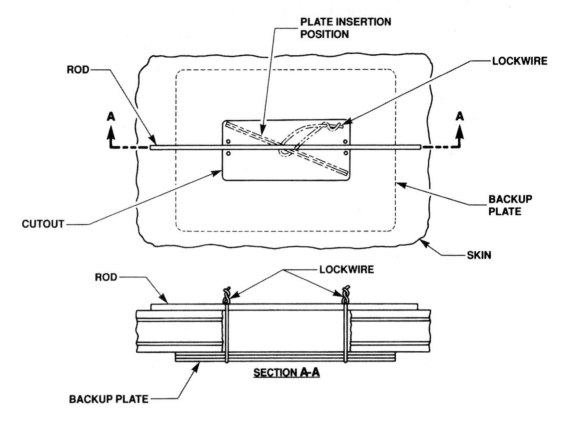

Figure 12-11. This is one method of curing a backup plate when one side is inaccessible.

16. Cut required number of plies to fill hole and for the repair plies, keeping in mind the orientation of each ply.

17. Lay plies in place to repair area. The final ply, sometimes known as a sanding ply, is placed over the entire area.

18. Pressure is applied and it is cured per manufacturer's instructions [See Figure 12-12 on page 12-16].

EDGE REPAIR

Edges are usually damaged by either being crushed or punctured.

1. This type of damage is removed using the specified scarf or stepcuts.

2. New plies are inserted along with and overlaping the patch on both the top and bottom of the part.

3. The repair plies are left longer than the edge of the existing structure, then cured.

4. Once the part has been cured, the edge can be trimmed to the correct length and shape.

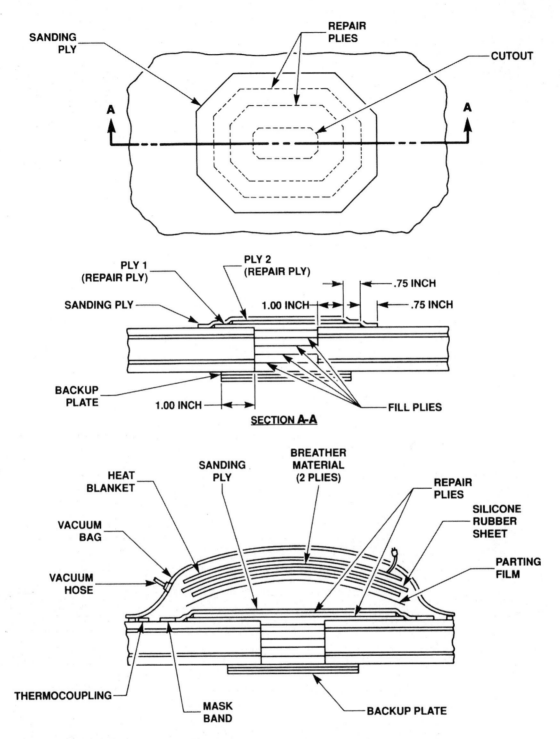

Figure 12-12. With damage extending through the laminate, this is what the stack-up and vacuum bag would look like.

EDGE DELAMINATION

Minor edge delamination sometimes can be repaired by injecting resin into the delamination, clamping the edge, and allowing the resin to cure [Figure 12-13].

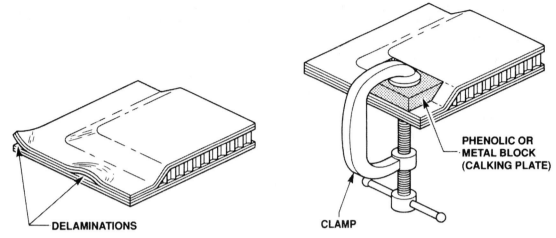

Figure 12-13. A typical edge delamination repair.

HOLES IN LAMINATES WITH LIMITED SURFACE AREA

If the damage is in a place where steps cannot be made 1/2-inch per ply and still stay on the composite, this type of repair is done. Instead of all the sanding being done from the top, some of the steps are done on the underneath side. This makes the area of the repair much smaller with the same amount of bonding area.

1. Step cut the damaged area as shown in Figure 12-14.

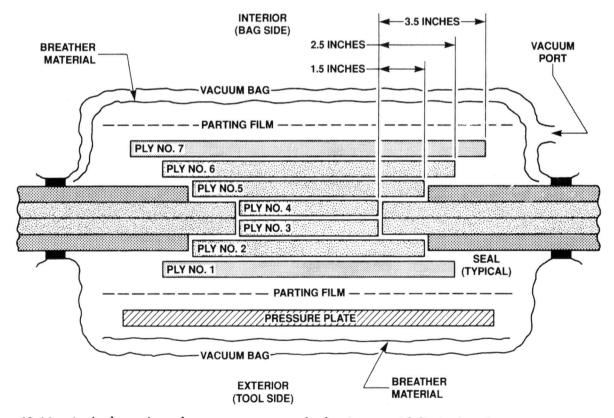

Figure 12-14. a typical repair and vacuum sequence for laminates with limited surface area.

2. A temporary stepped aluminum plate could be made to fit the cavity where plies 3, 4, 5, and 6 are shown.

3. Cover aluminum plate with parting film.

4. Clean area with solvent.

5. Another temporary aluminum plate should be made two inches larger than ply number 1, which is also covered with parting film.

6. Clamp aluminum plate in place to provide a solid backup surface for plies 1 and 2.

7. Impregnate fabric with resin system approved by the manufacturer or use pre-preg material.

8. Cut out plies to match cutout areas.

9. Apply repair plies numbers 1 and 2 and hold them in place with the other aluminum pressure plate.

10. Carefully remove the tapered aluminum pressure plate, and insert the other repair plies making sure ply orientation is correct.

11. Cover with parting film or peel ply and apply pressure.

12. Cure and finish in accordance with manufacturer's instructions.

REPAIRS TO SANDWICH STRUCTURES

Sandwich structure panels are vulnerable to impact damage primarily because these structures involve relatively thin face sheets.

1. Delaminations may occur at the point where the core is laminated to the skin.

2. Punctures to one side that damages the face sheet and core may be repaired a number of ways, depending on size, extent of damage, and location of the damage.

DELAMINATION AT THE CORE — SKIN TO CORE VOIDS (DELAMINATION)

A minor delamination between the skin and core can be addressed by resin injection similar to the way a laminate ply delamination is repaired. Holes are drilled into the skin, then resin is injected into the delamination cavity. The repair is then clamped and cured. [Figure 12-15]

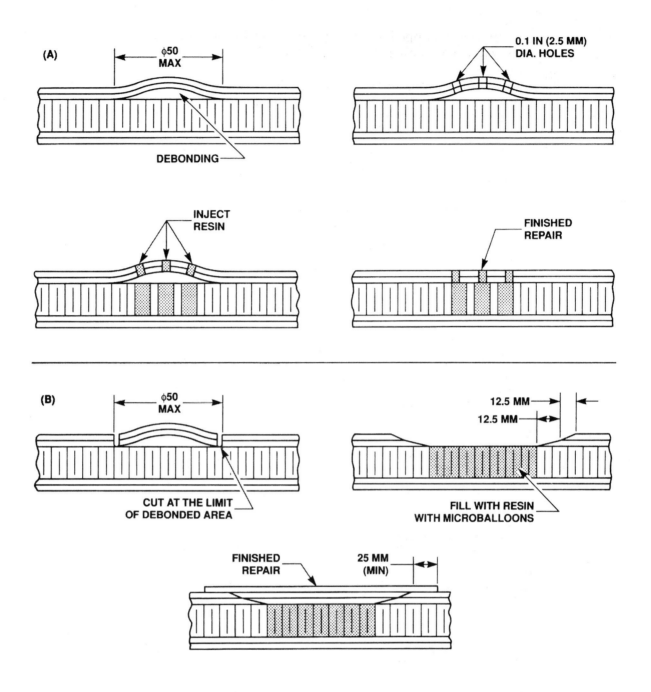

Figure 12-15(A). Delamination injection repair for a skin-to-core void. (B) Scarfed repair for a skin-to-core void.

A more extensive way to repair a skin to core delamination is to cut out the delaminated skin, scarf back the laminate skin, fill the core area with a potting compound, and install repair plies. The repair is then cured with heat and pressure. This same repair may be accomplished without filling the core, but rather by adding a layer of adhesive to the top of the core material and then laying the patches in place and curing. Keep in mind that the specific repair procedure depends on the manufacturer and their recommendations.

SMALL PUNCTURES THROUGH SKIN AND INTO SANDWICH STRUCTURE

This type repair is usually done if the damage is less than 1" in Diameter, and in a less structural area.

1. Determine the extent of the damaged area.

2. Clean out the hole by vacuuming any loose fragments, water, oil, or grease.

3. Prepare hole filler of resin and milled glass fibers.

4. Work paste into the hole.

5. Cure resin in accordance to manufacturer's instructions.

6. Sand surface with a fine sandpaper.

7. Wipe surface clean using an approved solvent.

8. Refinish surface.

DAMAGE TO ONE FACE AND THE CORE

If the damage is extensive and cannot be repaired by potting, the following repair procedure may be used:

1. Prepare the surface.

2. Remove core of honeycomb by routing.

3. Remove damage of laminate by scarfing or step cutting the plies.

4. Clean area by vacuuming and wiping with solvent.

5. Cut honeycomb plug to size, keeping the ribbon direction the same as the original.

6. Butter the interior ply with resin and install the honeycomb plug.

NOTE: Some manufacturers may call for a layer of adhesive to be laid into the hole and a foaming adhesive to be used around the core edge.

7. Prepare patches and apply to the sanded area.

8. Apply pressure and cure.

9. Refinish. [Figure 12-16A]

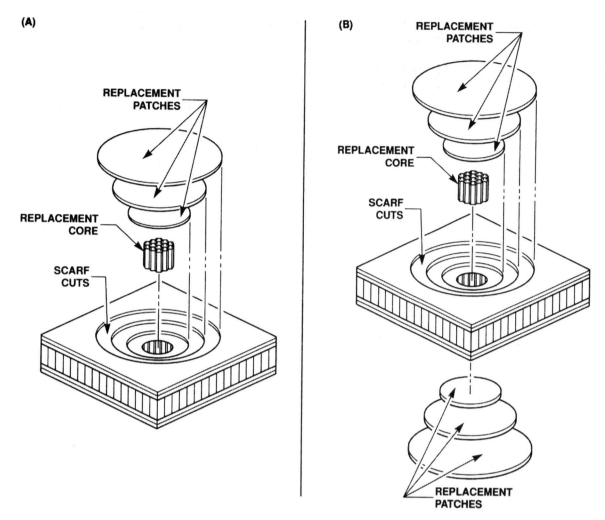

Figure 12-16(A). A honeycomb core replacement with laminate patches to one side. (B) With laminate patches to both sides.

REPAIRS TO BOTH FACE SHEETS AND HONEYCOMB CORE

When both sides are accessible, and damage is all the way through the part:

1. Prepare surface.

2. Rout out core.

3. Scarf both sides of face sheets.

4. Cut core to size, keeping ribbon direction the same as original.

5. Prepare patches for one side, making sure ply orientation is maintained.

6. Vacuum bag each side of the repair while curing only one side.

7. Remove the vacuum bagging when it is completely cured and prepare the patches for the other side.

8. Apply the patches on the other side and vacuum bag this side, then cure.

9. Refinish both sides of the repair. [Figure 12-16B on page 12-19]

REPAIR TO BOTH FACE SHEETS AND HONEYCOMB CORE

If one side of the damaged area is inaccessible, the repair can be completed using a pre-cured patch, which is bonded to the opposing side and cured. The core is then inserted and the plies are laid into the step cut, or scarfed out area.

1. Prepare the surface.

2. Remove the damaged core by routing.

3. Clean out the core area.

4. Apply adhesive to the backside of a pre-cured patch. The patch may have a hole drilled into it to facilitate applying pressure.

5. Insert the patch to the inside of the repair and apply pressure by using a cleco and some metal clamps.

6. Once it is cured, sand the top laminate by scarfing or step cutting.

7. Install the new core material.

8. Prepare the repair patches and apply to the sanded area.

9. Apply pressure and cure.

10. Refinish.

TRAILING EDGE REPAIR

The trailing edges of airfoils are susceptible to damage because they are very thin at the ends, can be easily bumped, and may collect water in them.

1. Route out the core of the trailing edge and scarf or step cut the damaged plies.

2. Install a new core material.

3. Prepare the patches and install over the sanded area.

NOTE: *The patches will extend past the trailing edge of the part. They will be trimmed off to the correct length after the curing operation.*

4. Apply pressure. If vacuum bagging is used, a self-enclosed bag should be used all around the trailing edge. A caul plate or pressure plate should be used to prevent the soft edges from curling up during the cure.

5. Cure the part. Sometimes the resins on either side of the part may cure at different temperatures. In this case, two heat blankets should be used, each at a different temperature and controlled separately.

6. Refinish the part. [Figure 12-17]

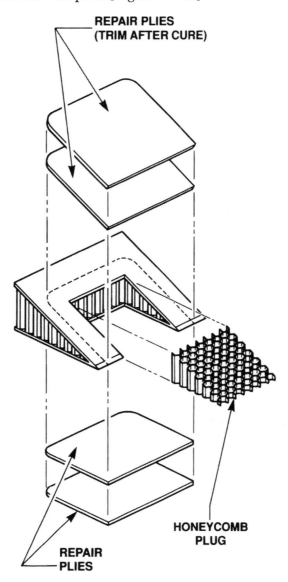

Figure 12-17. Trailing edge repair using a honeycomb filler plug

REPAIRS TO STRUCTURAL RIBS

Many manufacturers do not approve the repair of many parts, such as structural ribs, due to their critical nature. The most common problems associated with such repairs concern the failure of the fix due to severe flexing and stress. The repairs made to a structural rib are sometimes considered temporary until the entire rib can be removed and replaced.

These examples of repairs assume that the rib is made of a sandwich structure using a cellulose acetate foam core and a carbon/graphite laminate skin. Some Structural Repair Manuals recommend the use of fiberglass as a repair material instead of carbon/graphite. The fiberglass is used in the repair because the rib takes so much stress that if it is reinforced with carbon/graphite, it may continue to crack on the outer edges of the repair. Fiberglass is not as stiff as the carbon/graphite, so if it is used instead of the carbon/graphite, there is less chance of these imposed stresses.

CRUSH DAMAGE

If the edge of the rib is crushed, and the manufacturer does not want the technician cutting into the structural materials, the SRM may state that the foam and repair plies should be applied without removing the damage.

1. Remove damaged material and replace foam core with a syntactic foam. This foam may be in a liquid form and can be injected or brushed into the cavity.

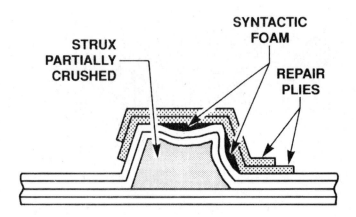

Figure 12-18. A typical crushed rib repair

2. After the foam has cured, sand the foam into the shape of the original part.

3. Prepare the repair patches and apply them over the foam.

4. Apply pressure and cure. [Figure 12-18]

END OR EDGE DAMAGE

The end or edge of the rib is usually where it fastens to other components. It may be somewhat fragile, and may become easily damaged in this area.

1. Remove damaged core material and scarf or step sand the laminate plies.

2. Fill the damaged core area with syntactic foam.

3. Allow the foam to cure and sand down to original contour of the part.

4. Prepare the new laminate patches.

5. Apply the patches to the sanded area.

6. Apply pressure and cure.

MID-RIB DAMAGE

Reinforcing ribs are often damaged in the process of loading or unloading an aircraft. In such instances, a temporary repair may be allowed.

1. The damaged foam core is scarfed out to an angle.

2. Scarf or step cut the laminate surrounding the core.

3. Syntactic foam is applied to the area and allowed to cure.

4. New repair plies are prepared and laid into the scarfed out area.

5. Pressure is applied and it is allowed to cure.

REPAIR OF DAMAGE TO COMPOSITE SKIN AND RIB

1. Remove surface coating and clean surface with solvent.

2. Sand skin plies to a 45-degree angle to remove damaged area. On rib area, remove any damaged area of core. Clean.

3. Impregnate fabric with properly mixed resins or use pre-preg fabric as per manufacturer's instructions.

4. Cut fabric replacements for filler plies to replace the removed damage.

5. With an approved filler, fill the damaged area of honeycomb.

6. Place filler plies over core.

7. Place a layer of parting film over area and apply pressure and heat the part to cure.

8. Sand the area lightly and clean with solvent.

9. Repair plies are made by tapering up from the damaged area. The first repair ply is made to extend 4-3/4 inches beyond the damaged area all the way around the patch.

10. Each ply thereafter is one inch smaller all the way around.

11. An overall repair ply is used for the entire repair.

12. Once the repair plies are installed, pressure and heat should be applied to cure. [Figure 12-19]

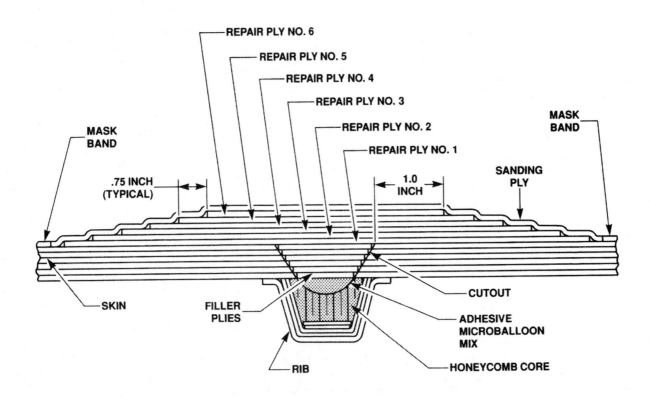

Figure 12-19. Repair to composite skin and rib

REPAIRS TO MISLOCATED, OVERSIZED, OR DELAMINATED DRILLED HOLES

One of the problems with drilling composites is that if too much pressure is applied while drilling, the fibers of each layer can delaminate, causing a void. The backside laminate layer may also breakout during the drilling operation. Before a fastener can be installed, these voids must be repaired.

1. Lightly sand the outer area approximately one-half inch around hole. [Figure 12-20]

2. Blend chopped fibers with mixed resin, and fill the hole.

3. Prepare patches.

4. Apply pressure and cure.

5. Re-drill holes to correct size or location.

A problem that can be tricky to fix occurs when drilling a mislocated hole, filling it, and having to drill the hole one-half diameter from where the original hole is. The filled hole will be softer to drill than the original structure, and the drill bit will want to wander over to the softer resin mixture. If you have access to a drill press, this problem will be eliminated, however, all parts cannot be put into a drill press. The best solution is to practice to learn how to get the drill to go where you want it to drill and not

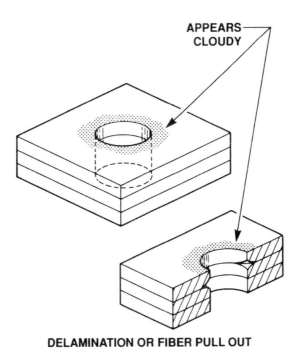

Figure 12-20. Typical drilled hole damage that must be repaired before a fastener can be installed.

wander into the soft resin. A drill block can also be used to keep the drill from wandering. [Figure 12-21 and 12-22]

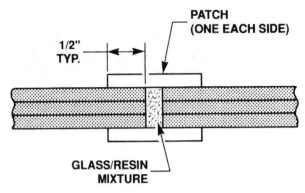

Figure 12-21. A mislocated drilled hole is filled and repaired in this manner

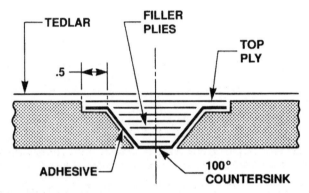

Figure 12-22. An example of a typical mislocated hole repair using reinforcing plies to fill the hole

REPAIR OF LOOSE OR MISSING FASTENERS

1. Standard aircraft procedures should be used for replacement of loose or missing fasteners. Washers should be used under the expanded side of the fastener. This is to prevent delamination at the edges of the fastener holes.

2. If the hole or countersink is oversize, the next larger fastener/countersink size may be used.

Most fasteners are installed wet with some type of adhesive. [Figure 12-23]

RADOME REPAIRS

Repairing radomes can be quite an involved task. Radomes are made to protect the aircraft's radar antenna from the flying environment. It needs to be almost transparent for the radar signal emanating from the aircraft, and the signal returning back to it. If there is a defect or improper repair in its field of vision, it may distort the readings and give inappropriate information to the pilot. The biggest problem with the radar is that it is in the front

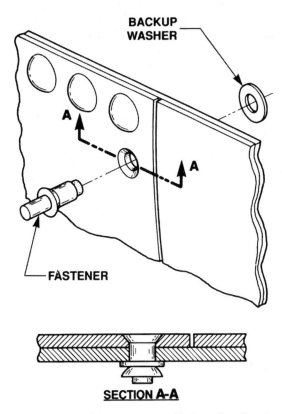

Figure 12-23. An oversize fastener installed with a backup washer to prevent delamination at the edges of the fastener hole.

of the aircraft, and rocks, birds, rain, snow, and hail can damage the structure. Static discharge may also present a problem if it burns small holes and chips in the paint. These are very small, but large enough for moisture to penetrate the fibers causing delamination of the skins. If the moisture fills some of the honeycomb cells, it could freeze at altitude and expand causing delamination of the skin.

Inspection of damage to a radome is important before and after a repair is made. Before the repair, the extent of damage must be determined. The test may be a simple coin tap test to check for delamination, or a transmissivity check on specialized equipment. A moisture meter may also be helpful in detecting moisture within the fiber structure of the radome. The extent of the damage is important to check. Many times, too many repairs, or repairs that are too close together, may cause the maintenance technician to opt for sending the structure out to a repair station specializing in radome repair. These shops have the molds to completely replace skins and cores to build up a damaged radome back to optimum condition. Be sure to check your Structural Repair Manual to see if the damage is within the limits.

When performing a repair to a radome, it is very important to follow the instructions exactly as the manufacturer states to do the repair. If the electrical properties are altered, it may cause a loss of signal, and can produce numerous problems that may appear to be deficiencies of other components within the radar system. Make sure you use the exact type and thickness of fabric, honeycomb, and resin specified by the manufacturer in the repair. The thickness of the repair can effect the quality of the repair.

Although the FAA does not require transmissivity tests before returning a repaired radome to service, other types of electrical test procedures may be found in most of the Structural Repair Manuals. These checks can insure that the repair does not affect the transmissivity, reflection or the diffraction of a signal. These checks may need to be made after the repair, and also after the painting of the surface, because the paint type or thickness of the paint can also interfere with the transmission of a signal. Repair stations set up to do many radome repairs have extensive testing equipment to check the soundness of the repair, and the signal transmissivity.

AC 43.13 is a very helpful advisory circular on aircraft radome repair, issued by the FAA.

One of the most common applications of polybutadiene resin is in the preparation of pre-preg materials for use in radomes. The operation of radar systems in both aircraft and marine environments presents a list of contradictory requirements. The radome structure must be very thin in order to ensure the maximum efficiency of the radar. At the same time, the radome must be very strong in order to endure the server impacts that occur. For example, in an aircraft during a hail storm. The radome must be stable over a wide range of temperatures so that it does not expand or contract significantly to cause mechanical problems, or cause a distortion of the radar signals. The radome must also be resistant to exposure to ultraviolet light and the corrosive action of water.

As the electrical performance of radar systems has improved, the performance capabilities of radome materials have also improved. For example, the use of advanced radar systems that operate in the K-band or 10.9-36.0 Ghz has proven that the standard epoxy-E-glass radome composite system is too opaque. Polybutadiene resins are the preferred choice of matrix materials in such an application because of their very low dielectric constant and low power dissipation factor. In addition, when subjected to high voltage arcing, polybutadiene resins resist forming carbon compounds that obscure radar signals. The mechanical characteristics of polybutadiene resins make them strong enough to enable the fabrication of thin radome walls that still withstand the stringent structural demands of a high-speed aircraft.

PROPELLER REPAIRS

With the introduction of composite structural fibers, many propellers are fabricated from composite material. Always use the manufacturer's repair manual to see if the damage is repairable or not. The following is a guide to repair propeller blades. Identify the materials used in the blade. The composite materials may vary from blade to blade. Inspect the area, typically by coin tapping, to see the extent of the damage. Identify where the damage is located. Damage to the tip of the blade may have larger areas that can be repaired, rather than the root where it is very structural. If the damage is to the root area, you may only be allowed to repair a small area of damage.

CAUTION: *When a deice boot must be removed, do not use strong solvents that could penetrate into a foam core. The solvents could dissolve the foam causing greater damage.*

Trailing edge damage is common, and a basic repair procedure might be to remove the damage by step sanding or scarfing. The part would be cleaned with a solvent, and replacement fiber reinforcements placed in their correct orientation with the proper resin system. This is then vacuum bagged and cured following the manufacturers requirements.

Erosion shields sometimes become disbonded, and a simple way to apply adhesive to the disbonded area is to drill a small hole into the erosion shield at the end of the disbond. Vacuum bag over the drilled hole, and pull a vacuum while applying the mixed adhesive to the edge where the disbond starts . Remove the vacuum when resin is pulled into the hole which was drilled. The entire area is then vacuum bagged to provide pressure while the adhesive is curing.

HOMEBUILT AIRCRAFT REPAIRS

With the decline of manufactured general aviation aircraft in recent years, the homebuilt industry has grown at a phenomenal rate. These aircraft are built by individuals at home or airports using many composite designs. The builders themselves are technically the manufacturers of the aircraft. If a person has built a homebuilt aircraft, the repair to that structure should not be a problem. However, many of these aircraft are being sold and bought by people who did not do the manufacturing of the aircraft, and consequently, repair technicians are called in to do the repair. These aircraft typically do not have a Structural Repair Manual to follow, and finding the correct procedures may be next to impossible.

The following is a guide to basic procedures for repairing homebuilt aircraft components. The composites used are typically fiberglass, foam, and Nomex honeycomb. Some of the later versions use some carbon graphite. Before beginning on a repair, identify the type of material that the structure is made of. Use the same weight and weave of fabric as the original structure, if possible.

1. Remove the paint and test the area for delamination by coin tapping the area and listening for a difference in tone. (Remember that a difference in tone is not always a sign of delaminations, but could be a change in core structure or materials. Mark out the area that is damaged. Check for core damage. If the core is damaged, it may have to be removed and a new core inserted. If the damage is small, the core may be filled with a potting compound and sanded to shape.

2. The damaged skin must be removed, and the surrounding area step or scarf sanded. To accomplish the proper step cuts in the laminate, each successive layer of fiber and matrix must be removed without damaging the underlying layer. Great care must be exercised during sanding to avoid damaging the fibers surrounding the area being removed. Sand down about 1/4-inch all the way around the damaged area for each ply.

3. The sanded out area is cleaned with a solvent to remove any excess sanding dust or grease that might be on the surface.

4. The plies are marked out on a clear piece of plastic, noting the weave direction of each ply. The patches made from the reinforcing material for the repair must carry the stress loads that were originally carried by the fibers that were manufactured into the part. There should be one fabric bonding patch ply of the same thickness and ply orientation for each damaged ply removed. Whenever repairing a composite componenet, the fiber orientation of the new patches must be in the same direction as the original structure.

5. Lay a clear piece of plastic material on top of the repair area. Trace the shape of the repair cutout onto the plastic. Note the warp orientation on the plastic for the particular layer being traced.

6. The resin system should be compatible with the structure. Most home built parts do not use a polyester resin system on the structural components. A two-part epoxy system should be weighed out to the proper ratio and mixed together. Impregnate the fabric with the mixed resin system. Place another clear plastic piece over the wet fabric, and cut the repair patches to the correct shape outlined on the plastic.

7. After the patches are cut out, they are laid onto the sanded area. Remove the plastic backing and place down using the correct fiber orientation.

8. If a room temperature cure "homebuilt epoxy" system is used, the resin usually cures very quickly. If this is the case, the repair cannot be vacuum bagged because it cures so quickly. The vacuum bagging cannot be applied in time, and the part will not benefit from the vacuum. Instead, a layer of peel ply will help to hold down the repair plies during the cure cycle and give the repair a finished look which requires little sanding except to feather out the edges.

9. If the type of resin used is a slower cure type (over 2 hours), then there is plenty of time to vacuum bag the repair. It will also help squeeze out much of the excess resin to give a stronger repair. Vacuum bag the repair using peel ply, bleeder, bagging film, and sealant tape.

10. Cure the repair. The surface of most homebuilt parts are finished with a resin mixture that has microballoons to make a slurry. This is used all over the surface to smooth out any defects. To help match the repair with the existing part, a slurry is made and spread over the repair area. This can have a layer of peel ply added to create a smoother, finely etched area that will require less sanding. Then the part is painted with the same type of paint that was used on the original aircraft.

AUTHOR'S NOTE

This book is intended to familiarize the technician with basic repair techniques, terminology, tools, and materials frequently used in composite repair. After being properly trained and the knowledge gained from this publication, a technician should be able to easily translate the manufacturer's instructions into airworthy repairs.

The following information is from an article that I wrote after the crash of American Airlines flight 587. It provides some of my personal observations of the composite aviation industry at the present time as it relates to the ongoing investigation into the cause of this tragedy. It is not my intention to cast blame or to make assumptions about any organization's role in the accident. It is, however, an overview of the crash investigation as it relates to advanced composites manufacturing and technology at the time of printing of this book.

Composites represent new materials and techniques that must be mastered by those who want to stay in tune with the aviation industry. One characteristic of the aviation industry is that it is always changing, always improving. As a result, it requires that the best people in the industry are also improving. Aviation produces some of the most beautiful, intriguing, and inspiring, machines made by man. These are the best machines. The best maintenance professionals are needed to inspect, maintain, and repair these machines.

When I learned of the recent accident of an Airbus, (American Airlines flight #587) I was very saddened as most of the world was. When I found out that one of the possible reasons for its failure was a composite repair, I was heart broken. This was the first time a composite had failed, and it was from a repair. (The NTSB has not completed its investigation, and I am writing this assuming that the composite repair failure was a factor.) This is my interpretation of the facts in this investigation, and just that - my interpretation. I studied the information coming out of the NTSB to try to understand what exactly happened. Here is a summary of items that have been determined up until the printing of this book.

Airbus manufactured the aircraft around 1988. In the manufacturing of it, there was a delamination (void between the fabric plies) on the vertical tail, close to the attach point. The manufacturer fixed the delamination using a mechanically fastened doubler that was reinforced with resin. This was the manufacturer's approved repair. The aircraft was delivered to American Airlines as new, with no mention of the repair, no inspection required of it. Around 1994, the aircraft withstood major turbulence, which was reported by the pilots. Inspection of the aircraft did not find any problems. On November 12, 2001, flight #587 took off from Kennedy International Airport with 260 people on board. There seems to have been a lot of turbulence from the wake of another aircraft, a JAL 747. The tail section broke away from the Airbus before crashing into the ground.

I knew the composite industry was in trouble when Dan Rather tried to explain composites as "a plastic material that is used structurally." The word "plastic" makes many people think of cheap toys that break easily, not a good word to use around aircraft, especially with the general public.

So, why do manufacturers even use composites?

- High strength to weight ratio (which means more payload)

- Their ability to withstand stresses (flexibility and stiffness)

- Can be formed into one complex piece, aerodynamically contoured shapes

- Composites don't corrode like aluminum

- Reduced wear

Sounds like an ideal aircraft manufacturing material!

Or is it?

Problems with Composites:

- Some may wick in moisture (aramids)

- Some exhibit dissimilar metal corrosion when bonded to aluminum (carbon/graphite)

- They are hard to inspect

- They may be difficult to repair properly without the proper training

- Finding the proper composite materials in small quantities may be very difficult

- Drilling into a composite may cause the structure to become weaker

George Black, an NTSB member, had this to say about the repair area from Flight #587: "Prior to its delivery to American, the left center fitting was found to be delaminated. It was repaired by the manufacturer—whether Airbus or a Subcontractor is not known, however. This was done to increase the thickness of the fittings and add reinforcing rivets. The fin was released with a specification that no additional special inspections were needed, according to the manufacturer."

Why do I question the repair? The repair made to Flight #587 by the manufacturer was a bonded on doubler reinforced with rivets to a structural composite component. Repairs that involve drilling through the composite component may weaken the part more than the original damage (in this case a delamination). A bolted on repair is usually considered temporary until a more permanent repair can be made. Reinforcing rivets added to a composite structural component? If you look at the pictures from the NTSB of the crash site, the holes, which were used to mechanically fasten the repair patch, can be seen. It looks like the perforation around a stamp—easy to tear.

(Photo courtesy of NTSB)

A doubler attached to the area may stiffen the part in an area where flexibility may be required, especially when higher loads are imposed (such as compensating for the turbulence caused by the 747 taking off ahead of it).

Did the manufacturer know in 1989 that drilling many holes into a composite component might weaken it?

The following 2 paragraphs are from the first edition of the book Advanced Composites. This book had an original copyright date of 1990. I was in the process of writing the book when the Airbus was being manufactured. If I knew this information, you would think a manufacturer of composite aircraft would also know this information.

The bolted and bonded on surface patches are not the preferred type of patch because the original strength may not be restored.

When the proper facilities, curing and bagging equipment are not available for on-line work, a pre-cured patch inserted with blind fasteners may be used. This type of repair usually does not give the maximum strength. Because it is not a flush repair, it may cause vibration when performed on critical parts. This type of repair may be considered a temporary repair until the damage can be scarfed down and the patches correctly laminated on with heat and pressure.

Usually the patch uses some type of mechanical blind fastener, which is drilled through the patch into the surface of the original part, to hold the patch in place while it is further stabilized with an adhesive.

There are many problems a technician faces when working in the composite repair field. Because the materials are new, many support resources are not in place. Here is an outline of what I see as lacking for the maintenance professional when facing a composite repair:

Small Quantities of Materials: It is difficult to find small quantities of some of the materials required. The weavers don't want to sell a few yards, so other distributors buy full yards and sell smaller quantities for repair use. The tracking of a specific material is very hard.

Certification of Materials: Because these other distributors are selling the materials, a certification of materials is required to trace the materials back to the weaver. There is no marking on the fabric. WHY? As AMTs, we know that the fabric used in covering a dope and fabric aircraft is required to have a marking on edge every three feet. This was put into effect in the 1940s. Yet today, the weavers are refusing to stamp the edges. It would be great to see a TSO number, weave number, or anything to identify it on the fabric.

Standardization of Materials: Speaking of TSO numbers, it would be nice if the weavers would standardize their weaves and assign a standardization number to each weave. That way, when a repair called for a 584 carbon, we know we could also use 584 graphite, or a G105, or a MI-1029 depending on the weaver, all of which are the same materials. When we ask for the compliance papers, we get the BMS (Boing Material Specification) number. If we are working on something other than a Boeing, we have no idea what that BMS stands for, and therefore require more paperwork from someone to write a clarification that indeed this material does in fact meet the specifications of a 584 carbon.

Standardization of Terms: It's so cute when I get a request for a quote and the items listed are: Baby blanket, gorilla snot, sticky tape, etc. When I question the person about it, they are always very defensive about it: "We used these terms when I worked at McDonnell Douglass." So, if you use these terms, others around you will be impressed with your professionalism. No, it's not very professional. Consistency begins with terminology. Standardization of terms is important for communication between maintenance people, parts people, buyers, etc. If the communication is poor, the resulting material may not be what you want. If you are an instructor, please don't use cute terms when teaching your students. Thanks.

Updated Structural Repair Manuals: When working in the field, I am extremely disappointed with some of the SRMs for composite repair. On one aircraft delivered to a commuter airline, there was one page saying that an update would be out soon. There was nothing showing the components that were made of composites (as I remember about 40 percent of the airframe), there were no lists of materials to repair with, no damage limitations. This update came two years later. Many times it is the maintenance professional that suggests types of repairs to be done, submits it to a tech rep, which then becomes the approved repair in the update. Many students who have graduated from my course are doing this in the field, using the illustrations from the book Advanced Composites.

The Number of Thermocouples Used: Here's a pet peeve of mine. How can the recording of the temperature prove the repair was done correctly? Many FAA professionals and shops are requiring numerous thermocouples in the repair. The repair done on Flight #587 could have used 10 thermocouples to record the temperature, but it failed. If the repair is not the correct repair, the wrong type of repair materials were used, all the oil or water was not cleaned from the repair area, if it was improperly bagged, if it was improperly sanded, or any other number of reasons, the repair could fail. It is not the number of thermocouples that determines a correct repair.

Training: One of the most common problems associated with the use of aircraft composites is that there are too few technicians trained in the techniques and materials of composite repair. As more manufacturers equip their aircraft with composite parts, the need for trained aviation technicians to fabricate, inspect, and maintain these aircraft also increases. The availability of trained technicians to provide airworthy repairs has not yet caught up with the industry demand. Although anyone with an airframe license is authorized to perform a repair to a composite component, some specialized training is usually needed to ensure a complete and airworthy job. This training is of increasing significance because many advanced composite materials are being used to fabricate structural components and primary control surfaces.

We can't do anything for the people who were on Flight #587. My hope is that we can work together as manufacturers, FAA personnel, airlines, industry trainers, and maintenance professionals to continue to make aviation one of the truly great industries.

Composite Terminology

A – Stage — The initial stage of mixing the two parts of a thermosetting resin system together. The material is soluble in some liquids and fusible.

AMM — Aircraft Maintenance Manual – May also be called an MMM or Manufacturers Maintenance Manual. This is a manual developed by the aircraft manufacturer that includes information prepared for the AMT or technician who performs work on units, components, and systems while they are installed on the airplane. It is normally supplied by the manufacturer and approved by the FAA as part of the original process of certification. It will contain the required instructions for continued airworthiness that must accompany each aircraft when it leaves the factory. An Aircraft Maintenance Manual can also be a manual developed by a Part 125 operator as part of their specific operating manual. As such, the FAA does not specifically approve the manual.

Accelerator — A chemical additive that quickens cure, or a chemical reaction.

Additives — Materials that are mixed into a two-part resin system to improve the properties of the system.

Adhesive — A substance, that is applied to two mating surfaces to bond them together by surface attachment.

Adhesive Film — Premixed adhesives cast onto a thin plastic film. Requires refrigerated storage.

Advanced Composites — A fibrous material embedded in a resin matrix. The term "advanced" applies to those materials, which have superior strength and stiffness and the process in which they are manufactured. Advanced composites are generally the ones used structurally on an aircraft.

Alloy — A blend of polymers or copolymers with other polymers or elastomers. Also called polymer blend.

Anisotropic — Fibers are placed in different directions to respond to the stresses applied in different directions.

Aramid — A type of fiber that is an Aromatic Polyamide. Kevlar®

is the brand name, which is manufactured by Dupont. There are other companies that also weave aramid fabrics for aircraft use.

Area Weight — The weight of fiber reinforcement per unit area (width ? length) of tape or fabric.

Aspect Ratio — The ratio of length to diameter of a reinforcing fiber.

Autoclave — A large vessel used to cure laminates and bonded parts, using pressure, vacuum and heat in an inert atmosphere.

Autoclave Molding — A manufacturing method that uses an autoclave. The composite assembly is placed into an autoclave at 50 to 100 psi to consolidate the laminate by removing entrapped air and excess resin.

Axial Winding — A manufacturing method using filament-winding equipment. In axial winding the filaments are parallel to the axis.

B-Stage — The intermediate stage in the reaction of the two parts of the resin system after being mixed. The resin system reacts to heat by softening. The resin in a prepreg material is usually in the B-stage before the curing process.

Bagging — Applying an impermeable layer of film over an uncured part and sealing the edges so that a vacuum can be drawn.

Bag Side — The side of a part that is cured against the vacuum bag.

Balanced Design — In filament winding, a winding pattern so designed that the stresses in all filaments are equal.

Balanced Laminate — Each layer except the 0/90∞ are placed in plus and minus pairs around the centerline. These plies do not have to be adjacent to each other.

Basket Weave — In this type of woven reinforcement, two or more warp threads go over and under two or more filling threads in a repeat pattern. The basket weave is less stable than the plain weave but produces a flatter and stronger fabric. It is also a more pliable fabric than the plain weave and maintains a certain degree of porosity.

Batch (or Lot) — Material that was made with the same process at the same time, having identical characteristics throughout.

Bearing Area — The cross-section area of the bearing load member on the sample.

Bearing Strain — The ratio of the deformation of the bearing hole, in the direction of the applied force, to the pin diameter.

Bearing Stress — The applied load in pounds divided by the bearing area.

Bias — A 45° angle to the warp threads. Fabric can be formed into contoured shapes by using the bias.

Bi-directional Cloth — A cloth in which the fibers run in various directions. Usually woven together in two directions.

Bi-directional Laminate — A laminate with the fibers oriented in more than one direction.

Bismaleimide (BMI) — A type of polyimide resin that cures at a very high temperature, and has a very high operating temperature range in the 550 – 600∞ F range, and some around the 700°F range. These are more difficult to cure because moisture emissions during the cure may cause voids or delaminations.

Bleed — An escape passage at the parting line of a mold (like a vent, but deeper), which allows material to escape, or bleed out.

Bleeder — A layer of material used during the manufacture or repair of a part to allow entrapped air and resin to escape. It is removed after curing. It also serves as a vacuum valve contact with the part.

Bleedout — Excess resin that flows out during the curing process, usually into a bleeder cloth. Sometimes appears during the filament winding process if the fiber has been through a resin bath.

Blister — Undesirable rounded elevation of the surface of a plastic, and somewhat resembling the shape of a blister on the human skin.

Bond Ply — The ply or fabric patch which comes in contact with the honeycomb core.

Bond Strength — The stress required to pull apart two plies or from the ply to the core. The amount of strength of the adhesion.

Boron Filament — A strong, lightweight fiber used as a reinforcement. A tungsten – filament core with boron gas deposited on it. It has a high strength to weight ratio.

Braiding — Weaving of fibers into a tubular shape instead of a flat fabric.

Breakout — When drilling or cutting the edges of a composite part, the fibers may separate or break.

Breather — A loosely woven fabric that does not come in contact with the resin and used to provide uniform venting and pressure under a vacuum cure. Breather material is used under the vacuum valve to allow the air to be evacuated inside the vacuum bagged part. Removed after curing.

Bridging — This term can refer to plies of fabric over a curved edge that don't come in full contact with the core material. It is also used to describe excess resin that has formed on edges during the curing process.

Buckle Line — On a honeycomb core, it is a line of collapsed cells with undistorted cells on either side. It is usually found on the inside of the radius on a formed core.

Buckling — A failure of the fabric in which it deflects up or down rather than breaking.

CMM – Component Maintenance Manual — A manual developed by the component manufacturer and frequently adopted by an airframe manufacturer. A CMM is most frequently not approved by the FAA. Blanket approval comes through the AMM or SRM.

C-Stage — The final stage in the curing of the mixed thermoset resin system. It cannot be softened by heat and is insoluble at this stage.

Carbon Fiber — Produced by placing carbon (an element) in an inert atmosphere at temperatures above 1,800°F. Used as a reinforcing material. Carbon fiber is a lightweight, high strength and high stiffness fiber. The material can be graphitized by heat-treating at a very high temperature.

Carbon/Graphite Fiber or Fabric — A fiber used in advanced composites comprised of carbon filaments which may be woven together. The terms carbon and graphite have been used interchangeably for years. The Americans prefer the term graphite, while the Europeans prefer carbon. Depending on the manufacturer of the aircraft, different terms may be used. The term Carbon/Graphite is used throughout this book to include both terms.

Catalyst — A substance which initiates a chemical reaction.

Catalyzed Resin — A term used to describe the resin mixture after it has been mixed with the catalyst or hardener. It may still be in the workable state.

Caul Plates — Smooth plates used during the cure process to apply pressure in a uniform manner.

Coefficient of Expansion — A measure of the change in length of volume of an object.

Coefficient of Thermal Expansion — The change in unit of length of volume accompanying a change of temperature.

Cocured — Laminates are cured and also bonded to another prepared surface.

Cohesion — The tendency of a single substance to adhere to itself. The force holding a single substance together.

Coin Tap — The use of a coin to tap a laminate in different spots to detect a change in sound, which would indicate the presence of a defect.

Composite — Two or more substances which are combined to produce material properties not present when either substance is used alone.

Compression Molding — A manufacturing method that uses a two-part mold that is in the shape of the finished part. Resin and fibers are placed into the mold cavity, the mold closed, and cured with heat to produce the final component.

Compressive Strength — The resistance to a crushing force.

Contaminant — An impurity or foreign substance present in a material or environment that affects one or more properties of the material, particularly adhesion.

Continuous Filament — An individual reinforcement that is flexible and indefinite in length. The fibers used to weave fabric are considered continuous filaments.

Core — The central member of a sandwich part (usually foam or honeycomb). It produces a lightweight, high strength component when laminated with face sheets.

Core Crush — Compression damage of the core.

Core Depression — A gouge or indentation in the core material.

Core Orientation — The placement of the honeycomb core to line up the ribbon direction, thickness of the cell depth, cell size, and transverse direction.

Core Separation — A breaking of the honeycomb core cells.

Core Splicing — Joining two core segments by bonding them together, usually with a foaming adhesive..

Crazing — Region of ultrafine cracks, which may extend in a network on or under the surface of a resin or plastic material.

Critical Strain — The strain at the yield point.

Cross Linking — With thermosetting and certain thermoplastic polymers, the setting up of chemical links between the molecular chains.

Cross-ply Laminate — A laminate with plies usually oriented at 0° and 90° only.

Cure — To change the physical properties of a material by chemical reaction, by the application of catalysts, heat and pressure, alone or in combination.

Cure Temperature — The temperature that the resin system attains for its final cure. It does not include the ramp up or down.

Curing Agent — A catalytic or reactive agent that causes polymerization when added to the resin. Also referred to as a hardener.

Delaminate — The separation of layers due to adhesive failure. This also includes the separation of the layers of fabric to a core structure. A delamination may be associated with bridging, drilling, and trimming.

Denier — A numbering system for filaments in the yarn used for weaving. The number is equal to weight in grams of 9,000 meters of yarn.

Disbond — The separation of a bond from one structure to another. Many times this term is used for referring to the separation of the laminate skin to the core structure. It is also used for a separation from a fitting to the skin.

Doubler Plies — A patch that extends over the sanded out area to the existing structure which strengthens the repair. A doubler can also be used where fasteners are applied or where there are abrupt load transfers.

Drape — The ability of a fabric or pre-preg to conform to a contoured surface.

Dry Fiber — A condition in which fibers are not fully encapsulated by resin during pultrusion.

Dry Laminate — A laminate containing insufficient resin for complete bonding of the reinforcement.

E-Glass — A type of fiberglass. The E stands for electrical. It is used primarily when there could be interference to radio signals such as with a radome.

Eight-harness Satin — A type of fabric weave. The fabric has a seven-by-one weave pattern in which a filling thread floats over seven warp threads and then under one. Like the crowfoot weave, it looks different on one side than on the other. This weave is more pliable than any of the others and is especially adaptable to forming around compound curves, such as on radomes.

Environmental Stress Cracking (ESC) — The susceptibility of a resin to cracking or crazing when in the presence of surface-active chemicals.

Epoxy Resin — A common thermoset material used in aircraft construction. Used as the bonding matrix to distribute the stresses to the fibers, and hold the fibers together. When mixed with a catalyst, they are adhesive, resistant to chemicals, are water resistant, and unaffected by heat or cold. One part of a two-part system, which combines the resin and the catalyst to form the bonding matrix. In composites, the term "resin" is often used to describe the two parts mixed together.

Fabric — Individual fibers woven together to produce cloth. Unidirectional or matted fibers may be included in this classification.

Fabric Warp Face — The side of a woven fabric in which the greatest number of yarns is parallel to the selvage.

Faying Surface — The surfaces of materials in contact with each other and joined or about to be joined.

Fiber — A single strand of material used as reinforcement because of its high strength and stiffness.

Fiber Bridging — Reinforcing fiber material that bridges an inside-radius of a pultruded product. This condition is caused by shrinkage stresses around such a radius during cure.

Fiber Content — The amount of fiber in a composite expressed as a ratio to the matrix. The most desirable fiber content is a 60:40 ratio. This means there is 60% fiber and 40% matrix material.

Fiber Direction or Orientation — The orientation of the fibers in a laminate to the 0º reference designated by the manufacturer.

Fiber Reinforced Plastics FRP — Term used interchangeably for advanced composites

Fiberglass — A glass fiber produced by spinning molten glass into long continuous fibers, used as a fiber reinforcement.

Fiberglass Reinforcement — Fiberglass used as reinforcement in a plastic matrix.

Filament — The smallest unit of a fibrous material.

Filament Winding — A manufacturing method in which a long continuous fiber is wound around a mandrel to produce a structure.

Fill Threads — Also known as the Weft or Woof. These are the crosswise fibers woven at 90° to the warp fibers.

Filler — Material added to the mixed resin to increase viscosity, improve appearance, and lower the density and cost.

Filler Ply — An additional patch to fill in a depression in the repair, or to buildup an edge.

Film Adhesive — A synthetic resin adhesive, usually of the thermosetting type, in the form of a thin, dry film of resin.

Four-harness Satin — A fabric weave. Also called crowfoot satin because the weaving pattern resembles the imprint of a crow's foot. In this type of weave there is a three-by-one interlacing.

Finish — A material that is applied to the fabric after it is woven to improve the bond of the fiber to the resin system.

Gel Coat — A coating of resin, generally pigmented, applied to the mold or part to produce a smooth finish. Considered as a nonstructural finish.

Gel Time — The period of time from the initial mixing of the reactants of a liquid material composition to the point in time when gelation occurs, as defined by a specific test method.

Glass Cloth — See Fiberglass.

Graphite — A carbonized fiber used as a reinforcement. The graphitization is accomplished by heating the carbon fiber to temperatures up to 5400°F. See Carbon Fiber and Carbon/Graphite Fiber.

Hand Lay-Up — Assembling layers of reinforcement by hand. This includes the working in of the resin yourself, as well as using a pre-preg fabric.

Hardener — Used to promote or control the curing action.

Harness Satin — A weaving pattern producing a satin appearance. See also eight-harness satin and four-harness satin.

Honeycomb — A core material resembling natural honeycomb to produce a lightweight, high strength component.

Hot Bond Repair — A repair made using a hot patch bonding machine to cure and monitor the curing operation. Hot bonding equipment typically includes both the heat source and the vacuum source.

Hybrid — The combination of two or more types of reinforcing materials into the composite structure.

IPC – Illustrated Parts Catalog — A required document which is produced by the manufacturer. It has the parts and their part numbers exploded for identification. It does not contain FAA approved data.

Impregnate — In reinforcing plastics, to saturate the reinforcement with a resin.

Inclusion — A physical and mechanical discontinuity occurring within a material or part.

Interlaminar Shear — Shearing force that breaks the bond between two laminates where they interface.

Kevlar® — Trademark of DuPont. A strong, lightweight aramid fiber used as a reinforcement fiber.

Laminate — A structure made by bonding together two or more layers of material with resin. It contains no core material.

Laminate Ply — One fabric-resin or fiber-resin layer that is bonded to adjacent layers in the curing process.

Lap Joint — A joint made by placing one adherents partly over another and bonding the overlapped portions.

Lay-up — Reinforcing material that is placed in position in the mold.

MMM – Manufacturers Maintenance Manual — See AMM or Aircraft Maintenance Manual.

Mandrel — the forming shape used in the filament winding process.

Mat — Used typically in the mold making process. Chopped fibers are held together with a binder. When the resin matrix is applied, the binder melts. Typically used with polyester resin systems.

Matrix — The material that bonds fibers together, and distributes the stress evenly to the fibers. Typically in advanced composites, the matrix is a resin.

Metal– Matrix Composites – MMC — Fibers bonded together with a metal as the bonding material.

Microballoons — Very small glass or phenolic spheres used as a filler.

Modulus — The ratio of a stress load applied to the deformation of a material.

Moisture Absorption — The pickup of water vapor from air by a material, in reference to vapor withdrawn from the air only, as distinguished from water absorption, which is the gain in weight due to the absorption of water by immersion.

Mold — The hollow form used to give shape to a laminate part while curing.

Mold Release Agent — A lubricant used to prevent the part from sticking to the mold.

Nomex® — Trademark of DuPont. A nylon paper treated material that is made into a honeycomb core material.

Nondestructive Testing (NDT) or Nondestructive Inspection (NDI) — Inspecting a component for damage without permanently damaging the part.

Orientation — The alignment of the fibers (0,45,90) to the baseline set by the manufacturer for a particular component.

Out Time — The time a pre-preg is exposed to ambient temperature, namely, the total amount of time the pre-preg is out of the freezer. This may include shipping time as well as the time it takes to cut off a small piece from the roll.

Parting Agent — See mold release agent.

Parting Film — A layer of thin plastic to prevent bagging materials from sticking to the part. It may be perforated to vent excess resin. It is removed after cure. May be used instead of Peel Ply.

Peel Ply — A layer of fabric used in manufacturing to vent excess resin up into the bleeder material. It prevents bagging materials from sticking to the part, and it leaves a very finely etched surface for painting. It is removed after cure.

Peel Strength — The amount of strength it takes a part to resist the stress applied when peeling apart two plies.

Perforated parting film or Release Film — A thin layer of plastic film used to prevent bagging materials from sticking to the part. The perforations allow some resin to flow through small holes in the plastic. Used in the same way as peel ply.

Phenolic Resin — A thermosetting resin produced by the condensation of an aromatic alcohol with an aldehyde, particularly of phenol with formaldehyde.

Pin Holes — Small holes caused by the mold used.

Plain Weave — A weaving pattern in which the warp and fill fibers alternate; that is, the repeat pattern is warp/fill/warp/fill.

Ply — One layer of reinforcement in a laminate.

Polyacrylonitrile (PAN) — The base material used in manufacturing some types of carbon fibers.

Polyester resins — can contain substantial amounts of several components other than the basic primary resin ingredients. A typical polyester formula might include the basic resin material, a catalyst, fillers, and accelerators. These components can be used in varying quantities to change the performance of the cured resin. Polyester resins can be formulated to produce greater or lesser resilience. For example, polyester used for helmets, automotive parts, & some nonstructural aircraft parts need greater resilience. Fabricators produce low-shrinkage polyester resins by using thermoplastic components such as polystyrene or polymethacrylate as the basic resin. Weather resistant resins can be formulated for use in gel coats by replacing some of the basic styrene resin with methyl methacraylate. Fire resistant polyesters are made by using fire retardants, such as tetrachlorophthalic, tetrabromophthalic, or chlorendic dibasic acids.

Polyvinyl Chloride (PVC) — A thermoplastic material composed of polymers of vinyl chloride. Some aircraft structures use PVC foam for the core material. The foams come in many different weights and densities.

Postcure — During the curing cycle of a manufactured component, the postcure is an additional elevated temperature soak to improve the mechanical properties.

Pot-Life — The length of time that the resin, mixed with catalyst, will be in a workable state.

Preform — A preshaped fibrous reinforcement of mat or cloth formed to the desired shape on a mandrel or mock-up before being placed in a mold press.

Pre-Preg — Reinforcing material that is pre-impregnated with resin/catalyst mixture. The resin system is in the B-stage and requires refrigerated storage. When heated, the resins begin to glow and will complete the cure when the temperature is elevated to it's cure temperature for the proper amount of time.

Process Control Record — A record of the materials and processes used in making the repair.

Puckers — Local areas on pre-preg material where the material has blistered and pulled away from the separator film or release paper.

Pultrusion — A manufacturing process that pulls the resin impregnated fibers through a shaping die to form a shape. The curing process also is done while it is in the die.

Puncture — A break in the skin that may or may not go through to the core material, or completely through the part.

Ramp and Soak – A curing process in which the temperature is slowly raised at a given rate to the final cure temperature and held for a specific amount of time. After that time, the temperature is slowly lowered to room temperature. For example, if the final cure temperature for a part is 250°F, the temperature would be ramped up to 250° at a rate of 8° per minute. Once it reaches 250°, the temperature is held there for 1 hour and 30 minutes, and then the temperature is lowered to 80º at a rate of 5º per minute. This process is typically done by using a temperature controller which is found on hot patch bonding equipment.

Reinforcement — Material used to strengthen the matrix. Fiber reinforced plastic is an example. Fibers are used to reinforce the plastic material.

Release Film — A layer of plastic material which is used in the vacuum bagging process that does not allow resin to bleed through it. It will not bond to the part when the resins cure. Perforated release film will allow some resin to bleed through.

Resin — A type of Matrix system used when mixed with a hardener or catalyst. The term resin is sometimes used to describe the matrix.

Resin Rich — An area which has an excess amount of matrix. A resin rich laminate usually is more brittle and weighs more than laminates with the proper amount of resin.

Resin Ridge — A ridge of excess resin that contains only resin.

Resin Starved — An area which is deficient in resin. A resin-starved part will not exhibit the structural strength that a part made with the proper amount of resin.

Resin System — A mixture of resin and ingredients required for the intended processing method and final product.

Resin Transfer Molding (RTM) — A manufacturing process in which the resin/catalyst mixture is pumped into a two-sided mold where a fabric reinforcement has been placed. The part is then heated and cured.

Ribbon Direction — On a honeycomb core, the way the honeycomb can be separated. The direction of one continuous ribbon.

Roving — A bundle of filaments that are twisted together for weaving into fabric.

S-Glass — The S stands for structural fiberglass. This type of fiberglass is used for much of the structural strength in advanced composite structures. A magnesium aluminosilicate composition that is especially designed to provide very high tensile strength glass filaments.

SRM – Structural Repair Manual — A manual which is developed by the manufacturer to cover all items not listed as minor maintenance, including instructions for structural repair, major component removal, installation, and adjustment, setup, etc. It contains manufacturer-approved data for major repairs and replacement.

Sandwich Structure — A thick, low density, core (Usually foam or honeycomb) between thin faces of high strength material.

Scarf Joint — An angled joint made by cutting away material and mating the new surface with the existing angular cut.

Sealant — A material applied to a joint in paste or liquid form that hardens or cures in place, forming a seal.

Secondary Structure — In aircraft and aerospace applications, a structure that is not critical to flight safety.

Selvage Edge — A manufactured woven edge on fabric that runs the length of the fabric or in the warp direction. It is removed for all fabrication and repair work.

Separator — A permeable layer that also acts as a release film. This could be in the form of a peel ply or a porous Teflon®-coated fiberglass. Often placed between the lay-up and bleeder to facilitate the excess resin wicking into the bleeder. It is removed from the laminate after cure.

Shear — An action or stress resulting from applied forces that causes or tends to cause two contiguous parts of a body to slide relative to each other.

Shelf Life — The time span that a product will remain useful. This should be listed on the label. Temperature during storage will affect the shelf life.

Solvent — A liquid used for dissolving and cleaning materials.

Starved Area — An area in a plastic part that has an insufficient amount of resin to wet out the reinforcement completely.

Starved Joint — An adhesive joint that has been deprived of the proper film thickness of adhesive due to insufficient adhesive spreading or to the application of excessive pressure during the lamination process.

Stiffness — The relationship of load and deformation. The ratio between the applied stress and resulting strain.

Storage Life — The period of time during which a liquid resin, packaged adhesive, or pre-preg can be stored under specified temperature conditions and remain suitable for use. Also called shelf life. The storage life should be printed on the label.

Strand — Normally, an untwisted bundle or assembly of continuous filaments used as a unit. Sometimes a single fiber or filament is called strand.

Stress — The internal resistance or change in shape and size expressed in force per unit area. A stress concentration is an area where the level of an applied stress causes a notch, void, hole, or inclusion.

Stress Corrosion — Preferential attack of areas under stress in a corrosive environment, where such an environment alone would not have caused corrosion.

Stress Crack — External or internal cracks in a plastic caused by tensile stresses less than that of its short-time mechanical strength. The stresses that cause cracking may be present internally or externally or may be combinations of these stresses.

Structural Adhesive — Adhesive used for transferring required loads between two cured parts. An adhesive can also be used to bond metal to a composite structure.

Structural Bond — A bond that joins basic load-bearing parts of an assembly. The load may be either static or dynamic.

Strux — A foam like material used to form structural sections for stiffening.

Surface Treatment — A material (size or finish) applied to fibrous material during the forming operation or in subsequent processes. The process used to enhance bonding capability of fiber to resin.

Symmetrical Laminate — A laminate in which the stacking sequence of plies below its midline is a mirror image of the stacking sequence above the midline.

Tack — Stickiness of the adhesive of a pre-preg material.

Tape — A term used for thin unidirectional material which is usually no wider than 12 inches. The material may or may not be a prepreg.

Tape Laying — A manufacturing process where prepreg tapes are laid across or overlapped to build up a shape. The parts are sometimes vacuum bagged and cured. This process may be automated by the use of tape laying equipment.

Tedlar® — A material used on the surface as a waterproof barrier.

Telegraphing — Dimpling of the fabric into the honeycomb core.

Tensile Strength — The pulling stress sustained by a specimen before it fails.

Thermal Stress Cracking — The crazing and cracking of some thermoplastic resins from overexposure to elevated temperatures.

Thermocouple — A wire assembly used with a control device to sense temperature readings.

Thermoplastic — A plastic material used in advanced composites as a matrix material. Heat is used during the forming operation. It is not a permanent shape, however, if heated again it will soften and flow to form another shape (Plexiglas windshield).

Thermoset — A plastic material used in advanced composites as a matrix material. Heat is used to form and set the part permanently. Once cured, it cannot be reformed by applying heat. Most composite structural components are made of thermoset plastics.

Thixotropic — An agent used to thicken a resin system without adding weight. It makes the resin system less dense. Thixotropic agents include chopped fibers, microballons, and fiber flox. Some agents give more strength than others do.

Tool — The mold used in manufacturing a composite component.

Tooling resins — Resins that are used to make molds.

Toughness — A measure of the ability of a material to absorb energy.

Tow — An untwisted bundle of filaments

Tracer — A fiber, tow, or yarn added to a pre-preg for verifying fiber alignment for distinguishing warp fibers from fill fibers.

Unidirectional — A fabric, tape, or laminate with all the major fibers running in one direction, giving strength in that direction.

Vacuum Bagging — A means of applying atmospheric pressure to a part while curing by sealing the part in a plastic bag and removing all air.

Viscosity — The resistance to fluid flow. Resins have a viscosity rating which correspond to how thick they are.

Void — An empty area in the composite laminate. The term void may be used in place of delamination.

Volatile Content — The percent of volatiles that are driven off as a vapor from a plastic or an impregnated reinforcement.

Volatiles — Materials, such as water and alcohol, in a resin formulation, that are capable of being vaporized at room temperature.

Warpage — Dimensional distortion in a plastic object.

Warp Direction — The threads running the length of the fabric as it comes off the bolt. Parallel to the selvage edge.

Warp Face — The side of the fabric where the greatest number of yarns are parallel to the selvage edge.

Water Absorption — The ratio of the weight of water absorbed by a material to the weight of the dry material.

Water Break Test — Spraying water on a part to be bonded to assure there is no oil or grease contamination on the surface.

Water Jet — Used primarily in the manufacturing process as a cutting tool. A very high-pressure stream of water is used to cut through the component.

Weave — The particular manner in which a fabric is formed by interlacing yarns. Usually assigned a style number, which is used in ordering materials for the repair of a component.

Weft Direction — Fibers that are perpendicular to the warp fibers. Sometimes referred to as the woof or fill.

Wet Lay-up — A method of making a reinforced product by applying the resin system as a liquid when the reinforcement is put in place.

Wet-out — The saturation of an impregnated fabric in which all areas of the fibers are filled with resin.

Wire Mesh — A fine wire screen used to dissipate an electrical charge from lightning or static buildup. It is used for lightning protection usually directly under the top layer of fabric.

Working Life — The period of time during which a liquid resin or adhesive remains usable.

Woven Fabric — A material constructed by interlacing yarns, fibers, or filaments to form fabric patterns.

Wrinkle — A surface imperfection in laminated plastics that has the appearance of a crease or fold in one or more outer sheets of the paper, fabric, or other base. Also occurs in vacuum bag molding when the bag is improperly placed, causing a crease.

X-Axis — The axis or the direction of the laminate used as the $0°$ reference on a part.

Yarn — Twisted filaments, fibers, or strands that form a continuous length suitable for use in weaving into materials.

Zero Bleed — A laminate fabrication procedure that does not allow loss of resin during cure.